G000038785

A NEW MODEL ARMY

also by Michael Yardley

Poland: A Tragedy
Backing into the Limelight – a biography of T. E. Lawrence
[Sandhurst A Documentary]

A NEW MODEL ARMY

Michael Yardley

Dennis Sewell

© Michael Yardley and Dennis Sewell 1989

First published in Great Britain 1989 by
WH Allen & Co Plc
Sekforde House, 175-179 St John Street
London EC1V

ISBN 1 85227 121 3

Printed and bound in Great Britain by
Mackays of Chatham Plc, Chatham, Kent.

This book is sold subject to the condition that
it shall not, by way of trade or otherwise,
be lent, re-sold, hired out or otherwise circulated
without the publisher's prior consent in any
form of binding or cover other than that
in which it is published and without a similar
condition including this condition being imposed
upon the subsequent purchaser.

Contents

Acknowledgements vi
Introduction 1
1 The Evolution of the Modern Army 8
2 The Green Machine 25
3 The Regimental System 37
4 The Moral Dimension 47
5 A Game of Soldiers 74
6 Participatory vs Delegative Defence 101
7 The Unsinkable Aircraft-Carrier? 128
8 The Changing Face of War 150
9 The Future: The Challenge of Adaption 178
Conclusion 201
Index 207

Acknowledgements

This book has taken longer to write than either author had anticipated. In the past three years many people have helped: the serving soldiers, not named below, who have allowed us to interview them; the specialists who have let us pick their brains; the friends and family who have put up with and encouraged us. Maggie Lacchin even lent us a house when the project outgrew our own. To everyone, especially the understanding bank managers, thank you. Finally, we would like to say that the opinions expressed are our own.

Our Roll of Honour includes:

Attachés: German, French, Swiss, Norwegian, Swedish, Israeli. Dr Stephen Badsey, Capt. Brian Bunker (rtd), Dr David Chandler, Douglas Collard, James Leaton Gray, David Gwyn-Jones, Dr Tony Heathcote, Lt Col. John Hickey (rtd), Lt Col. Michael Hickey (rtd), Imperial War Museum, Derek Johns, Ian Kemp, Phillip Knightley, Maggie Lacchin, Prof. David Martin, Otto Mikkelsen, John Montgomery RUSI librarian, National Army Museum, Edgar O'Balance, Lt Col. Sam Pope (RM rtd), Mary Rees-Pyves, Alastair Rosenschein, US Information Service, Chen Wallace, Fiona Yardley, John Yardley, Vivienne Yardley.

. . . if the trumpet give an uncertain sound,
who shall prepare himself to the battle?

I. Corinthians 14.8.

Introduction

This is a book about the British Army as it is and as it might be. It is also a book about the British Army as it was. The amount of historical material presented in the following pages may surprise some readers, but to understand the British Army of today and to consider seriously the ways in which it might develop, it is important to know something of its past. The prevailing relationships between the professional Army and the person of the Sovereign, for example, can only be understood with reference to the great events and issues of Cromwell's Commonwealth, the subsequent restoration of the Monarchy, and the Glorious Revolution of 1688. We have borrowed the title *A New Model Army* from Cromwell. This does not mean that the book is intended as a set of prescriptive solutions to all the Army's problems. We do not attempt anything so ambitious as a comprehensive blueprint for reform, but we make a number of suggestions in what we hope will become an increasingly public debate.

There is a difficulty in writing about defence and particularly Army matters. For there exist – broadly – two types of reader: one is well versed in military history and strategic theory; the other may have a interest in the contemporary defence debate but does not always have much background knowledge. Because we believe that the subject of defence needs to be opened up to far wider discussion, we have set out to cater for both types and have included as much background material as we felt was needed to make the matters discussed accessible to the general reader. Accordingly, some may wish to take *Chapters 1, 2, 3,* and those pages dealing with the history of the troubles in Northern Ireland at a canter or even a gallop, as they are unlikely to find much there that is new to them. However, we hope those who are familiar with our Army and defence policy will find the arguments pursued in the rest of the book challenging.

For a long time the defence debate in Britain has been overshadowed by a dispute over the retention of various classes of nuclear weaponry. Consequently, the question of our conventional forces – particularly the Army – has received little public airing in recent years. The emergence of a number of factors seems set to change this state of affairs. Firstly, the initial success of the arms control process as manifested in the Intermediate Nuclear Forces (INF) treaty is changing the overall strategic framework within which NATO's armies operate; secondly, the commencement of the Conventional Armed Forces in Europe (CFE) talks at Vienna presages dramatic limitations in the number and types of weapon system with which our ground forces are equipped; thirdly, the costs of new defence technology are running far ahead of our ability to pay for them; and finally, Britain, together with a number of our European allies, is facing a significant drop in the number of people of suitable age for military service.

Accordingly, the time has come to think again about the sort of Army we want and need. Will the improving relations between East and West mean that we can make do with fewer soldiers, or will the phased abolition of nuclear weapons mooted in certain quarters require us to strengthen, rather than run down, our conventional forces? What changes will we need to make to our tactics to come to terms with the battlefield of the future where the kind of armoured warfare we have been preparing for during the past twenty or thirty years may have been rendered obsolete by a combination of new technology and treaty limitations?

These are some of the questions we set out to find answers to. As our book goes to press, it is clear that the pressure for change is increasing. As each month goes by there are fresh announcements of force reductions by the Warsaw Pact, and growing indications, particularly from West Germany, that NATO's traditional reliance on nuclear weapons is looking shaky.

However, the more one looks at the implications of these fundamental changes in the world situation for the British Army, the more it becomes clear that one is dealing with an institution which does not find it easy to adapt to change. This is not altogether surprising: the Army has always placed more emphasis upon tradition than innovation and it is in the nature of all-volunteer armies that a certain stasis sets in: those who are happy with the status quo are those who remain; those who do not like it either leave or will never have joined in the first place.

But it is not merely the Army's conservatism that we see as a stumbling-block to much-needed reform. We detect within the service a profound malaise that stems from the development of a value-system based not upon notions of right and wrong but upon what is expedient. For all its talk of 'standards', the military system is at heart narrowly pragmatic. Some readers may feel that we have laboured the moral theme in this book, but if the Army of a democracy does not conduct itself in an ethical manner, its usefulness as a guardian of democratic values is markedly reduced.

At the moment, the Army is broadly left to get on with its job without being subjected to much public or political scrutiny. This is not so much the fault of the generals (though they can be secretive) as that of the politicians – as Stephen Howe wrote in the *New Statesman's & Society* in January 1989:

> Labour's long internal debate on nuclear weapons has been conducted in two equally alienating styles: bitter denunciation and almost impenetrable code. The Tories have never seriously discussed defence in public. The centre parties are hopelessly divided and try to conceal the fact by undignified silence. With such a lead from the parties, it's no wonder that public attitudes on defence are in a mess. Few people know the most basic facts about the politics of defence, strategic doctrines or weapons systems. Defence is not seen as the most important issue, but it does generate powerful, irrational feelings.

A major factor in the Labour Party's last two disastrous defeats at the polls – and no doubt the reason for Neil Kinnock's recent conversion to multilateralism – was its failure to persuade people that it was willing to defend the country effectively. But there are also signs – not least the popular perception of a reduced threat – that the nuclear issue may not remain so potent an electoral weapon for the Conservatives as it has been. An opinion poll published in *The Guardian* in January 1989, only one month after Mr Gorbachev's surprise announcement of conventional force reductions, showed that just 4 per cent of those questioned believed that the Soviet Union represented a 'serious threat' to our security.

Against such a background of public opinion, it may become far more difficult to base an election campaign on a double-indemnity policy of keeping our independent nuclear deterrent while maintaining a high level of spending on conventional forces. Electoral politics apart, it is likely to become difficult even for a Conservative government to justify the permanent presence of 56,000 British troops in West Germany, especially if the citizens of that country become more insistent that we should pull out. Peter Millar, writing in *The Sunday Telegraph* in January 1989, noted that recent polls showed 75 per cent of Germans saw no serious threat from the east and that more than half wanted all nuclear weapons removed from their soil. He quotes German Admiral Elmar Schmähling (who has publicly expressed the desire for American and British troops to leave) as saying, 'The disquiet provoked by my statements is justified only because I am expressing what more and more Germans are thinking.' There seems little reason to doubt him. Currently 20 per cent of West Germans reaching the age of eligibility for conscription say they are conscientious objectors.

In Britain, where there is no compulsory national service, and where consequently any manpower problem will be even more sharply aggravated by demographic factors than it will be in Germany, the growing perception of the Army as something not as important as it once was is likely to make taxpayers increasingly reluctant either to fund the higher wages that will be needed to attract recruits or to afford the expensive technology the Army says it desperately needs. Already we spend something in the region of £19 billion annually on Defence and it has been estimated that this sum may rise to £27 billion or more by 1992.[1]

Some of the ideas in this book may appear radical, yet most of them have already been discussed quite widely (if discreetly) within the Army. The military bureaucracy, however, is adept at considering matters and then doing little about them. More than 200 'studies' have been carried out during the last ten years on subjects to do with British forces in Germany alone – but many, once written, have been merely shelved.

We accept the need for a powerful army, and a continued commitment to Europe, and have also looked beyond NATO's central front. Mindful of the fact that this country's last major experience of battle took place in an unexpected location – the Falkland Islands – and of the prevailing tensions in much of the Third World, we have examined the prospects for 'out-of-area' operations. Our capacity for mounting any kind of military intervention in distant corners of the globe is at the moment extremely limited. Is this something we should build up alone? Or,

1. See *International Defence Review*, January 1989.

as we begin to harmonize our foreign policies with those of our neighbours under the terms of the Single European Act, should we be looking towards the formation of an integrated European intervention force, following the lead of the new Franco–German Brigade?

We have also looked at the Army's role in fighting terrorism, with special reference to the past twenty years in Ulster. Unfortunately, terrorism suits modern conditions, and this essentially psychological technique is likely to become even more widespread and threatening. It is certainly the most active modern battlefield, and one upon which war is not only conceivable but all too regularly fought. Today we face terrorists armed and supported by foreign governments; tomorrow those terrorists may have chemical weapons or other no-less-terrifying instruments of war supplied by their sponsors. Indeed, existing groups could inflict far greater casualties with the resources they presently possess (as has been shown for example in Lebanon where extremist groups have been let off the political leash). Bearing the potential threat in mind we question whether the Army has been allowed to develop an effective counter-terrorist methodology – or whether the seemingly irreconcilable demands of policing and intelligence gathering have left the military hamstrung.

Moreover, we ask whether there may not be important lessons for us to learn from the successes of terrorists and guerrillas. They have shown that modern war may have become essentially an act of communication. We explore the idea that terrorists and guerrillas by their 'propaganda of the deed' have learnt to exploit the weaknesses of systems which may have grown too large or become too centralized in their command to be truly effective. Moreover, we believe that an ethically directed use of some of the techniques developed by insurgents might constitute a very powerful weapon indeed – one which could be deployed even on the central front of NATO. As Anthony Burton wrote in considering T.E. Lawrence and the development of politically motivated insurgency and psychological warfare:

> People in Western Europe – and more especially in Britain – have been accustomed to possessing military strength and technological proficiency . . . however . . . we shall become progressively weaker relative to the United States and the Soviet Union. We shall have neither the numbers nor the technology. This deficiency can only be repaired by greater attention to Lawrence's 'psychological dimension'. Hitherto we have studied guerrilla warfare primarily in order to defeat it; in our

> comparative weakness we shall have to study it yet more intensively so that we can utilise it in order to offer a potential aggressor a prospect of total opposition. In such a situation we must not 'let the metaphysical weapon rust unused' by adopting a narrowly military approach to our defence problems.'

This book inspects Britain's metaphysical arsenal and questions whether it is enough to keep our psychological weapons in mothballs or whether there is not an urgent need both to modernize them and to keep them more constantly deployed.

We do not consider the 'psychological' alone. Indeed, we are particularly concerned with the spiritual and moral dimension, for we believe that moral behaviour is, in the long term, more efficient. Some readers may feel they detect a contradiction here: on the one hand we suggest there is something to learn from the terrorists and guerrillas, on the other that morality is important. The point is that the lesson to learn from modern insurgents is not their amorality, but their flexibility and economy of effort.

Mao proved that, armed with patience, a powerful idea, and the support of the people, it is possible to beat an enemy with a greater industrial base. Yet, Mao, like Lenin, believed that the end justified the means. We believe the means must always advertise the end. The Army we would like to see built up would reflect the best values of our culture. In the dreadful eventuality of war our tactics must strive for the minimum loss of human life.

Not least of the problems the Army will face in the future will be finding a way of persuading its soldiers to fight when it is necessary for them to do so. The idea of 'Queen and Country' is irrelevant to many of today's youth. Moreover, thanks to the awesome power of modern weaponry, a soldier's mates – indeed his whole regiment – can be obliterated with a single round. As great a problem as persuading people to fight in war, is that of persuading them that they should learn to fight in peace. We may be recruiting many of the next generation of soldiers from a disillusioned and socially alienated underclass whose members are already cynical at 16. This could force the Army to pay attention to the broader development of its soldiers. If so, the Army may well find a new role as one of the major instruments of fostering the notion of responsible, participatory citizenship.

If it is to perform such an important task well, to become more flexible, dynamic and socially innovative, the Army will need to give its soldiers something they can believe in because it is inherently good.

It will be clear by now that what follows is not going to consist of unmitigated praise of the Army. There will be criticism, strong criticism in places, but it is intended to be constructive.

Finally, we should warn readers that the pace of change nationally and internationally has required constant revision of the text. It is possible that some of the factual information presented may well have become outdated before publication. Nevertheless we have tried to give our readers as broad and as up-to-date a picture as possible.

If this book prompts discussion outside and inside the Army, it will have served its purpose.

Michael Yardley
Dennis Sewell
London, June 1989.

1

The Evolution of the Modern Army

'An armed disciplined body is in its essence dangerous to liberty.'
Edmund Burke

Any exploration of the origins of the British Regular Army inevitably becomes something of an odyssey. Much has been written on the subject, and there is by no means a universal consensus of opinion about it. However, though certain points are open to debate (for example, no day can be easily selected as the one on which the Army was born), it can be said that the birth itself took place during the mid-seventeenth century, that pregnancy was difficult, and that one of the parents was the New Model Army – the force, raised by Parliament in 1645 to fight the Royalists in the English Civil Wars. The New Model Army was quite different from anything seen before in England. Companies of mercenaries and men-at-arm raised by feudal levies had often been employed by English kings, and a militia system had existed since Saxon times, but the New Model Army's relatively centralized administration, attempts at regular remuneration, systematic training, and size (initially 20,000 men, increasing to 70,000 by the end of the war), made it novel. After its decisive defeat of the Royalists, the well-organized legion went on to become, under a junta of major-generals led by Oliver Cromwell, the first national standing army in British history,[1]

1. Some might argue it was predated by the Yeomen of the Guard introduced by the Tudors, but this was a force on an altogether different scale.

and soon degenerated into an instrument of tyranny, by means of which Cromwell ruled autocratically for eight years as Lord Protector of the Commonwealth of England. It was not a happy episode in British history.

One of the the most obvious consequences of government by 'Old Ironsides' via a national, regular army was the transformation of a traditional English prejudice against soldiers and soldiery into the most active loathing of a standing army.

Thus, when Cromwell died in 1658 the standing army's future was far from certain. The regime he had built was destabilized, and the Army itself began to break up. Certain senior officers, realizing they could no longer perpetuate military rule and averse to the idea of continued dictatorship under Cromwell's son Richard, sought a return of the monarchy. They sent word to the exiled Charles Stuart, heir of Charles I. A bargain was struck. Charles agreed to meet the Army's arrears of pay and, in return, was assisted to the throne by the very organization which had defeated his father. Yet, there is a danger in over simplification.

However, under the terms of the Declaration of Breda of 1659 (the charter of the Restoration), he was also officially and immediately committed to disband the Army in response to widespread political objections to it. Despite its role in the Restoration, the standing force remained unpopular, most significantly with Parliament, the body which had originally brought it into existence, but which had turned against it as a result of Cromwell's actions. It might be thought that Charles, once safely enthroned, would have been anxious to comply with the Breda agreement and rid the nation of the remnants of the Roundhead menace. However, although he had committed himself unequivocally to disbanding the Army (a process which in fact had been started by the Army itself when the funds to pay the troops ran out), both Charles and his more martial brother, James, were anxious to avoid sharing the fate of their father. It had been the lack of a small standing force with which to repel the Scots' invasion of 1639 and the ensuing argument over the taxes needed to raise one which had brought Charles I into violent conflict with Parliament, triggered the Civil War and eventually led to the loss of his kingdom and his head. It is not altogether surprising, then, that Charles I's sons hoped for an occasion to prove to Parliament that a small regular contingent was necessary to maintain public order.

On 6 January 1661, one arose. At eleven o'clock on that Sunday evening Thomas Venner, a religious fanatic, led a march of his Fifth Monarchy Men (a group which believed that there had been four monarchies on earth and that the fifth would be the monarchy of

God, their name being taken from the forty-fourth verse of the Second Chapter of the Book of Daniel) through the City of London. As they made their way towards St Paul's Churchyard, they cried 'Live, King Jesus!', but it soon transpired that the spirit motivating them was far from holy. The frenzied mob grabbed a passer-by and interrogated him on his religious and political beliefs; the poor fellow made the mistake of affirming loyalty to his earthly monarch, as well as to the King of Heaven, and was beaten to death.

After the murder, Venner directed his gang northwards. They set up camp at Cane Wood near Highgate. But the remnants of the New Model Army were encamped within reach of London. On hearing of the disturbance, General Monk, the Commander-in-Chief, sent some troopers under the command of Sir Phillip Howard to flush out the insurrectionists but Howard's men soon withdrew, as Cane Wood was not good cavalry country. On the following Tuesday morning Venner's gang left their hides and rampaged through Aldgate and Leadenhall. After a skirmish with a troop of Monk's cavalry, they barricaded themselves in an alehouse, where they were all either killed or captured. Venner himself received multiple wounds, but was kept alive for the ritual of a formal execution.

This curious incident brought home to Parliament just how fragile public order had become. Despite the cost and political problems of a standing army, Charles II was able to argue that he required, at the very least, an expanded royal bodyguard as a guarantee of political stability. The King was also canny enough to make the occasion one of reconciliation between old enemies. For example, on 14 February 1661 at Tower Hill, only a few months after the Secretary of State had told the Commons, 'So long as the soldiery continues, there will be a perpetual trembling in the nation, for they are inconsistent with the happiness of any Kingdom',[1] Monk's men ritually laid down their weapons, to pick them up again in Royal service as the junior companion of two regiments of personal guards which Charles had brought with him from his exile. Some commentators choose this date as the birthday of the Army. Certainly, the nucleus of a new standing army, half ex-Roundhead, half Royalist, had been created, although its formal title was not the Army but the King's Guard.

During the reign of Charles II the constitutional relationship between this embryonic Army, the Crown and Parliament was deliberately kept ambiguous; it seemed that Parliament, while conceding the practical need for a standing force, did not wish to be

1. *Companion to the British Army*, David Ascoli, (Harrap, 1983).

too closely associated with it in public. Ultimate command of Guards and Garrisons lay with the King, but Parliament retained effective control, for it alone had the right to decide on numerical strength and to control their budget. In order to check the power of the King's standing army, Parliament refused to recognize it officially as such and instead encouraged the development of the militia – part-time, community-based forces which in the pre-Civil War era had been principally responsible for the nation's land-based defence.

Parliament's failure to articulate more plainly the constitutional position of the regular forces was imprudent considering the instability of the country at the time. When Charles II died in 1685 he left a force only 7,000 strong. However, the potential danger of a standing professional body without proper constitutional checks and balances soon became clear when his brother, James II, set out to expand the King's Guards into a fully fledged army. Just as Charles had used the Venner incident as a justification for a larger Royal Guard, so James used Monmouth's 1685 rebellion (when Charles II's bastard son made an attempt to seize the throne, but was decisively defeated at the battle of Sedgemoor) in the same way.

There was little doubt that James had a natural flair for matters military and was an excellent administrator, unlike his notoriously idle late brother. But James was undiplomatic, impelled – it was alleged by many – by the idea of imposing Louis XIV's brand of Catholic absolutism on a predominantly Protestant nation. When further finances for his new army which had grown to over 20,000 men were refused, James created a constitutional crisis by exercising his power to dissolve Parliament. The scene was set for another civil war.

However, war was avoided after a delegation of peers opposed to the King visited James's son-in-law, William of Orange, and offered him and his wife, Mary, the English throne. The offer was accepted, and William landed in England with a contingent of Dutch troops. The English commanders sent by James to fight him defected to the Prince of Orange, and the King was toppled in the 'glorious' and relatively bloodless Revolution of 1688.

With the arrival of William and Mary, some of the constitutional ambiguity of the past was clarified by the specific terms of the Declaration of Rights. By stipulating that 'The raising or keeping of a standing Army within the Kingdom in time of peace, unless it be with the consent of Parliament, is against the Law,' the principle was finally established that the Army, although raised in the sovereign's name, was in fact subordinate to Parliament. Amongst the many provisions of the Declaration was a clause stating that all (Protestant) Englishmen had the right to keep and bear arms for their own protection and as a check against tyranny.[1]

However, although it was unequivocal in some respects, the Declaration of Rights did not effectively define the status of the Army. In 1689, a mutinous incident occurred at Ipswich when some soldiers with Jacobite sympathies refused to embark for Holland to fight the French on William's behalf and set off home in the direction of Scotland. This prompted quick legislative action when it was discovered that the Army was regulated by no special set of laws in time of peace (indeed, despite the references to it in the Bill of Rights, it did not, in law, exist) and that there were, consequently, no legal grounds for proceeding against the mutineers. The ensuing Mutiny Act was of great significance because it made soldiers subject to a special legal code and, in so doing, established the Army on a statutory basis as an entity separate from the rest of society. Parliament had been forced to act in this case; generally it remained reluctant to become involved in military affairs. It disliked and distrusted the Army, and saw its own role as one of keeping the military in its proper place – if there had to be an army they would continually chastise it – rather than sponsor or guide its development.

Individual regiments were effectively the property of their colonels, run with little regard for those unlucky enough to be serving in their ranks. Officers had no formal training and, as they traded their commissions as commodities, bought promotion rather than earned it. (There were occasional exceptions, for example, the monarch sometimes awarded commissions to those he favoured.) Service in the ranks soon became the last refuge of the destitute and the low esteem in which the trade of soldiering was held, reinforced by parliamentary neglect, became a self-perpetuating condition that persisted into the twentieth century.

Nevertheless, it is interesting to note that, from the very outset, the Regular Army had a particularly strong association with the monarchy (to this day every soldier swears allegiance to the

1. There is a similar provision in the US Bill Of Rights which causes some controversy. Few people realize that it was preceded by and almost certainly based upon the clause in our own Declaration of Rights. It is important in both cases because it establishes the right of the individual to defend himself *in extremis* by force of arms – a fundamental right that has been greatly eroded in modern times.

sovereign rather than the government) and felt a natural antipathy towards elected politicians. All four regiments of Charles II's Guards are still with us today. The King's regiment of foot eventually evolved into the Grenadiers, and General Monk's infantry into the Coldstream Guards. The cavalry became the Lifeguards and the Blues of the now amalgamated Blues and Royals.

Britain's relationship with Europe has been another important factor underlying the development of the British Army. The political and social development of most of Europe during the last few centuries has been heavily influenced, in the case of some countries even dominated, by the presence of large standing armies. These were essential since with long, easily breachable, land frontiers, the countries of Europe could find themselves at war almost without notice.

By the second half of the nineteenth century, with conscription the norm among the large European powers, the central place of the Army in the politics of the state was confirmed. Many major political disputes involved the issue of the Army and who should control it. The one exception throughout this period was Britain, in which the Regular Army remained small and isolated from society. Although this situation was partly due to the national sentiment against large standing armies, the principal reason for its long persistence was geographical: Britain is an island. Moreover, from the Middle Ages, English domination of the British isles had never been seriously threatened by its other inhabitants. Union with Wales came in 1536, with Scotland in 1707, and with Ireland in 1801 (modified in 1922 with the creation of the Irish Free State). The main threat to Great Britain, as the British Isles were called by the middle of the eighteenth century, came from the major European powers.

Accordingly, Britain's strategy, which evolved between the fifteenth and eighteenth centuries, was fundamentally maritime. Although militia forces, and later a regular army, were maintained, the chief concern became the maintenance of a fleet capable of defeating that of any other power. Thus, the Royal Navy developed as the principal armed service, and was given priority in money and attention. Almost as a by-product of the concentration of effort and resources into the Navy, Britain acquired a trading empire with colonies and way-stations for the fleet.

These required garrisons to protect them, and infantry battalions would be despatched from England and, later, from British India, to man them. Often troops would remain in station for twenty years or more in their role as armed policemen: unlike the other armies of Europe, imperial policing became the British Army's main task.

Although crucial, maintaining the fleet and the colonial garrisons was not of itself enough to ensure Britain's long-term security. Britain depended for her survival and growing prosperity on her invulnerability as an island, but she could never allow any other country to become so powerful as to dominate Europe, and so develop the resources to challenge the Royal Navy. Britain therefore pursued a policy of identifying the strongest power and opposing it by supporting coalitions of rival states with money and troops. Thus, Spain was opposed in the sixteenth century, France in the seventeenth, eighteenth and early nineteenth, and Germany in the nineteenth and twentieth centuries.

As long as Britain was safe from invasion the British could afford to engage in protracted war with every confidence in winning. The regiments of an army could be created and disbanded as necessary around a nucleus of permanent troops, and the Army needed to be no larger than was necessary to demonstrate Britain's commitment to her allies. This was the pattern of wars from the start of the War of the Spanish Succession (1702–14) to the end of the Revolutionary and Napoleonic Wars (1789–1815). During this period the Army was occasionally expanded on a large scale to 100,000 men – during the Seven Years War (1756–63) and at the height of the Napoleonic Wars to a quarter of a million – but it was always rapidly run down with the coming of peace.

The Regular Army, therefore, evolved as a disparate group of individual regiments (of one or two battalions), used to long service in isolated locations. After the Napoleonic Wars (1800–15) it consisted of about eighty battalions, a total strength of about 70,000 men.[1] By the middle of the nineteenth century 80 per cent of the

1. These figures do not however include the forces of the East India Company. Until the Indian Mutiny in 1857 there were both British regular troops and the very substantial forces of the East India Company serving in the Indian sub-continent. The Mutiny brought pressure for change, and the company forces of European origin were absorbed into the British Regular Army and the native troops and their European officers – now granted Queen's Commissions via the Viceroy – brought under the control of the Crown in India though they remained in three separate 'armies', those of Bengal, Madras and Bombay. Service of any sort in India was looked down upon by officers based at home; when transferred to India, British battalions often underwent a complete change of officers. With a few exceptions, those with money and ambitions stayed at home. Service in India did, however, offer those officers who could not afford regimental life at home the opportunity for an exciting life without the need for a private income. In 1902 there was a major reorganization and the armies of Madras, Bengal and Bombay were brought together into a single 'Indian Army'.

Regular Army was stationed overseas, and imperial policing, coupled with occasional internal policing, completely dominated its development.

It is not altogether surprising, therefore, that the Crimean War found the Army wanting. Communication and control had become confused, for example whilst cavalry and infantry came under the control of the Commander-in-Chief (except those in India), artillery and engineers came under the Master-General of Ordnance, who was also responsible for the supply of weapons and ammunition. Since incumbents of the latter office guarded their empires as jealously as did commanders-in-chief theirs, this did little for military efficiency. Arcane customs and tangled structures clogged the Army at every level.

If inter-arms communication was bad, inter-service communication was worse: the Army and the Navy were often not even on speaking terms. Luckily, save for the Crimean War, the British Army was not called to commit troops to a major European conflict between 1815 and 1914. The Crimean fiasco did at least show up some of the Army's weaknesses such as its medieval tactics, poor officer training, incompetent logistics supply, almost non-existent medical facilities and the lack of inter-service co-operation. Luckily the war did not threaten the survival of the nation. A new style of press coverage was one of the reasons for these shortcomings coming to light.[1]

Although there was confusion, mismanagement and an innate conservatism in the higher echelons of the Army, the period from Waterloo (1815) to the Great Exhibition of 1851 was a dynamic and prosperous phase for the British Empire.

By 1845 the United Kingdom, confirmed after the decisive victory against France as the dominant world power, produced 25 per cent of the world's annual economic output. This feat was achieved partly because Britain was isolated from war, and so had minimal defence costs, and partly because its industrial revolution began some fifty years before those of the rest of Europe.

It was, in many respects, a golden age for Britain. But towards the end of the century, technological developments in warfare eroded the credibility of the maritime defence strategy on which her

1. William Howard Russell who covered the Crimea for *The Times* is often referred to as the first modern war correspondent. The impact of his reports was very great, arguably causing the fall of the government. Experience of the press in the Crimea and later in the South African campaign explains the enormous efforts made to keep the British press away from the front line in 1914.

prosperity was based. Using the new technology of railways for rapid mobilization, and breech-loading rifles for firepower, the state of Prussia was able to upset the balance of power in Europe by defeating other states so rapidly that Britain, with her ineffective Army, was unable to respond effectively. The defeat of Austria in six weeks in 1866 and the defeat of France in two months in 1870 established Prussia as the centre of a new, unified German Empire, and the most serious challenger for the domination of Europe to emerge since Napoleon's France. Britain had been forced to watch helplessly as this happened because, having no large standing army, she had no option of military intervention. She had stopped Bonaparte, but she could not stop Bismarck.

The proven effectiveness of modern armies, coupled with a continuing problem in recruiting the troops for imperial policing, led to a series of reforms of the British Army by the Liberal Secretary of State for War and former officer, Edward Cardwell, in 1870–1. These were continued by his successor but one, Hugh Childers from 1880–2. The structure of the infantry regiments was rationalized so that each had two regular battalions, one at home and one stationed abroad. The reorganized regiments of foot were simultaneously linked by name to specific counties representative of their main catchment areas, with local militia and volunteer units affiliated as supplementary battalions. New sub-districts were created, each with a regimental depot which served as administrative headquarters, recruit training centres and bases for the militia.

Before Cardwell's reforms, the militia and volunteers had come completely under the control of the county Lords-Lieutenant overseen by the Home Office. The Regular Army establishment had fought from the early nineteenth century to bring the militia under their own control, finally achieving this goal not so much because of the persistence of their lobby, but because Cardwell thought it essential that militia, volunteers and regulars should be brought closer together if a large and efficient force were to be fielded quickly in time of war.

As well as establishing the policy of territorialization, Cardwell's reforms gave Canada, Australia and New Zealand responsibility for their own defence, improved equipment, shortened service in the ranks, and developed the Regular Reserve made up of former short-service regulars (whose terms of service were changed to 6 years with the colours and 6 with the reserve). Against extraordinary opposition from the Army, Cardwell also managed to achieve the abolition of purchase.[1]

Taken together these changes laid the framework for the modern Army, at least in respect of the infantry.

Even after the Franco–Prussian War (1870–1871) many people of influence in Britain continued to regard France as the dominant European power and believed it was in Britain's interests to remain aloof from Europe. However, following the exposure of British weakness in the Second Boer War of 1899–1902, in which the nation had felt diplomatically isolated and militarily impotent (despite a temporary doubling in size of the Army), efforts were made to end the 'glorious isolation' from European affairs which had characterized the nineteenth century. Britain entered into a series of diplomatic agreements (amongst them the *Entente Cordiale*) whose practical effect was to commit her to the French side in the First World War.

Another important consequence of the Boer War, reinforced by the perception of the possibility that Britain might become embroiled in a continental war, was a renewed impetus towards military reform. A number of official commissions were set up in the first years of the new century, and during the period 1904–8 many of the eccentricities and inefficiencies of the British High Command (which had so hampered the South African expedition and which Cardwell's reforms had not addressed) were done away with. One of the most important innovations was the creation of a co-ordinated General Staff system copied from the Prussian model. The post of commander-in-chief was abolished and replaced with a new Army Council with seven members.

When the Liberals came into power in the winter of 1905, Richard Haldane was appointed Secretary of State for War. His brief was to continue reform and to reduce military expenditure. He quickly formulated a new plan for the Army. It created separate directors for operations, staff duties, and training; military organization was standardized throughout the Empire; and manuals of staff procedures and responsibilites were issued. Haldane also made specific

1. The argument advanced by those in favour of retaining purchase was that the system ensured officers had a commitment to the established social and political order. Cardwell won the day but not without the Treasury having to spend £6 million in compensation. The officers would accept nothing less than the market rate, which was over £1,000 for an ensign's commission in the Guards, and as much as £10,000 for a lieutenant-colonelcy. These were huge sums at a time when common soldiers often had less than a shilling a day to spend.

and far-sighted preparations for war. These included – after his discovery that the Army as it stood would take two months to get 80,000 men to France – the creation of an Expeditionary Force of 7 divisions (6 of infantry and 1 of cavalry) each with its own support services, which together could be mobilized within 12 days. He reorganized the volunteers and Yeomanry into a new Territorial Force of 14 divisions of infantry and 14 brigades of cavalry) and transformed the old militia into the Special Reserve whose function would be to reinforce the Expeditionary Force in time of war.[1]

To ensure a ready supply of officers for his new Army and to increase its contact with the wider world, Haldane set up the Officer Training Corps (which still operates at many public schools and universities). To make command and control of infantry regiments more effective, he introduced a new structure whereby the eight-company battalion which had been the norm throughout the nineteenth century was replaced by a streamlined organization of four enlarged companies, each commanded by a senior captain or a major. By any standards Haldane's achievement was enormous. Britain,the dominant naval power, had acquired a formidable Army only a few years after the South African *débâcle*, and at decreased cost – proof that it is not always money which is at the root of defence problems.

When the assassination of the Archduke Franz Ferdinand at Sarajevo sparked off the 'war to end all wars', Britain was relatively well prepared. Apart from significant numbers of trained reservists, about a quarter of a million regular troops were ready for action. The Expeditionary Force itself, numbering about 120,000 men, was an exceptional formation, highly trained and boasting excellent morale. However, it would soon suffer very heavy casualties.

Nevertheless, for the first two years of the war there was no shortage of replacements, as hundreds of thousands of ordinary citizens came forward to join up. In spite of the number of casualties on the Western Front, it was not necessary to introduce conscription in Britain until January 1916.

By the end of the war the British Army consisted of 71 divisions (excluding imperial contingents amounting to another 3½ million

1. The Special Reserve should not be confused with the Regular Reserve. The latter, which still exists, is not an active formation but a list of those former regulars with a contractual obligation to return to regular units in time of war. Haldane's Territorial Force and Special Reserve were active groups which coexisted as part-time alternatives to Regular Army service. The function of the Special Reserve was to reinforce Regular Army regiments in war; the Territorial Force mustered its own regiments.

men). Altogether 5 million British troops served in the war, 1 million of them at any one time (after early 1916) on the Western Front – the only occasion in British history when such a huge Army has been created.

Britain had taken a leading role – the leading role in 1914 and 1917 – in confronting and defeating the Army of the major European land power of the day. For Britain, the war was like no other. It was a depersonalized conflict in which individual merit or military skill paled into irrelevance before the awesome power of new technologies which brought death that was sudden, arbitrary and unavoidable. It was a war in which proud but bewildered generals fell back upon tactical rigidity when their 'modern' ideas failed; a static war (after the relative mobility of operations in the opening months ended in the creation of trench-lines as equally matched contingents from both sides met each other) where the advantage was usually with the defence, and in which the combat aeroplane, the tank and chemical munitions made their debut, and in which 'scientifically' formulated principles for the manipulation of information were developed. It was a total war in which, for the first time, much of a nation's private industry was moblized towards the single aim of victory, and airships attacked concentrated civilian targets. Fundamentally, it was a war of attrition where being a winner was less important than not being a loser.

It was also a war in which the British Army was greatly changed, if only for the duration of hostilities. Because of the scale of the conflict, divisions rather than regiments often became the basic tactical unit, and new specialist corps of technical specialists – such as machine-gunners, cyclists, aviators and tank operators – were set up. It was a war in which artillery in particular took on a new importance, since even limited offence was impossible without it; and in which effective battlefield communication became extremely difficult.[1]

Perhaps the most important lesson that Britain learnt from its eventual victory was that the cost was too high. Nearly a million British troops were killed in action, a horrifying proportion of the young male population (16.2 per cent of men between the ages of 20 and 24). At the end of the war Britain had confirmed its rule over an empire larger than at any time in her history, and the prospect of an

1. Ian Hogg makes the interesting observation that this made the First World War unique: in the past verbal communication had usually been possible, in the future radio communication would be perfected. *The British Army in the 20th Century*, Ian Hogg, chapter 4 (Ian Allen, 1985).

early return to the continent seemed remote. Conscription was abandoned as the Army returned to its pre-war job, policing the Empire, with its standing strength reduced to something just below its level in 1914. It was not long before the government announced the Ten-Year Rule, later subject to multiple extensions, by which no plans would be made in preparation for war in the absence of an apparent threat.

Although the presence of a war memorial in every town and village was indicative of the closer relationship between Army and people that had been forged on the anvil of total war, the politicians during the 1920s and 1930s utterly neglected the nation's land forces. The exciting, new Royal Air Force, which had been formed in 1918, and the Royal Navy were treated better (although they still suffered as a result of the prevailing anti-war sentiment and economic crisis).

One of the many mistakes made in this period was the failure to develop the tank. Some visionaries like General Fuller and Basil Liddell Hart wrote in the 1920s of a new sort of war – later to be called blitzkrieg – in which tanks would not act in support of infantry, but as a fighting force in their own right, used to strike deeply and very rapidly into the enemy lines. Though the Army retained its tank corps, it failed to give it an adequate tool for its job. Meanwhile, the fashionable argument in the thirties, ironically also championed by Liddell Hart,[1] was that in any future war Britain should rely principally on the French Army for ground troops while itself supplying air- and sea-power to the Alliance. The acceptance of this line of thought, the effects of the memory of Flanders, and the harsh economic circumstances of the Depression go some way to explaining the extraordinary weakness of the British Army at the outbreak of the Second World War.

Only in the spring of 1939 did Chamberlain's government agree to set about re-equipping and enlarging the British Army. Conscription was reintroduced in May, four months before the outbreak of war, but initially only five divisions were sent to France; and, although Britain had invented the tank in the First World War and

1. The paradox is partly explained because Liddell Hart changed his mind about tank warfare. According to Sir Michael Howard, writing in *The Spectator* on 25th February 1989, 'By 1939 he was arguing that the growing power of the defensive had made blitzkrieg impossible; that mobility favoured the defence more than it did the attack and that the anti-tank gun was now an effective counter to the tank. Any offensive was likely to be disastrous. In consequence it would not only be unnecessary but unwise to commit a British army to the Continent in support of the French.'

experimented with them during the 1920s and 1930s, the British Army had no fully equipped armoured divisions at the outset of the war and no adequate tank in production. The Army, still without a proper doctrine for tank warfare, went to war with three types of tank: cruisers, for independent roaming around the battlefield, light reconnaisance machines, and those built especially for acting in support of infantry. As Ian Hogg notes, 'these divisions persisted for most of the war years, wasting untold hours of design and manufacturing effort, when every other combatant had given up such fine distinctions and had developed what might be called 'general purpose tanks'.[1]

More positively, the Army began to re-equip and organize its infantry for a mechanized role. The change of philosophy found practical expression in the introduction of a new lightweight machine-gun, the Bren, to be used by individual infantry sections (sub-units of the platoon) and a small tracked vehicle to carry it and them across the fast-moving battlefield. The Bren-Gun Carrier was arguably the first British armoured personnel carrier. As a result of these technical developments, ordinary soldiers began to find themselves with more responsibility, a trend continued to this day.

In September 1939, the British government decided to spend a year creating an Army of 60 divisions. The idea was to take the offensive together with the French some time in late 1940 or early 1941. Unfortunately, the collapse of France in May and June 1940 ruined the plan. It also removed any land front on which Britain might have deployed the Army (except for the relatively minor theatre of North Africa). Instead, fearing a repetition of the casualties of the First World War, the government confirmed its acceptance of the principle that the Navy and Air Force should become the main focus of effort.

Although more than 3 million Britons had donned khaki uniforms by 1945, there were only 12 divisions in north-west Europe, 4 in Italy and 2 in Burma, and most of them were perpetually short of troops.[2] Moreover, the British Army frequently came off worse when it actually engaged the enemy. This, however, was not so much because of a deficiency in numbers (indeed it was often the Germans who were outnumbered on the battlefield), but more a

1 . *The British Army in the 20th Century,* Ian Hogg, chapter 5, p. 81. (Ian Allen, 1985).
2 . This is currently an area of some debate amongst historians, but it appears that two things are agreed: firstly that proportionately more troops were held back than in the First World War, and secondly, that the 'tail-to-teeth' ratio was also much higher than in that war, i.e. more resources were tied up in support activities.

consequence of a professionally minded enemy having learnt to integrate its armour with infantry and artillery. Although the Allies gradually learnt the lesson, they never achieved the same degree of inter-arms co-operation with the possible exceptions of the Soviets and Patton's 3rd US Army.

As a result of the policy of limited land-force commitment, British casualties were far lower than they had been in the First World War (about 520,000 in total, with approximately half that number killed). However, this inability or unwillingness to commit armies to the Continent on the scale of those of the First World War had some negative consequences. It gave the Americans, with over 60 divisions in northern Europe in 1945, the upper hand in deciding strategy and, it may even be argued, facilitated the Soviet occupation of eastern Europe. This is not to say that British forces did not play an important role; of course they did. Moreover, alone amongst the Allies, Britain endured the whole war and, the Army, though far smaller than in the First World War, was again principally an army of citizens, rather than professionals. To an even greater extent than in the First World War traditional regimental organization gave way to larger formations which better matched the new operational requirements.

It is estimated that 50 million people died in the Second World War – three times as many as in the First World War. About 15 million were military casualties and 35 million civilian. It also transformed political conditions in Europe partly because of the bankruptcy of so many of the participants: the war was five times more costly than the 1914–18 conflict. The emergence of the two superpowers of the USA and USSR rendered the problem of the old balance of power in Europe irrelevant. The conflict in Korea against an aggressive Communist state brought the point home, and introduced a new power into the equation – Mao's China. With the Suez *débâcle* of 1956 the decline in Britain's position as a major world power became inescapable.

During the mid-to-late 1940s, the threat of an evermore powerful Soviet Union, problems in India, Palestine and other parts of the Empire led Britain to retain conscription in peacetime. Although the greatest commitment in numbers was still to imperial policing, British troops fought in a conventional war in Korea and the new strategic situation brought Britain into the NATO alliance in 1949, with a pledge to maintain a large army on the European mainland. The existence of nuclear weapons was another factor to be taken into account, and the question of whether or not it was even possible to fight a conventional war in Europe again became debatable. The rapid introduction of nuclear weapons by the US and later the UK during this period was not just a result of the demonstration of their destructive power at Hiroshima and Nagasaki in 1945, or of mere technological momentum. As well as being an international status symbol, they were seen as a cheaper alternative to conventional forces which would allow national resources to be directed away from the military. Their introduction further separated the professional military establishment which would use them from the nation at large.

The radical change in British fortunes and strategy after 1946 did not produce an equivalent reform of the Army. During and immediately after the war, it appeared that some of its social values might be changing, but when conscription ceased in 1963, the Army, still smarting from post-war attempts to reform its structure and its regiments, returned to an all-regular force which retained many of its pre-war prejudices.

The Army of the 1960s and early 1970s found itself uncomfortably out of step with the society from which it was drawn. Despite its involvement in the Ulster crisis from 1969, it became the victim of a series of cost-cutting exercises designed to release funds for social programmes and industrial development. This situation resulted in a steady lowering of morale which came to a head with the pay crisis of the late 1970s.

During this period the Army's commitment to NATO superseded all other considerations. The British Army of the Rhine (BAOR) took the greater part of any available resources, and training for a European war took precedence even over fighting the counter-insurgency campaign in Northern Ireland. So that, when in 1982 the Army, rather to its surprise, found itself fighting in the South Atlantic, many were concerned that soldiers who had been prepared only for the European battlefield might not fight well in a completely different tactical environment. But though those units that had been trained for mechanized warfare performed markedly less well than the Royal Marines and the Paras, the Falklands War proved that there was enough flexibility in the system to cope with unexpected demands.

Nevertheless, the fact that we were able to defeat a 3rd division force in 1982 should not be overstressed. The Army of the 1980s is not a product of sustained, rational planning. Rather it has developed in a higgeldy-piggeldy fashion – often in reaction to, rather than in anticipation of, the wars it has been called upon to fight.

Although there have been occasional reforms during the intervals between wars, more usually the Army's condition in peacetime has been one of neglect.

2

The Green Machine

'Large organization is loose organization.
Nay; it would be almost as true to say that
organization is always disorganization.'
G. K. Chesterton

Today's Army is made up of about a quarter of a million men and women, of whom 157,000 are regulars; the rest are divided between the Territorial Army (TA), the Home Service Force (HSF) numbering only 3,000[1]and the Ulster Defence Regiment (UDR) of whom there are almost 6,500. It is difficult to discuss how the Army works, what its function is or how it may change over the next decades, without understanding a little of its organization and that of the Ministry of Defence (MoD), together with some of the political and legal controls to which both are subject.

The traditional wariness of the British towards standing armies in peacetime still finds its expression in the close and detailed political control exercised over the armed services, although the fears of contemporary politicians are directed rather more at the danger of defence expenditure running out of control than the possibility that the armed forces might overthrow the prevailing constitutional arrangements.

The precise mechanisms for the political control of the armed forces are complex. The Army used to have its own headquarters at the War Office in London, but in 1963 this was combined with the Admiralty and the Air Ministry into the tri-service Ministry of Defence, under a single Secretary of State for Defence, who exercises political responsibility for the Army and the other two

1. Though it is useful to make a distinction, the Home Service Force is officially part of the Territorial Army.

services. Standing above the MoD and its Secretary of State are the Prime Minister and the Cabinet where many vital defence policy decisions are made. Parliament exercises its influence by debating the defence estimates annually, allotting one day to a special Army debate and monitoring the activities of the MoD in the Commons Select Committee on Defence.

The armed forces are also subject to specific legal controls. The modern version of the Mutiny Act, which originally established a standing army in law, is known as the Army Act, 1955. This must be confirmed every five years by Parliament (although it is a mere formality, there being no discussion or divisions). Common law is also important, giving the Crown the prerogative to use armed force to repel attack on the kingdom in cases of invasion, insurrection or riot.

In addition to our treaty obligations which affect the peace- and wartime deployment of our troops abroad, there are a number of Acts (notably the Emergency Powers Act, 1920 and the Emergency Powers Act, 1964) governing any internal use of the armed forces, either in natural emergencies (Military Aid to the Civil Community); in cases of strikes and other events which might threaten the supply of essentials of life (Military Aid to the Civil Ministries); and in cases where peace and public order are threatened, such as in Ulster since 1969 or during the Iranian Embassy siege in London in the spring of 1980 (Military Aid to the Civil Power).

The Army Board is the committee at the head of the Army Department at the MoD. It is the body which is officially responsible for running the Army's affairs. There are separate departments and boards for the other two services and a defence procurement executive common to all services. The Army Board's members include the Armed Forces Minister and the Minister of State for Defence Procurement as well as several senior civil servants (a Second Permanent Under-Secretary, the Controller Research and Development, and the Deputy Under-Secretary (Army)). In addition to the officially designated bureaucrats and politicians there are five very senior soldiers: the Chief of the General Staff (CGS) – the professional head of the Army, the Assistant Chief of the General Staff (ACGS), the Adjutant-General (AG), the Quartermaster-General (QMG), and the Master-General of Ordnance (MGO). However, the day-to-day management of the Army is delegated to a smaller Executive Committee of the board made up of its Army officer contingent and the Second Permanent Under-Secretary.

Because each service is still administered by its individual service department, the old clearly defined 'principalities' and the jealousies that go with them have not yet disappeared. Over the years many attempts have been made to reconcile the differences between the three services; although they do now talk to one another, each still has its own priorities, its own agenda and its own particular outlook. Because of these strong inter-service rivalries, the life of a member of the General Staff is bedevilled by office politics and department intrigues. Consequently, there have been calls to simplify the system further by dismantling the individual service departments altogether and uniting all functions within the Defence Staff. This may well be on the agenda in the next few years.

The real business of soldiering is conducted away from the MoD in the garrisons and the camps. There the Army divides itself into 'arms' (those who expect to be involved in combat), and 'services' (which are responsible for providing specialist skills and logistics support). For example, the Infantry, Cavalry, Artillery, the Royal Signals and the Royal Engineers are counted among the arms, while the Royal Army Ordnance Corps and the Royal Electrical and Mechanical Engineers are services. It is beyond the scope of this book to examine each of the branches of the Army in detail, but it is worth looking in outline at the organization of some of the major arms.

The Royal Armoured Corps (RAC) consists of 17 regular and 5 territorial regiments. (The two regiments of Household Cavalry which, bar their ceremonial duties, have a similar role to Royal Armoured Corps regiments, are not technically part of the RAC.) The majority of the regiments in the RAC are historic cavalry regiments which have names like the 9th/12th Lancers, the Queen's Dragoon Guards and the 13th/18th Hussars. The remainder are the four Royal Tank Regiments which evolved out of the First World War Machine-Gun Corps. Of the 19 regular armoured regiments, 15 are roled as heavy armour, equipped with main battle tanks, and 4 as 'recce' regiments with fast, ultra-light aluminium-armoured vehicles. Regiments are periodically re-roled, exchanging their main battle tanks for recce vehicles or vice versa.

The RAC has its main centre at Bovington in Dorset and another major training facility at Catterick in Yorkshire, troops at Wimbish near Saffron Walden in Essex, and at Tidworth in Wiltshire. As armour is best suited to the defence of NATO's central front, most of the RAC is in Germany, though there are two armoured recce squadrons in Cyprus: one serving as part of the UN peace-keeping force, the other tasked to protect the two British Sovereign Bases (parts of the island which remained under the Crown when the rest of Cyprus was granted its independence).

All cavalry regiments are made up of squadrons: a headquarters squadron and a number of 'sabre' squadrons (the actual fighting squadrons armed with tanks or armoured recce vehicles). The regiment is commanded by a lieutenant-colonel (known as 'the Colonel') and the squadrons by majors (known as squadron leaders, though this is an appointment and not a rank, as it is in the Royal Air Force). Squadrons are differentiated from one another by letters (A, B, C, etc.) and are, in turn, subdivided into troops, which are numbered. The private soldiers are called troopers, and if you were to ask one about his job, he might say something like, 'I'm in 2nd Troop, B Squadron, 17th/21st Lancers.' The number of soldiers serving with any regiment varies slightly according to role and other circumstances, but a rough guide would be 400–500 men per regiment, 100 per squadron and 15 per troop. As far as its heavy armoured regiments are concerned, there are two types, the type 57, with 57 tanks in four squadrons, and the type 45, with 45 tanks in three squadrons.

There is a completely different terminology in the Infantry. The Infantry has 38 infantry regiments. Within these there are 55 regular battalions and 41 Territorial Army battalions. It is the battalion that lives together (and, when necessary, fights together) and approximates to the cavalry regiment. Each regiment except the Paras, the Ghurkas and the SAS is placed under one of six administrative divisions (Guards, Scottish, Queen's King's, Prince of Wales' and Light), with each infantry division comprising 6–9 regular battalions. The infantry divisions are not the same as the divisions which are fighting units, but are exclusively administrative entities, an attempt to share the overheads of training establishments between a number of battalions. Thus, each infantry division maintains a depot, the point of intake for new recruits.

The battalion is the focus of regimental soldiering for the infantryman. A standard, non-mechanized British Army Infantry Battalion numbers about 650 soldiers ranging in rank from lieutenant-colonel to private. It is organized as follows:

a) At the most basic level there is a *'fire team'* of four soldiers commanded by a lance corporal.

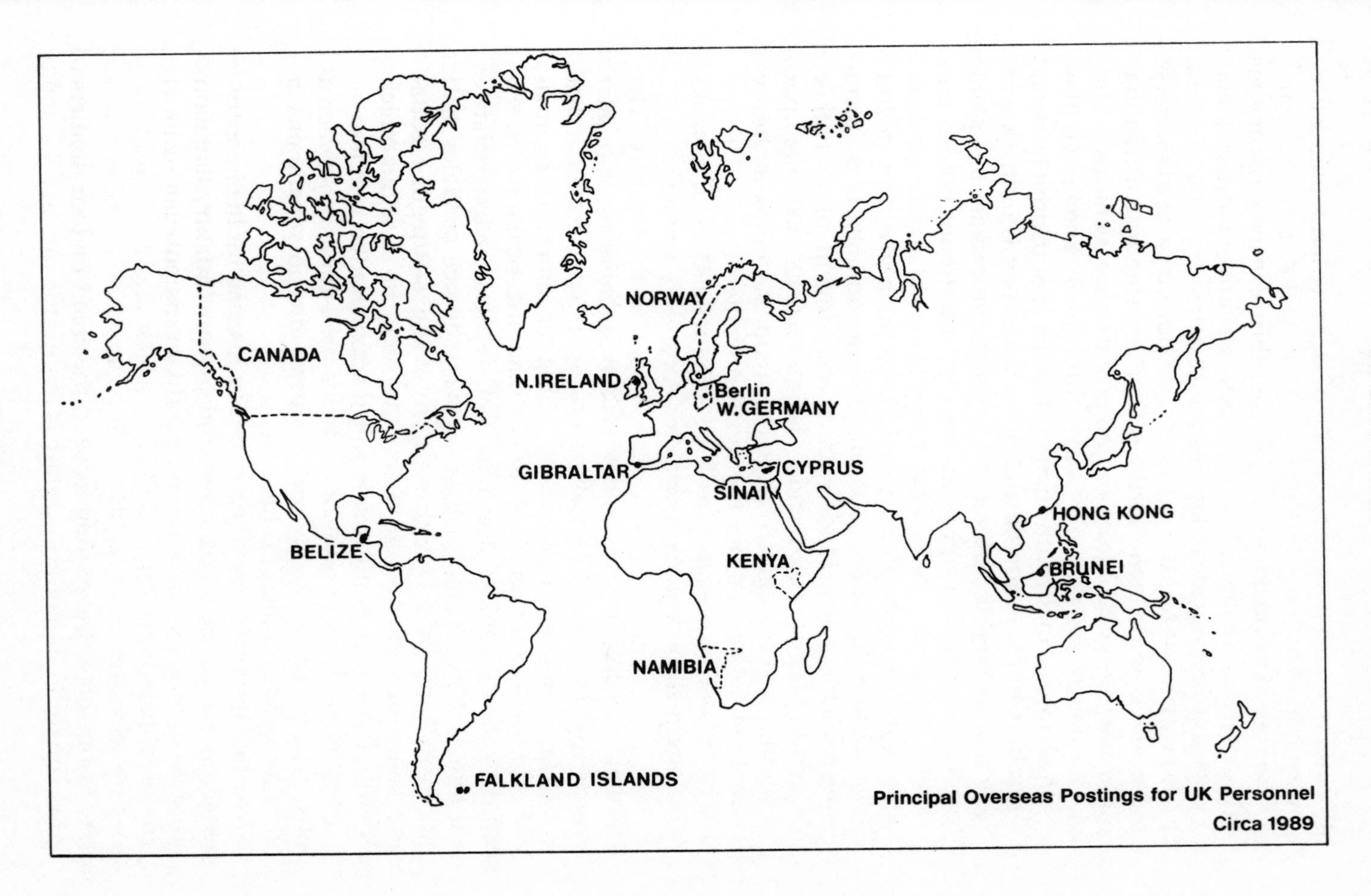

Principal Overseas Postings for UK Personnel
Circa 1989

b) Two fire teams make up a *section* of eight men commanded by a corporal.
c) Three sections make up the *platoon*, this is usually commanded by a second lieutenant or lieutenant with the help of a platoon sergeant. (Sometimes platoons are commanded by a sergeant.)
d) Three platoons form a *company* which has a captain as second-in-command and a major as the officer commanding. It also has a company sergeant major and a small headquarters staff.
e) An infantry *battalion* may have three or four rifle companies which are armed with standard rifles and medium or light machine-guns. In addition there is a fire support company which contains a mortar platoon, an anti-tank guided missile platoon and a reconaissance platoon. Finally, there is a battalion headquarters company which comprises a signals (communications) platoon, a supply platoon (called the quarter-master platoon), the motor transport platoon, the assault pioneer platoon (responsible for field defence works, laying mines, etc.), a catering platoon, pay section, clerical section (called the orderly room), Provost (regimental police section), medical section and light aid detachment for the repair of vehicles.
f) The whole organization will be commanded by a lieutenant-colonel with a senior major as his second-in-command.

Other persons of importance within a battalion will be the quarter-master – the officer, always commissioned from the ranks, in charge of stores in peace and bringing up rations to the front in war; the padre; the medical officer; and the families officer – a retired officer, usually a major, with special responsibility for accommodation; the adjutant, a captain who acts partly as a staff-officer assisting the CO and is also in overall charge of discipline; and last, but certainly not least, the regimental sergeant major (RSM) – the senior non-commissioned officer in the battalion.

There is a variety of nomenclature for the ordinary soldier in the infantry: he may be a rifleman, a guardsman, a private or some other name, depending on his unit.

Another important distinction in the infantry is between those battalions which are mechanized and those which are not. Mechanized infantry are equipped with lightly armoured vehicles such as armoured personnel carriers (APCs) which allow foot-soldiers to keep up with armour in highly mobile operations and which decant their troops on to the ground close to the area in which they are to fight. The trend in modern warfare is to give the infantry the ability to fight from vehicles known as armoured fighting vehicles (AFVs), which are powerful pieces of equipment, bristling with cannon, machine-guns and even, in the US Army, small missiles. All infantry battalions stationed in Germany are mechanized, whilst those in the UK are equipped with lorries, or wheeled armoured personnel carriers called Saxons.

This distinction between mechanized and non- or partially mechanized mirrors the traditional split between light and heavy infantry. However, any battalion except the Parachute Regiment may now be given a mechanized 'heavy' role. Even men of the Royal Greenjackets, traditionally lightly armed skirmishers of the historic 'rifle regiments', can find themselves in APCs.

The other arms and services which do not have a regimental system along the lines of the cavalry and infantry are known as corps. They have borrowed some elements of regimental style to foster a sense of family in their organizations, but the nature of their work as specialists often means that they do not live and work as a unit. For instance, each cavalry regiment has a complement of the Royal Electrical and Mechanical Engineers (REME) to look after its vehicles, but they will be too few in number to set up separate living or social arrangements. There will also be members of various small corps to look after pay, catering, health, etc. attached to any cavalry or infantry unit.

The Royal Artillery calls itself a regiment but is really a corps divided up into a number of regiments which themselves are made up of batteries. The 'Gunners' have a language and habits of their own, much of which is entirely incomprehensible even to other serving solders. As the old Gunner saying has it: 'The infantry don't understand their orders, the cavalry ignore them . . . the artillery make their own arrangements.' They are one of the most technically sophisticated arms, and probably the first to make a reality of the notion of the computerized battlefield. As a result, they recruit some of the brightest soldiers which, bearing in mind that they are the only branch of the Army to be equipped with nuclear weapons, may be cause for some comfort.

Soldiers in all regiments or corps can be divided into three strata: officers, non-commissioned officers (NCOs) and private soldiers. Officers hold the Queen's Commission, all (with the exception of Quarter-master Commissioned Officers) attend Sandhurst and are in charge. Their ranks run from second lieutenant (who together with lieutenants are called subalterns) to field marshal, an essentially honorary rank given for life to the Chief of the Defence Staff. NCOs range from lance-corporal through corporal, sergeant, staff sergeant, company (or squadron) sergeant-major to regimental sergeant-major (who may also be called warrant officer first class).

The terms of service for officers and men are radically different. Officers may hold regular, short-service or TA commissions. The short-service officer signs up for three years, and can extend this for a few years thereafter, whilst the regular has the chance of a career that will last until the age of 55. In the ranks, however, there is little need for older soldiers and the retiring age is 40. In practice, many of those who sign on at 18 leave after three years, though those who have been given junior NCO rank will often stay for six or nine years. The Army is, consequently, a more youthful organization than most, with the overwhelming majority of its members under the age of 32.

So far we have described the Army in administrative or social terms; now we need to examine the ways in which the 'building blocks' of regiments and battalions are combined for operations. Modern warfare requires soldiers on the battlefield to be arranged in 'mixed-arm' groupings so that commanders can co-ordinate the use of infantry, armour, artillery and, often, air-power to the best tactical effect. How this is done will depend on the task that the commander has been asked to carry out: fighting the Soviets in Europe, for instance, would impose very different requirements from patrolling the streets of Belfast or Derry. In addition, fashions in military thinking, like any fashions, are ephemeral: the history of the Army can truly be said to be a history of reorganizations.

One subject of several reorganizations has been the brigade. This has traditionally been the basic mixed-arm formation in the British Army and has consisted of a brigade headquarters which commands infantry, armour and artillery, signals, support and logistics elements. It is a flexible arrangement which allows for variation in the proportion of armour to infantry, according to role. In 1977, as part of the Army's response to the cost-cutting 1975 Defence Review, all brigade headquarters were closed down. The theory current at the time was that a division (a grouping of two or more brigades with additional support) could be commanded from the top as a single unit. This arrangement was not effective and the brigade was soon re-invented under another name, the field force. Finally, in 1982, the Army openly recognized its mistake and the brigade was formally restored. Although there is constant tinkering with the system and formations seem forever to be being phased in or out, at the last count there were 26 brigades in the British Army.

One of them, 1st Infantry Brigade at Tidworth, forms the UK Mobile Force. In time of war this would be sent to Denmark on requisitioned Danish car ferries to guard NATO's Baltic approaches. Presently numbering about 10,000 men, on mobilization it would be strengthened to around 15,000 men with a Territorial Army component, making it only slightly smaller than a typical division in Germany. Britain's strategic reserve is the 5th Airborne Brigade which includes two battalions of the Parachute Regiment and a battalion of Gurkhas. This is the core of Britain's 'out of area' capability, supposedly able to take on tasks anywhere in the world, but we will argue later that this force is inadequate even when acting together with 3rd Commando Brigade of the Royal Marines (with which it sometimes trains, building upon a close relationship established in the Falklands conflict).

The UK also has a commitment to the multinational Allied Command Europe Mobile Force (AMF). The UK supplies this brigade-sized unit with an infantry battalion, a logistic support battalion, four Puma helicopters and supporting arms and services: in all about 2,300 personnel. The AMF is specially equipped for arctic conditions as it is thought its deployment in the northern regions is most likely. However, it is ready to go anywhere. In the event of an attack, or the threat of an attack on one NATO country, each of the others would send its component of the AMF to the point of danger so that forces of all nations may become early casualties of the fighting. Its value would be more political – as a symbol of the unity of NATO – than military.

Within the brigade, formations such as the battlegroup (an infantry battalion with a squadron of tanks), or the combat team (an infantry company with a troop of tanks) can rapidly be constituted on an *ad hoc* basis and the Army spends much of its time on exercise developing co-operation at this level.

In terms of training, and to a certain extent in terms of equipment, the Army may be divided into two groups: those whose role in war is to help defend Europe as part of Britain's NATO commitment, and the rest, who may be preparing for or already performing a variety of tasks such as defending the UK, serving overseas in Belize, Brunei, Gibraltar, Hong Kong, Cyprus or the Falklands, helping to train armies in Africa and other parts of the globe, or forming part of Britain's 'out of area' capability, prepared to fly anywhere at short notice. Nineteen thousand British troops currently serve outside UK or BAOR commands.

Approximately 56,000 British regular soldiers are stationed in West Germany, forming the British Army of the Rhine (BAOR). In addition, there is a brigade in Berlin of about 3,000 men which is not technically part of BAOR. The main fighting component of the Army's forces in Germany is the 1st British Corps (I Br Corps). This consists of three armoured divisions (the 1st, 3rd and 4th Armoured Divisions), to be reinforced by the 2nd Infantry Division, whose HQ is at York in peacetime. There are many other units, normally based in the UK, which would reinforce I Br Corps in the build-up to war. Some are small support units but others are full brigade strength and are designed to fill brigade-sized 'slots' currently left open in the divisions already in Germany. These reinforcements are made up of both territorial and regular units and would be further strengthened with reservists. Once mobilization had been completed, the number of British troops committed on German soil would number about 150,000.

The administrative organization that looks after the Army in the UK and would manage the British end of the reinforcement operation is United Kingdom Land Forces (UKLF). Based in Wiltshire, UKLF is divided into ten geographical military districts: Northern Ireland, Scotland, Western, Eastern, South-East (Aldershot), South-West, North-East, Wales, North-West and London District. Each district is responsible for all regular and territorial administration and training within its boundaries, including the various Army schools and colleges, and for operations within its boundaries, in the event of war.

Although officially part of UKLF, Northern Ireland District is managed as a separate command. The Army is represented in the province by the 39th Infantry Brigade in Lisburn and 8th Infantry Brigade in Londonderry, and a new brigade recently formed to cover the border. Apart from specialist intelligence and support units (including a small number of SAS), the troops on the ground consist of 6 permanent battalions, 3–4 more on short tour and the Ulster Defence Regiment of 2,800 regular and 3,700 part-time men and women soldiers. Those on short tour leave their wives and families behind in barracks, often in Germany. This has led to a number of social problems and the Army has had to reconcile the competing interests of military efficiency (which requires that soldiers are on the streets for long enough to acquire the special skills needed in Ulster) with showing due regard to soldiers'

UNITED KINGDOM
MILITARY DISTRICTS
SCOTLAND
H.Q. EDINBURGH
LONDONDERRY
NORTHERN
IRELAND
BELFAST
H.Q.LISBURN
NORTH
WEST
NORTH EAST
H.Q. YORK
H.Q. PRESTON
H.Q. SHREWSBURY
WESTERN
EASTERN
H.Q. COLCHESTER
WALES
H.Q. BRECON
LONDON
H.Q. ALDERSHOT
H.Q. BULFORD
H.Q. UKLF WILTON
SOUTH EAST
SOUTH WEST

families for whom prolonged separation can cause significant strain. We will be looking more closely in a later chapter at Operation Banner, as the system of short-term 'roulement' service in Northern Ireland is known, but at this point it should be noted that it has not only been infantry battalions who have served in an internal security role in the province: gunners, signallers, sappers (Royal Engineers) and many others also served as surrogate infanteers.

Though too often forgotten the Ulster Defence Regiment is an important part of the British Army and serves permanently in Northern Ireland. Despite its shortcomings (the greatest of which is the fact that it is not representative of the whole Northern Ireland community, being firmly weighted in terms of membership, on the Protestant side of the sectarian divide), the UDR is, in many ways, a model of an integrated full- and part-time organization. It may well offer lessons for the rest of the Army in this respect.

The part-timers of the mainland Territorial Army do not undertake tours of duty in Northern Ireland, something that goes some way towards undermining the 'one Army' concept that the MoD has been struggling to establish for some time. The minimum requirement in the TA is that each soldier should complete approximately 40 days' training per year. Many train far more than this, and because quite a large number are former regulars, TA soldiers should not be lightly written off as unprofessional. However, the TA has a high wastage rate and consequently training can become repetitive, leading to a vicious circle of increasingly dull soldiering resulting in progressively shorter engagements. Officers may pay lip service to the 'party line', but many regular NCOs and soldiers feel they have little in common with units where the majority of those serving may have had less than 150 days' military experience. Furthermore, society at large affords the territorials little respect. As a result, the TA is finding it increasingly difficult to attract and keep good recruits.

3

The Regimental System

'I hope you won't disband the regiments too quickly, I want plenty of brass bands for my funeral.'

Winston Churchill (to Harold Macmillan)

The key to understanding the Army's culture is the regimental system. The Army still makes the regiment the focus of emotional attachment and individual loyalty. Those with direct experience of the system, who are amongst the few who might adequately explain it to outsiders, naturally find it difficult to discuss in purely logical terms. Even for those who have been part of the system, the barriers to describing it do not end with the challenge of objectivity. There are semantic hurdles to be overcome as well. The phrase 'British regimental system' is often used carelessly, particularly by those who have not considered properly what it means. For them it is like the proverbial elephant: hard to describe but recognizable when encountered.

Unfortunately, the conceptual complications extend well beyond the all too promiscuous use of the word 'regiment'. When one starts to investigate the British regimental system, two things become clear: it may not be as uniquely British as many believe (the Danes, Dutch, Norwegians and Swedes operate similar systems), nor is it (at least as it has developed since the Second World War) anything like as systematic as the name suggests. Often when senior British officers refer to the regimental system, they appear to mean the British Army as it is. For them the regimental system represents a cluster of attitudes rather than a specific structure. Amongst the many associations evoked by the phrase 'regimental system' are the idea of a professional military caste and the belief that major structural or social change would destroy the regimental icon. Meanwhile the habitual use of the term can distract attention from the fact that the regimental organization of the British Army has become rather confused of late (indeed, curiously reminiscent of the pre-Cardwell era).

However, when the Army uses the word regiment to outsiders it is usually referring to the single or multi-battalion infantry regiment of 650–2,100 men, or the armoured regiment of about 500 men and 50 tanks. A reasonable, but imperfect (not least because it only mentions the cavalry and infantry arrangements in any detail), definition of the regimental system of the British Army is:

That form of professional organization in which:
1) the basic administrative unit (and building-block of larger formations) is the regular armoured regiment of about 500 men or the regular infantry battalion of about 650 men, in both cases commanded by a lieutenant-colonel;
2) individual soldiers identify with this unit of 500 or 650 as their tribe or clan (tribe, clan and family are all words frequently used by the Army to describe its regiments); and where, when this unit is only part of a regiment (as in the case of one battalion of a multi-battalion regiment), there is a secondary focus of loyalty to the larger, parent regiment;
3) the regiment, large or small, is associated with one specialist role (e.g. armour or infantry) rather than being an integrated multi-arm formation;
4) units generally have an affiliation with a specific part of the United Kingdom (especially for recruitment purposes) and where, in the case of many regular infantry regiments (the Foot Guards are all notable exceptions) they may have one or more Territorial Army battalions sharing their regimental identity;
5) there is a corpus of sacred history, a hoard of sacred possessions (e.g. the paintings and silver of the officers' mess), a special dress code (e.g. the scarlet tunics and bearskins of the Guards), a totem (usually called the colours), and a rigid hierarchy within which an individual's place is clearly known to himself and others;
6) the individual, commissioned or not, enters the regiment after the rite of passage of training and must then undergo a period of semi-official apprenticeship or probation;
7) the origins of hierarchy are often perceived as feudal, with all members being categorized as officers, non-commissioned officers

or other ranks (similar classifications being applied to their dependants as well), and with the social organization and practice of the regiment generally mirroring that of 'old England' (or Scotland or Ireland), an attractive mythical land to which a living link is maintained through the person of the Sovereign;
8) the royal connection is firmly maintained and individual regiments have developed particularly (many would say, splendidly) arcane customs.

The roots of modern regimental organization may be traced both to companies of armed men that medieval landowners were obliged by the feudal system to commit periodically to the king's service, and to the bands of mercenaries which offered themselves for hire when the feudal levies were insufficient or unreliable.

The word regiment is derived from the Latin *regimen*, a rule or system of order, and was first applied to French cavalry units in the mid-sixteenth century. The term came into common use in this country during the Civil Wars (1642–45 and 1648–49). It had a special significance when applied to the innovative Parliamentarian forces of 1645 and after. Regularly recruited, the regiments of the New Model Army consisted of ten companies, each of about 120 men, commanded by a colonel assisted by a lieutenant-colonel, a major and seven captains, with all officers acting as company commanders. This sort of organizational system was retained by the Regular Army after the Restoration.

From then, whenever the Crown thought it necessary to raise a regiment, a warrant would be issued to a colonel-designate (typically a senior landowner, a member of Parliament, or a Lord-Lieutenant), together with a lump sum to cover the initial costs of raising the regiment and the promise of a capitation fee thereafter. The colonel raised further revenue from the sale of commissions and supplemented this by practices such as maintaining dead men on the books of each company and 'shaving' deductions for food and keep. In return for their fighting services, soldiers received a wage. The Crown supplied their weapons, but often it was the colonel who supplied distinctive uniforms, just as a large landowner might dress his servants in livery. The finery of a regiment could become a status symbol for its colonel, and some colonels, especially the richer ones, vied with one another to create the most splendid uniforms. Indeed, until the reign of George II (1727–60), a regiment of infantry or cavalry was effectively the colonel's property. He named it, and designed its colours or guidon. It was he who dictated how it would be run.

The power of the Crown over the regimental colonels was not fully established until a Royal Warrant of 1751 confirmed a numbered order of precedence in the Army.[1] Although this had the positive effect of imposing some order on what had become a very confused state of affairs, the attempt to regulate the regiments also encouraged snobbishness about their new numbers (a low one being perceived as more desirable than a high one). Thus the 1st Life Guards was the premier regiment, and the artillery were less important than the 49th Regiment of Foot. Although the numbering system has long been abandoned, its effects are still felt. The regimental system implies not just an internal hierarchy within the regiment, but also an external hierarchy which places the regiment itself in a ranking order of the whole Army. When this hierarchy contradicts or has an unfair effect upon the more legitimate hierarchy of operational effectiveness, problems must arise; but this is an issue which the Army is loath to address.

Since about 1714, and despite considerable opposition, the regiments stationed in Britain had lived within the community, being billeted at inns and farms. This changed in 1792 with the decision to build barracks on a wide scale – a consequence of the French Revolution. The fear was that soldiers billeted within the community might be subverted by radicals. The Army remained outside society for the whole of the nineteenth century. Most commentators would agree that it was during this period that it developed into the institution that we recognize today.

Until Victorian times regiments were created and disbanded according to immediate necessity, but from the seventeenth century onwards, the trend was towards an ever-larger peacetime Army. Moreover, the expansion of the British Empire meant that a regiment might spend ten or twenty years at one overseas station. In 1859, following the Indian Mutiny, the senior 25 infantry regiments of the Army each formed a second battalion, and Cardwell's reforms led in 1872 to all the infantry regiments from the 26th to the 109th Foot (with two exceptions) being paired and the

1. There were in 1751 altogether two regiments of horse guards, three regiments of dragoon guards, fourteen regiments of cavalry, three regiments of foot guards, forty-nine regiments of infantry, and one regiment of artillery, in that order of precedence.

joining to them of local militia and volunteer battalions. Cardwell's admirable reforms allowed for the cross-posting of officers and shared administrative costs. As Antony Sampson writes:

> Regiments in their modern sense were invented – like the civil service – in the dynamic 1870s. They were the administrative unit devised by Colonel Cardwell, the Secretary of State for War, as a way of ruling the empire: there were seventy-five regiments each with two [regular] battalions – one at home, the other guarding a distant outpost – and in their static isolation they developed powerful and splendid characters of their own, which were not necessarily very relevant to military efficiency.[1]

In 1881 a decade of great reform was completed by the adoption of county titles for the majority of infantry regiments, replacing their cherished numbers.

Cardwell's scheme was not, however, applied to the cavalry. (An attempt was made to group the cavalry regiments in threes, but it was rejected.) The cavalry, which rarely served overseas except in India, remained as single regiments, although a few adopted regional titles and all tended to favour one particular region in recruiting.

In the 1870s the influence of the Victorian ideology of service and philanthropy began to be felt amongst many regimental officers. Previously it had been generally accepted that they took virtually no interest in the everyday lives of their men – something encouraged by the nature of imperial soldiering. When a regiment was posted overseas, rapid transfers often resulted in a virtually new set of officers going with it. Flogging and fierce discipline were the order of the day. After the 1870s, isolated with their men within the society of the regiment, officers began to develop a greater concern for their soldiers' welfare. Meanwhile, the institution of the Officers' Mess became more important, and for the same reason – the enforced isolation in which they lived. By the end of the century, it was not unknown for senior regimental officers to remain voluntarily unmarried (although, of course, not chaste) for the sake of continuing to live in the Mess. It provided, as indeed it still does in

1. *The New Anatomy of Britain*, Anthony Sampson, pp. 306–307 (Hodder and Stoughton, 1971).

many cases, the opportunity for its members, even those of relatively modest means, to live the life of country gentlemen. Fierce snobbery and strange rituals of initiation developed: the practice of barely speaking to a new subaltern for his first half-year with the colours was typical. New arrivals could also expect a baptism of fire in the form of an elaborate practical joke, which of course had to be 'taken like a man' to ensure social acceptance. A few years after arriving many officers would go through not dissimilar rites of passage to gain entrance to their regimental freemasonic lodge.[1]

The regiment appeared to translate rural social relationships between the landowning class and its peasantry into military life. The system was essentially 'feudal' in the sense that it was, or was perceived as being, based on land. Today many senior officers acknowledge the feudal origins of their regiments' hierarchies and customs, but also argue that since the system works, there is no reason to change it.

However, some commentators have argued that the feudalism of the modern (post-1870) regiment owes rather more to the Gothic Revival and an idealized notion of knighthood than to true feudalism, and is best understood as a form of Victorian paternalism. Evelyn Waugh recognized something of this in his novel *Put Out More Flags*:

> 'It's an odd thing,' Basil began, 'that people always expect the upper class to be good leaders of men. That was all right in the old days when most of them were brought up with tenantry to look after. But now three-quarters of your officer-type live in towns. *I* haven't any tenantry.
> The Lieutenant-Colonel looked as Basil with detestation.
> 'No, no, I suppose not.'
> 'Well, have *you* any tenantry?'
> '*I*? No. My brother sold the old place years ago.'
> 'Well, there you are.'[2]

In fact, it was in the period 1870–1914 that the regimental ideal, as this century knows it, was perfected. Sadly, it was also the period in which Britain's transition from a rural, county-based society to an urban, technological society was completed, and in which the

1. Freemasonry appears to have taken hold within the Army during the second half of the nineteenth century. It remains a powerful force in the Army (as it does in the police, the Security Service (MI5), and the Judiciary to the present day).
2. *Put Out More Flags*, Evelyn Waugh (Penguin, 1969).

nature of warfare changed as small colonial conflicts gave way to clashes on a titanic scale.

As we trace the development of the traditional regimental system it is worth considering some other possibilities for the organization of fighting men. One which might have developed in the mid-eighteenth century was a unified Corps of Marines under the Royal Navy. Although above all a maritime power, Britain never evolved large marine forces (such as the US Marines). Countries which have had to create their own armed forces in the twentieth century, such as Israel, have tended towards a unified Defence Force of which ground, air and naval forces are each a part. That is not to say that the experiment is always successful. In 1968 the Canadians – whose Army follows the British regimental system – also unified their armed forces in the face of considerable hostility from the services themselves. This experiment is now broadly judged to have failed.

There have also been some interesting modifications to the regimental system in the British Army. During the second Boer war military formations were created based on volunteers, taken *en masse* from small, cohesive social groups – for example, specific trades or professions. The idea was developed on a much larger scale in the First World War as the Pals' Battalions. These units, such as the Bradford Pals, reflected an urban rather than a rural social structure. The main drawback of the Pals approach was that heavy casualties could have terrible consequences for a small community.

The First World War also saw, for the first time in British Army history, regional divisions. The 51st Highland Division and the 36th Ulster Division were probably the best-known examples. The Territorial Army still has a 51st Highland Brigade and a 52nd Lowland Brigade, while the two armoured brigades of the 1st Armoured Division in BAOR are called 7th and 22nd Armoured Brigades, after the two brigades of the 7th Armoured Division of the Second World War (the Desert Rats), testimony to the fact that there have been some successful attempts to make formations larger than the regiment the foci of individual attachment and loyalty.

Yet another development of the First World War was the creation of modern specialist corps such as the Royal Flying Corps, Tank Corps, and Cyclist Corps, a pattern repeated in the Second World War with the Observer Corps, Reconnaissance Corps, Intelligence Corps and others, together with the imposition of a Royal Armoured Corps structure on the cavalry and tank regiments.

Whatever their value in war, only a few of these new corps survived into peacetime in the face of traditional regimental competition.[1]

An important deviation from the regimental system which occurred in the Second World War was the creation of new élite forces, whose high morale derived not from tradition but from special selection (as with the Parachute Regiment and the Commandos), or special training and personal inspiration (as with the Chindits and the Special Air Service (SAS)). The large-scale use of selection to create divisions of high fighting value was a feature of the German military system. The British did not generally adopt this approach (except possibly with the Guards Armoured Division). Instead, some divisions simply emerged as being of high fighting value.

Another successful WWII experiment was the battlegroup, the *ad hoc* specialist formation of all arms, often named after its commander. This system commonly employed by the Axis was copied by the Allies. The Americans institutionalized the battlegroup in their armoured divisions by scrapping an old brigade structure and replacing it by three Combat Commands of all arms, subdivided into teams as necessary. Something like this appeared in practice in British armoured divisions in 1944 but was never given official sanction. The present 1st British Corps armoured divisions are structured in this fashion, with slight variations in brigade structure, with the battlegroups beneath them (approximately two battalions in size) structured as required.

After the war an effort was made to reorganize the infantry regiments into larger administrative brigades (a group of battalions smaller than a division). In 1948 the Brigade of Guards, the Light Brigade, the Green Jacket Brigade and eleven regional brigades, with distinctive titles such as the Forester Brigade or the Home Counties Brigade, were formed. Each regiment within these brigades was progressively reduced to one battalion by the early 1950s. (The regimental system seemed then altogether less sacred than it is today.)

Towards the end of the decade the Army introduced brigade cap badges – a major step in the British context – making it quite clear that the brigade was intended to be the basic formation of the

1. The Germans in the Second World War even created special battalions to use as fighting troops men with common illnesses or disabilities, e.g. foot battalions, and stomach battalions, and combined these into Static Divisions without intrinsic transport, intended for defence only. Above these came the Infantry divisions, but it was widely recognized that the Panzer (armoured) divisions got the best men as well as the best equipment.

future. Nevertheless, regimental organization survived, albeit in a confused form – the rational systems of Cardwell and Haldane had degenerated into a situation where individual infantry regiments might have one, two or three battalions. But the brigade concept lasted only four years, so great was the outcry from those in whom the regimental system had worked its alchemy. Ironically, the emotional attachments which had been so carefully and so deliberately fostered in order to secure loyalty and obedience had rebounded to frustrate plans for change.

In 1962 serious reform was abandoned. Taking the course of least resistance, it was announced that the infantry regiments should be invited instead to move voluntarily towards the large regiment model. As one old soldier told us, 'The regimental system was too strong, so the War Office accepted defeat.' In 1968, the same lobby ensured the rejection of the Corps of Infantry concept, whereby all the regiments would be brought together within a single monolithic structure. What has survived is a patchwork of regiments of varying numbers of battalions, arranged within administrative divisions to share the costs of recruit training and sundry common services. By 1971 there were 6 large infantry regiments each comprising 3 battalions, and each created by the amalgamation of 4 regiments; 11 of 1 battalion by amalgamation of 2 regiments, and 11 of 1 battalion continuing from before 1957. Against the odds and despite periodic calls for a more cost-effective structure, our confused regimental organization persists.

The explanation of the regimental system's past success and present survival lies in a combination of factors: that the regiment has provided a group small enough for the individual to relate to directly; that the internal structure of the regiment has its roots in the British class system (which is also a stubborn survivor); that the collective body of the regiment is guaranteed a continuity more lasting than the career of the individual member; and that it is a convenient arrangement for the policing operations which the British Army is often called upon to undertake. Its principal practical disadvantage is that many of the things which go towards maintaining *élan* in the regiment may also lead to friction when dealing with those outside it. A related problem arises when individual officers rise beyond the confines of their own regiment and aim to fill posts in the higher command structure. Their outlook may colour their judgment, leading them to promote the interests of their own military family at the expense of those of the Army as a whole. Though past attempts at reforming the system have largely been prompted by the desire to save money or by the natural military inclination towards tidiness, in recent years there have been calls to scrap the system on the grounds that it is not well suited to the demands of modern warfare. Those who raise this argument point to the need for infantry, tanks and artillery to work closely together.

Furthermore, the regimental system as currently operated, demands extremes of conformity amongst all ranks, which may stifle initiative and lead to a narrowing of outlook. Some cite positive aspects to this. Michael Howard notes the specific loyalty to the regiment, rather than to the Army in general, as a factor promoting political stability: 'The regimental system may isolate the military but it also tames them, fixing their eyes on minutiae, limiting their ambitions, teaching them a gentle, parochial loyalty difficult to pervert to more dangerous ends.'[1]

Yet, there is no reason why some of the less desirable characteristics of the regimental system could not be reformed without losing the family identity and continuity which is at the core of its strength. This could be done regardless of the specific task assigned to a unit and regardless of whether it was organized on a single or mixed arms basis. The fact that problems persist suggests either a failure of imagination or an unwillingness to contemplate even modest reform on the part of those senior officers who reserve to themselves the right to initiate any changes in the Army's social institutions.

1. Howard 1962, p. 81.

4

The Moral Dimension

'When I went to Sandhurst we were not taught to behave like gentlemen, because it never occurred to anyone that we could behave otherwise.'
Major-General J. F. C. Fuller

The Army may like to say that it is a mirror of society, but a soldier is far from being simply a civilian in uniform. He is a member of an organization historically distinct from – and sometimes shunned by – civil society. It is an organization which has learnt to enjoy its own company and which cherishes its separateness. Moreover, it is an organization which has always been expected to perform the extraordinary function, from time to time of killing people and destroying property. This above all else separates the Army from the rest of society. The experience of two world wars, the growth of an anti-war political movement, as well as what is often mistakenly believed to have been more than forty years of peace have led many to have qualms about maintaining such a body.

It is clear that we will need an Army for the foreseeable future. It is also clear that the most careful thought should be given to the Army's ethical development as well as to its military training. Every organization acquires its own particular culture, which can often enhance its operational effectiveness by providing a secure social framework within which its members can pursue commonly agreed ends. However, there is always a danger that, if an organization's distinguishing qualities are too strongly emphasized, its members will become defensive in their relations with the outside world and begin to place greater emphasis on its internal priorities at the expense of those of the community it exists to serve.

What are the ethical and spiritual values to be preserved and encouraged in an Army? What value should be placed on them? Is the Army fostering the right values among its officers and men, or is it tolerating or encouraging values that will prove dysfunctional in the long run? Will the changing circumstances of the 1990s require not only a new type of soldier, but also a new set of ethical standards for the profession of arms? Can the Army, as it is presently constituted, realistically hope to bring about whatever transformation is necessary? These are the questions we will be considering in this chapter. In order to answer them we will first examine some of the attitudes and ways of behaving that prevail in today's Army.

The Officer Corps

The Army has chosen to ignore many of the fashions of the past forty years. Particularly in its social arrangements, it has succeeded in maintaining a remarkable consistency during a period of enormous upheaval and change. A soldier from the late 1940s, transported to today's Aldershot, would find little unfamiliar in the pattern of modern Army life. Certainly he would find that the old dispensation under which the military world divided itself, like Gaul, into three parts – officers, NCOs and men – is still intact.

This is not to say that the Army is not aware that the generation which has grown up since the abolition of National Service sees Army officers only as a series of absurd stereotypes. Indeed, to counter such perceptions the Army has made use of the most up-to-date communications techniques. One advertising campaign that appeared in the colour supplements of Sunday newspapers a few years ago featured thirty or so faces beneath the caption 'Spot the Colonel'. Standing out amongst the ruddy and bewhiskered visages was a youthful 37-year-old who was, of course, the only real colonel on the page. To reinforce the notion that ours is a modern Army, images of helicopters, tanks, missiles, radar, computers and so forth, accompanied by associated 'techno-babble', have been used to considerable effect. The technology may look impressive but the truth is that an Army is not made up of tanks and guns and missiles but of flesh and blood.

The Army has not always reacted well to the social changes in the world outside the barrack gates. Arguably its most obvious failure has been in not properly coming to terms with the radical changes that have taken place in the British class system. This has had far-reaching effects on the recruitment and training of officers and on the regimental system itself. Instead of one Army with a common aspiration to excellence, we still have a small number of fashionable regiments whose members look down their noses at the others who, feeling inferior, often display a sullen, envious self-consciousness. Meanwhile, the relationship between officers and men has become more ambiguous in recent years.

The Army originally based its hierarchical structure on the assumption that the upper classes possessed a natural authority and the working class displayed a natural deference. It was as if society divided itself neatly into officers and men. This was always something of a sham, but it worked. For example, Sandhurst was developed in the early nineteenth century partly because the Army had run out of genuine gentry and aristocrat officers. It had to take in the middle class and turn entrants from this background into 'officers and gentlemen'. After the Second World War it became clear that the Army would have to recruit its officers from among the lower-middle and working classes. This posed two immediate problems: firstly, how to persuade the men to accept the authority of those whose qualifications for officer status were not immediately apparent; and secondly, how to minimize the social tensions within the officer corps between those from a traditional – that is, upper- or middle-class – background and the new breed of grammar school, or more recently, comprehensive school officers.

The Army has not, of course, been alone in having to contend with the problems of class and class-consciousness. Every institution in Britain has had to deal with them over the past forty years and in many respects the Army has followed the civilian model in its approach. In keeping with the general meritocratic trend, the Army's first response was to redefine the nature of an officer. It began to emphasize ability and education at the expense of birthright and evolved a set of personal qualities that it felt it could insist on any officer displaying, irrespective of background.

Thirty years ago the novelist Simon Raven wrote an essay about the Army entitled 'Perish by the Sword'.[1] The Army he was describing was the Army of the 1950s but many of its features are still in evidence today. Here he describes what he calls the Warminster virtues – that set of values associated with the Army's School of Infantry at Warminster in Wiltshire:

1. *Encounter*, XII, May 1959.

> How much, in the last resort, was thought to depend on superior qualities of morality and character! . . . it was the catchwords with quasi-moral implications ('guts', 'common sense') that filled the air as the course went on. Another Warminster virtue was a peculiar brand of humour. This was not the ability to see oneself and one's activities in a detached and ironical spirit – that would have been fatal. Humour meant being cheerful in the face of unpleasant circumstances, rallying the men's spirits by laughing with them over some slapstick incident, submitting 'like a good sport' to an unjust punishment given to oneself by the Adjutant and 'laughing about it afterwards in the Mess'. This conception of humour (an obvious branch of 'guts') was in fact discreetly designed to counteract or totally extinguish any tendencies towards an objective (or intellectual) humour that might contain tinges of satire or cynicism – for such a thing would have been detrimental to another highly prized virtue, that of enthusiasm. About enthusiasm I can hardly trust myself to speak. It seemed to mean a sort of blind, uncritical application to any task, however silly or futile, that the neurosis or panic of a superior might suddenly thrust upon one . . . enthusiasm could involve a frantic expense of time and energy on some trifling project . . . the heartiness and hysteria . . . was of course distasteful to the more fastidious and sceptical officers for whose benefit yet another virtue, that of loyalty, had to be invoked. Loyalty meant that you were required in the name of the Queen and the honour of the Regiment, to conceal any impatience or amusement you might feel when the demands made on your enthusiasm became operatic, farcical or just plainly impossible of fulfilment.

Raven identified other Warminster values: 'courage under fire'; 'initiative'; and, perhaps most important of all, 'responsibility', which, 'Like the Holy Ghost . . . is supposed to be everywhere, and anything which is not material for the exercise of guts or enthusiasm (or one of the other Warminster qualities) is certainly in the realm of responsibility. It covers everything from making an intelligent assessment of how to move a Division down to being careful not to get drunk in the Sergeants' Mess.'

These Warminster values were essentially those of the middle-ranking public school of the first half of this century but remain part of the character template to which the Army believes officers should conform. Since Raven's time there has been an influx of officer cadets to the Royal Military Academy at Sandhurst with working-class manners and regional accents and the Army has responded to this phenomenon by devoting as much attention to modifying the social behaviour of its future officers as to developing what it sees as desirable personality traits. Accordingly, Sandhurst has learnt to employ an extraordinary process of social conditioning designed to turn working-class men into passable imitations of middle-class men. Quite how blatantly it does this can be seen in Michael Yardley's account of the Academy's training presentation, 'How to Behave in the Mess', published in the *Sunday Telegraph Magazine* in 1987:

> A loutish character comes on stage, a jock-strap stretched over his tracksuit bottoms and a Sony Walkman dangling from the convenient pouch. Normally an affable captain in the Royal Artillery, the slob is soon joined by his opposite archetype, a splendid vision in bowler, breeches and boots . . .
>
> All manner of characters soon appear to demonstrate the pitfalls inherent in the complex etiquette of the mess. They order the wrong drinks, have the wrong accents and wear trousers with checks so loud they would do an American golfer credit. A gushing Sloanish girl in Barbour and pearls asks if she might use the loo. The slob shouts across stage, 'There's some bird here who wants to sling her drizzle!' – thunderous applause. . . . The message of the officer's mess presentation is clear: don't be an oik, show proper deference to seniors and get a decent tailor.

The Army justifies this approach by saying that it is not primarily concerned with the *embourgeoisement* of its working-class entrants but with upholding what it calls 'standards'. These together with the Warminster values are spoken of as if they were moral virtues rather than behavioural characteristics. It is precisely in this failure properly to distinguish between the truly moral and the merely social that the Army has erred. The traditional notion of an officer and a gentleman was not simply a matter of social distinction but one of moral scrupulousness. Gentlemanly qualities (derived as they were from the idea of chivalry) were to do with service, an unselfish regard for the comfort and convenience of others, and dedication to high ideals. But in an interview with one of the authors, Major-General Keightley, then Commandant at Sandhurst, explained the purpose of the Academy's social training thus:

> We're not trying to teach them to look down their noses at all Communists and that sort of thing but we teach them what would be expected of them in an officers' mess. In the show *South Pacific* there's a marvellous song called 'You've Got to be Carefully Taught'; it was applied to an American sailor not marrying a Filipino girl. You've got to get that right and behave as the officers you are with would expect.[1]

1. *Sandhurst: A Documentary*, Michael Yardley, p. 196 (Harrap, 1987).

Another former Commandant at Sandhurst used to begin his opening address to newly arrived cadets with the following words: 'Gentlemen, congratulations on adopting an honourable calling. When one looks about at the general dross that characterizes civilian life today, one can rightly regard oneself as fortunate to be shot of it.'

Nor is this general scorn for the outside world the preserve of the officer caste: amongst the NCOs and the private soldiers of today, civilian standards are perceived as being inferior to military ones. Most of us appear to the soldier as either workshy or incompetent and to the senior officer as venal or corrupt.

Since the Army now trains non-graduate Junior Officers in only three terms (under twelve months, nearly twice as quickly as it did fifteen years ago), and graduates in six months, it may be inevitable that confusion has arisen between real gentlemanly virtues and the easily mimicked trappings of Sloane Rangerdom. And though the Army may appear to offer class mobility unavailable elsewhere, the transformation of the working-class lad into the middle-class officer is imperfect. Many fail the social litmus test that has been perfected over decades. Consequently, men from 'non-traditional' backgrounds still find it very difficult if not impossible to become officers in certain regiments.

When officers really were gentlemen, snobbishness was considered a vice, but an unpleasant degree of snobbery has developed, particularly among younger officers in the more fashionable regiments. There has also been a marked deterioration in the way young Army officers conduct themselves, reflected in their lack of consideration and concern for others. Perhaps this is because the Army is too busy teaching its working-class officers unimportant social niceties to spare the time to insist that all officers should behave as *gentle*men.[1]

By focusing on officers' social presentation rather than their moral virtues, the Army is effectively reinforcing the class distinctions it pretends it seeks to eliminate. One result is a lack of social ease and cohesion amongst officers, but the problem runs deeper. Much of the malaise within the Army stems from the corporate values which the system encourages and reinforces through its methods of

1. However, one recent and far more positive trend at The Royal Military Academy is an appreciation of the value of academic studies. These have been cut back severely in recent years and the status of the academics has consequently diminished. The effects of cuts remain but the dynamic new Commandant, Major-General Graham, has made a special effort to overcome this problem, despite a ridiculously limited budget.

promotion and reward. Though there have always been ambitious officers, it used to be the case that the system frowned on careerism and would take active steps to limit it. Now the Army behaves like an American multinational corporation – taking a functional view of its human raw material and giving the impression that it is interested only in results. This has led to the emergence of the 'thrusting major' as a new military stereotype. This man has little loyalty to the Army and uses its facilities and resources simply to further his own career. He is also potentially mobile, and likely to opt for premature voluntary retirement as soon as he finds something sufficiently lucrative outside. This is a corrupting influence which undermines group loyalty and replaces it with a form of office politics where currying favour with superiors is more important than ability. One Captain who chose to leave the Army in 1989 confided in the authors that the working atmosphere generated by blatant careerism was the main reason that he and many of his fellows were applying for PVR (Premature Voluntary Release). 'If I'm going to work like a merchant banker, I might as well be one and get paid like one.'

Ambition is not the only vice that the Army has begun to foster in its officers rather than train out of them. Because it has chosen to opt for social conditioning and technical instruction in place of character training, it fails to identify and modify a whole range of dysfunctional psychological traits common among many people attracted to the military life.

In 1976 Professor Norman Dixon, then Reader in Psychology at University College London, published *On the Psychology of Military Incompetence*, a study of military organization in which, by comparing some of the best and some of the worst leaders in history, he was able to point to a number of psychological factors that are conducive to disaster in warfare. The book contained many lessons for the Army and, for a while, it enjoyed considerable popularity, particularly among instructors at Sandhurst and the Staff College. Yet today the Army still fosters many of the attitudes and qualities of mind that Dixon identified as potentially dangerous. Interestingly one of the traits Dixon remarked in the military incompetent was a high degree of sensitivity to any form of criticism:

> . . . their sensitivity seems out of all proportion to that of other public figures. In terms of fame or notoriety, well-known generals or admirals are on a level with film stars, politicians and even newsworthy academics; hence one would expect that they might come to accept the possibility of negative publicity as part of the game, a small price to pay

> for the 'perks' which they otherwise enjoy. This they seem unable to do. In fact, there is a distinctly paranoid element in the way some senior commanders have reacted to even the faintest breath of criticism.[1]

Clear evidence of this sensitivity is provided by the attempts to discredit Lieutenant Robert Lawrence, upon whom the award-winning television play *Tumbledown* was based. In 1988 he wrote a book, in collaboration with his father, pointing up various shortcomings in the Army's attitude to wounded men who had been brought home from the Falklands. Lawrence recorded, amongst other things, that he had been forbidden to wear uniform at a service of remembrance but was instructed to wear it for what was, in essence, a public relations event for a car manufacturer; that he had been the victim of bureaucratic muddle with regard to his treatment and rehabilitation; and, he alleged, was advised not to say goodbye to his men on his last day in his battalion on the grounds that the sight of a wounded man might be bad for morale. Lawrence subsequently became the target of a campaign of innuendo and downright character-assassination that was remarkable for the degree of spite and venom displayed. Some of the stories that appeared about him in the press appeared to be based on information provided by individuals still serving in the Army and even some widely-respected writers resorted to *ad hominem* arguments – citing Lawrence's alleged arrogance – in order to belittle the criticisms that he had made. Perhaps the most distasteful suggestion put about was that the head-wound Lawrence had received in the Falklands had so altered the balance of his mind that nothing he said should be treated seriously. Less directly offensive, but doubtless stinging to Lawrence, was the repeated insinuation that by making his complaints public, he had 'betrayed' his former regiment and the Army itself.

Apart from sensitivity to criticism, Dixon identified a number of other traits that characterize the military incompetent: anti-effeminacy; a liking for 'bull'; anti-intellectualism; and a tendency to display 'butch' behaviour patterns. Warning of the dangers of recruiting future leaders who demonstrate these traits, Dixon says:

> . . .by selecting and promoting on the bases of such . . . . criteria as size, strength, physical courage and prowess at games, the armed forces tend to ignore other attributes which really may be of even

1. *On The Pyschology of Military Incompetence*, Norman F. Dixon (Jonathan Cape, 1976).

> greater importance to a senior commander – intelligence, high educational level, resistance to break-down under stress and substantial reserves of moral courage.[1]

Furthermore, Dixon found that the checklist of factors that lead to military incompetence are similar to those identified by psychologists as characteristic of the immature 'authoritarian personality'.

Among other things, the authoritarian is likely to display a rigid, conventional social outlook, be inclined to reject and punish those who violate conventional values, be scornful of the imaginative and tender-minded, have an exaggerated regard for strength and toughness and believe that what goes on outside his own ordered world is dangerous and probably 'dirty' in a sexually corrupt way. Such people can be naturally drawn to certain military organizations where their anxieties and insecurities will be appeased and their own values reinforced. Dixon wrote on the 'authoritarian' types, 'They are taught to judge people for their usefulness rather than their likeableness. Their friends and even future marriage partners are selected and used in the service of personal advancement . . .'

As we have seen, this negative characteristic is enforced by those who believe, 'You've got to be properly taught'. And the Army promotes rather than discourages many of the other dysfunctional traits that Dixon identifies, such as social rigidity, conformism, the tendency to equate tenderness with weakness and anti-intellectualism.

Although there is an official definition of what constitutes good leadership at the Royal Military Academy Sandhurst, in the experience of both the authors – who attended Sandhurst as cadets and have since been back to conduct more than sixty interviews – no one there seems able properly to remember or recite it. When asked, the usual reply is something like, 'Well, the Sandhurst motto is "Serve to Lead" and that about sums it all up really.' This lack of clarity is, perhaps, due to the fact that the Academy has adopted a rather sterile functional model developed by the psychologist, Professor John Adair (See Fig. 1).

Where do today is officers come from? In the autumn of 1988 the MoD launched an advertising campaign to encourage more civilians to apply for commissions in the Territorial Army. Tommy Macpherson, chairman of the National Employers' Liaison Committee for the Reserves, described the purpose of the campaign thus: 'What we

1. Ibid.

Fig 1: Adair's Model of Leadership – the Checklist at Sandhurst.

PHASES	Achieve task (a)	Build/Maintain TEAM (b)	Develop/Satisfy INDIVIDUAL (c)
PLANNING	Define the task Obtain information Make appreciation Make a plan	Involve team in planning Detail groups Appoint sub leaders	Assess the skills potential of each man Use knowledge and expertise of individuals to assist in making your plan
BRIEFING	State aim Issue orders	Give clear orders Explain reason for task Set standards/priorities	Delegate Check the individuals understand the plan
CONTROLLING	Ensure that all activity is directed towards achieving the aim Monitor progress Re-plan if necessary	Co-ordinate Maintain standards	Maintain standards
SUPPORTING	Provide resources	Maintain team spirit	Encourage individuals Criticize constructively Look after administration
INFORMING	Keep yourself informed of progress in all areas	Keep team in the picture on progress Ensure communication within the team	Thank and praise
EVALUATING	Review tasking. Has aim been achieved?	Recognize success Learn from failure	Listen to feedback Assess performance

are after is the yuppie; or more precisely, the yuppie-at-arms.' No clearer statement could be made that the officer is no longer required to have the moral qualities of a gentleman.

In an average cavalry regiment (these are the more fashionable and upper-middle class) there will probably be one or two officers drawn from the aristocracy, perhaps cherishing associations with the regiment going back a number of generations. Then there will be a large group who are the sons of farmers or stockbrokers. These officers will have been educated at one of the better public schools and will have joined the regiments in which their fathers served. Finally, there will be a group of officers who are the sons of professional men or serving officers in the Army – they too will have gone to public school but it is possible their fathers did not.

The atmosphere in most of these regiments seems convivial and relaxed. The officers are on Christian-name terms with one another and the subalterns frequently affect a languid disdain for military matters. They like to appear great exponents of the cult of the amateur, believing that *élan* is the only necessary quality of an officer and that the minutiae of equipment and tactics are for the NCOs or the dull plodders in the 'fish and chip' regiments and corps. The relaxed style of cavalry officers has its roots in the fact that their only important role for many hundreds of years was to set an example of bravery to their men. Cavalry charges were led from the front and 'dash' was always the supreme virtue. Until the horse gave way to the tank, there was no need for them to display other military qualities. Being by nature and temperament unsuited to the 'Army barmy' way of life, they have to choose, once the fun of being a subaltern is over, between leaving the service or reluctantly adopting a more professional attitude. This choice has become coloured in the late 1980s by the fact that an easy translation to the City in one's late twenties is no longer there for the asking, so the thrusting major and even the thrusting captain can now be found in the smartest regiments.

Officers are rather different in the less fashionable regiments and corps. There, increasingly, they have an awkward and intractable problem: no one can easily distinguish between officers and men. Many working-class officers will tell you that the Army is 'just a job, like any other' but the men, like Corporal Y ask, 'Why should I take orders from him? He's no different from me.' The officers express hostility towards the cavalry and Guards, but oddly, the contempt displayed towards the more upper-class regiments is intensified when, with what seems like effortless superiority, cavalrymen or Foot Guards prove themselves more proficient in military skills. (The SAS generally has a high proportion of Guards officers on its strength.)

The Army's problem with its whole officer corps is how can a militarily necessary distinction be maintained between officers and men? Different parts of the Army have tried different approaches: the cavalry and Guards have attempted to maintain a form of class distinction while the corps and some infantry and artillery units have espoused meritocracy overlaid with a measure of social training. Both can be said to have worked only to the extent that from the private soldier's perspective there remains a broad homogeneity in the officer caste and we are still a long way from mutiny in the ranks. Nevertheless, class resentments are simmering, both within the officer corps and between officers and men, and are bound to undermine the necessary operational co-operation and trust between the various arms of the service.

There are examples of behaviour, or more accurately, misbehaviour that transcend the Army's social boundaries, but which are compounded by the failure of too many officers to lead by example. Drunkenness is a real problem. Soldiers have long enjoyed a reputation for heavy drinking and the Army is happy to extend a robust tolerance towards over-indulgence, assuming it can be contained within reasonable bounds. Yet anyone who requires evidence of how thin the veneer of civilization really is, need look no further than a soldiers' bar. Lieutenant R. described to us one of the least-pleasant duties of an Orderly Officer:

> Closing the NAAFI was the worst bit. The lads used to play a game when they were really pissed which involved sitting along the counter in a line. The first man would drink a pint of mixed white spirits. The cocktail would usually include gin, vodka and Bacardi rum. Once he'd drunk so much that his stomach couldn't handle it he'd vomit in front of the next in line who would duly lean down and eat the pile of sick off the counter. This would cause him to vomit in his turn and so it would go on. The next morning they'd come on parade really 'steaming' but there was a kind of unspoken understanding that so long as a soldier was not obviously still drunk, he was OK.

Officers are unable to do much to moderate this kind of excess as their own behaviour in the Mess is well known to the other ranks. On a typical Officers' Mess Dinner Night (a men-only occasion when everyone gathers in their scarlet-and-gold Mess kit) prodigious quantities of champagne, wines and spirits are drunk. By about 2 a.m., people will be swinging from chandeliers, playing 'Mess rugby' (a more violent version of the real thing, with fewer rules), ripping up the cloth on the billiard table and hurling the balls or whatever else comes to hand at one another's heads. Many end the night being carried to bed in an alcoholic coma. Others are likely to go on a rampage of violence and destruction. It is not unknown for firearms to be discharged, thunderflashes thrown into rooms and fire extinguishers set off. Hi-fis and televisions have been thrown out of windows and few Messes can honestly claim to have all their valuable pictures and silver intact. All this could be dismissed as harmless fun, but it is difficult to reconcile with the fastidiousness of Sandhurst's presentation of 'How to Behave in the Mess'.

In October 1981, shortly after resigning his commission, one of the authors, Michael Yardley, wrote an article on Army life in

Germany and the UK, entitled 'What shall we do with the drunken soldier?', which was published in the *New Statesman*. It focused on the problem of alcohol abuse and the Army's refusal to deal with it, but it also explored many other problems of an Army which seemed reluctant to embark on much-needed reform. What follows are modified extracts from the original piece:

> At 2 a.m. the Duty Officer's phone rang and I lifted it, half asleep, 'Guardroom Sir, we've got a tech stores man down here – says he's beaten up his wife.' I got there in a few minutes to find a very drunk man who had apparently ended an argument with his pregnant wife by kicking her in the stomach. He had got drunk, he told me, because he was fed up with his job and 'Anyway, that kid's not mine.' Neither the wife nor unborn child was seriously injured; but that night I decided to leave the Army.
>
> Incidents like this happened all the time while I was serving in West Germany. Human frustration manifested itself as violence or drunkenness, usually both, helped along by the cheap duty-free drink which the Army makes available as a safety valve. Fights, marital breakdowns, alcoholism and car crashes are among the direct and common consequences. Drinking may become the only escape from the soul-destroying life in hideous garrison towns like Sennelager or Hohne. Last year [1980] 8 members of the British Army were killed by terrorist action in Northern Ireland; 13 soldiers died while on duty in West Germany, 18 whilst off duty, most of them in car crashes . . . .
>
> Many of the soldiers I commanded, were not, frankly, very bright. I believe they were confused. They thought they ought to be rough and tough and showed it in the ways that came naturally . . . .You cannot really teach a man to kill unless you balance it with something more than booze and discipline. . . .
>
> Once they are in the Army and at a training depot, recruits find that life is a treadmill of drill, rote learning and petty punishment. The type of punishment deemed necessary to 'build a soldier' is sadistic, or simply stupid, and staff invent bizarre rituals for recruits like cleaning a latrine with a toothbrush. The 'difficult' recruit who fails to 'see sense' may well have it 'punched into him' usually by his peers rather than by his superiors and more often than not because of the imposition of collective punishments for individual transgressions. . . . the training of recruits was largely left to the non-commissioned officers, a pattern throughout the Army which the NCOs encourage. Indeed, the NCO usually regards the young officer as a nuisance to be endured. . .

Yardley concluded that the Army was faced with a crisis of moral authority in its officer class which had become quite incapable of doing anything other than tolerating and perpetuating an organizational culture that had been allowed to become excessively violent, aggressive and brutish.

Michael Yardley was not the only young officer at that time who had been confronted by such problems. Morale in parts of the Army by 1981 was at a very low ebb. The pressure for change might well have become irresistible had it not been for victory in the Falklands: a victorious army is seldom in the mood for a painful examination of conscience. However, the Army may be living on borrowed time. Generations of officers have genuinely cared for their men and have tried to do their best for them – often in the teeth of bureaucratic indifference. Nowadays, officers seem more selfish and neither Sandhurst nor 'the system' appears inclined to teach them to be less so. Few are prepared to put their own careers on the line for the sake of their soldiers and all the indications are that soldiers in the last decade of the twentieth century are going to need more care, not less.

Non-Commissioned Officers

The Army's abdication of responsibility for matters moral is, arguably, most conspicuously manifested in its failure properly to civilize a significant number of its soldiers before giving them non-commissioned officer rank. Sergeants and corporals too often regard toughness, often amounting to thuggishness, as the principal virtue. Discipline at platoon or troop level is often maintained by the threat of physical violence. The cult of aggression is nurtured despite the fact that it is of no military utility and constitutes a disciplinary liability.

The writer Tony Parker in his book *Soldier, Soldier* – an anthology of tape-recorded conversations with serving soldiers devotes a chapter to the most important NCO of them all: the Regimental Sergeant-Major (RSM).[1]

> The RSM's just about the most stupid man I've met in my life [Lance-Corporal L told Parker] . . . he shouts and screams and yells at people, he doesn't talk to them as if they were human beings at all. . . . He's like a character out of a pantomime and all he succeeds in doing is making himself look fucking stupid. . . . Some people will tell you those days are gone for good in the Army. In that case people like our

1. *Soldier, Soldier*, Tony Parker, pp. 114–116 (Heinemann, 1985).

> RSM should be got rid of, because they don't belong in any modern set-up.

Nor did Sergeant B offer Parker any more charitable a view of his RSM:

> . . . one day there was a fly in the clerical offices and he said to a man 'Get that fly killed, soldier'. They had some fly spray, this was in the summer: so the soldier gave it a squirt on the window, and it dropped down dead. There was a second or two's silence and then the RSM hit the bloody roof. He went absolutely raving mad at the soldier for letting the dead fly lie on the window ledge . . . and because there were a few drops of fly spray on the glass. Any normal person would have killed the fly himself in the first place . . .

Of course bullying Sergeant-Majors are not a new phenomenon and the Army (and good Sergeant-Majors) well know what to tolerate and when to draw the line. However, there is also a danger of breeding an attitude of mind which can have sinister results. One gunnery instructor used to address his student officers thus:

> Gentlemen this is APSE – Armour Piercing Special Effects – and it's filled with white phosphorous gas. Strictly, according to the Geneva Convention, you're not supposed to use phosphorous against troops. But because we don't give a toss about the Geneva Convention and because this is a particularly useful bit of kit, we will. Actually some clever bugger has got round the Geneva Convention by saying we're not using it against troops but against vehicles. What happens is that you hit the BMP [a Russian armoured personnel carrier] in the side and the phosphorous goes off inside and the cunts in the back get out a bit sharpish. This phosphorous stuff is bloody good kit – they reckon it burns right down to the bone and the medics can do fuck all to get it out.

Such an outlook is typical of the many NCOs who like to think of the world as a hard, tough place and look at things with a harsh, cynical realism. 'I don't know why we're bothering with all this crap about moving POWs [Prisoners of War],' Sergeant W said to one of the authors on exercise. 'In the next war we're not going to be taking any bloody prisoners anyway.' Another sergeant bragged how, in Northern Ireland, he had cut a man clean in half with machine-gun fire. (In fact the shooting itself was justified, it was the sergeant's enthusiasm which was distasteful.)

For the officers, however, the NCO class is invaluable: it is central to the Army's functioning. Captain P's is a typical view:

> The NCOs are the movers and the shakers. They get things done. Most of them, of course, are as thick as pigshit but there really is not

> substitute for all those years of experience. When a young officer arrives in his battalion he will need to rely heavily on his platoon sergeant and that officer/NCO relationship goes all the way up the line in regimental soldiering: the company commander will rely on his company sergeant-major and even the commanding officer has a similar sort of relationship with the RSM.

Although NCOs have played an important role for a long time, the last twenty years have seen an increase in what has come to be known as 'sergeant power'. In many battalions there are sergeant platoon commanders – doing the same job as second lieutenants but not enjoying officer status. Some countries commission good NCOs almost as soon as their worth is noted, thus diluting the quality of the NCO class as a whole. In Britain, however, few NCOs appear to want to be commissioned – mainly for social or class reasons such as not wanting to lose their friends or because they fear that they would feel out of place in the Officers' Mess. Indeed, many of them genuinely like the life of an NCO. Towards the end of their careers most good warrant officers (the most senior grade of NCO) are offered a chance of a quartermaster's commission and usually hold a captain's rank as they serve out their time running the stores or performing some other administrative duty.

One of the main causes of the increase in sergeant power has been that they have been the only ones really to understand the technology in what has become an increasingly technical Army. This has also meant that NCOs are becoming better qualified – many who entered the Army with no educational qualifications at all sign up for courses run by the Royal Army Education Corps. However, the acquisition of educational qualifications can make even a Guards NCO (usually the most traditional and conservative) a little resentful of young officers. One colour-sergeant told us, 'It was all very well when officers had ten thousand acres – and were creatures apart – but now I've got my A levels, which is more than some officers. Things have changed.'

Whereas promotion for officers, if not automatic, is relatively smooth and predictable at least until the rank of major, for NCOs it is a tough and competitive business. One blemish on his record can ruin a man's career for life. According to a Company Sergeant-Major in a Guards battalion (where competition is at its most fierce):

> If you're going to rise through the ranks to NCO, it's very much survival of the fittest. Officers don't have that inbuilt burning ambition [which we have] to fill someone else's shoes. They are more friends

> together than we are. As NCOs and warrant officers you tend to be more aloof anyway.

Moreover, the system as it stands can militate against the promotion of the more intelligent and sensitive NCOs. It is important to get noticed, but because the officers who will be responsible for confirming promotions do not necessarily know what goes on behind the scenes, the NCO who employs quiet persuasion may find that the very existence of the problems he is solving is not known to his superiors. Consequently, the noisy, politically astute careerist will often be preferred over the man of real integrity.

The NCO ethos finds its institutional expression in the Sergeants' Mess. The Army argues that it is induction into this NCOs' version of the Officers' Mess that files down the rough proletarian edges of the former corporal and acts as a rite of passage into the lower-middle class (which is where the Army believes that the more senior NCOs properly belong). The Sergeants' Mess usually has a lot of rules of the 'jacket and tie and no jeans' variety and contains living accommodation for bachelors, a dining room and a bar (for which the Army has usually provided one or two fruit-machines in order to lend it a pubbishness to contrast with the clubbishness of the Officers' Mess). Ruled with a rod of iron by the RSM, it has a very correct and proper atmosphere – it is certainly not the sort of place where the regurgitated vomit of one's drinking companions is eaten. Indeed, in the past few years the drinking problem among NCOs has diminished as it has become clear to many of them that a reputation for excessive drinking is likely to prejudice their career prospects.

Once it has achieved this superficial social transformation of its NCOs, the Army appears content. Again, no moral or ethical dimension is emphasized, and little is done to develop a more rounded, mature and integrated character in the NCO. No one seems prepared to make a priority of instructing young NCOs that it is not helpful to bully people, that aggressive behaviour is distasteful and that a callous attitude towards human life (even the lives of enemies) is unacceptable in the Army of a democratic and Christian society.

The Private Soldiers

The unreasonable and sometimes brutal habits of some NCOs may, to an extent, be encouraged by the Army, but at least the authorities do try to modify the worst aspects of private soldiers' behaviour. Often they are not provided with the ideal raw material. The Army has to compete with industry and the dole. Many recruits have little formal education and increasingly many arrive without benefit of constructive parental guidance.

On arrival at the Army's induction centre at Sutton Coldfield in the West Midlands the potential recruit undergoes a series of aptitude tests. These determine whether or not he is suitable for military service at all (the Army can afford to be selective in periods of high unemployment) and, if so, to which branch of the Army he is most suited by virtue of his intelligence or previous working experience. The brightest tend to be sent to the more technical arms: the Royal Electrical and Mechanical Engineers and the Royal Signals; many of the less able end up in the infantry.

All recruits must pass through 13 weeks of basic training. For most this will be the first taste of real discipline they will have had in their lives and it is certainly a tough period. The Army says that this process is one of 'breaking down and building up': fostering a sense of team spirit at the expense of egotistical individualism. The reason behind it is the high degree of interdependence and mutual reliance that is a characteristic of soldiering, particularly in battle. Certainly, the British soldier is not known for letting down his mates when under fire nor for abandoning his responsibilities when he finds them inconvenient. Indeed, many have been surprised at how, in war, men who have led otherwise petty or venal lives have found themselves capable of extraordinary acts of courage and sacrifice.

Of course, basic training itself is not enough to explain this: the Army weaves a complex web of attachments to motivate people to risk their lives, but the process begins with an imposed discipline designed to generate the self-discipline which is essential for the conquest of fear. However, unless the martinet-like corporals who are charged with supervising this process at the various depots really know what they are doing (which includes knowing where to stop), they can easily bring about precisely the opposite effect to that which the Army intends. Instead of developing an attachment to the team, the recruit can become withdrawn and isolated, anxious only to stay in the background, carefully avoiding the corporal's eye lest trouble should ensue. This is the antithesis of true character-building. It results in the withering away of personal initiative and generates a reluctance to volunteer for any duty, however necessary for the well-being of the group or the achievement of the collective aim. The threshold at which this reaction is likely to occur may well be lower today than when the basic training regime was devised. The breakdown of communities and families in our inner cities has tended to produce a recruit far less socialized than at any other time in our history.

Once he is with his regiment, the single soldier will live in the block, usually in a room shared with four or five others. Bathroom and lavatory facilities are communal and the troops eat together in the cookhouse. Life in the block can soon become dull and troublesome: there are frequent inspections and each soldier is obliged to do his share of housework. This leads many of them into early marriages and the illusory delights of the married quarters 'patch'.

It is usually just after they have set up home that soldiers' financial problems begin. Many buy cars, hi-fis and electrical appliances on the 'never never'. Alas, never seems to arrive all too soon with a flurry of writs and repossession orders that the junior officers spend a long time sorting out on behalf of their men.

Marital infidelity is another constant problem and can cause serious disciplinary difficulties, particularly when a wife starts to sleep with a man who outranks her husband. Indeed, behind the seeming tranquillity of the patch, all kinds of sexual depravity can be found. One of the authors recalls an occasion when he caught a group of soldiers *in flagrante*:

> I was with another officer searching for some men who were late for duty one Sunday afternoon. Having been tipped off that they had been seen entering the home of a civilian who lived locally, we went to the house and rang the bell. The door was answered by a small, rather timid man who invited us in. 'We're looking for some soldiers,' my colleague explained, giving their names. 'Oh yes, they're here,' the man told us, 'upstairs – screwing my wife.' A few moments later, nine rather shame-faced soldiers appeared with the fattest and ugliest woman I have ever seen. She was quite clearly drunk and farted noisily as she come into the room. My brother officer and I politely declined the glasses of sweet sherry offered to us and left with our men. Later I asked one of the boys what he could conceivably have found attractive in the woman. 'The more gopping the slag is, Sir,' he replied, 'the better she is at it.' Another of the group remained sullen for days – he hadn't, it transpired, 'shot his load' by the time of our arrival. He subsequently became known amongst the officers as Coitus Interruptus – and this nickname was leaked to the ranks by an indiscreet subaltern, which further added to the man's misery.

Abroad, and especially in Germany, the great problem is boredom. Unable to speak the language, many soldiers and their wives fail to appreciate the opportunities that the country offers and develop a nostalgic yearning for home. The Army does its best by offering language training and providing sports facilities including skiing and sailing (which soldiers could not easily afford to try out in other postings) but, it seems, the problem is an intractable one. More than half the UK service and attached civilian personnel serving in Germany are accompanied by their families who make up a total of more than 80,000 dependants. Obviously, opportunities for the wives to find jobs are limited, though it has been argued that they are further limited by agreements between the British and West German governments on the number of German civilians to be employed at British military facilities. (This question is currently under review by the MoD and some action is likely, not least because the Public Accounts Committee of the House of Commons drew particular attention to it in their report on the 'Costs and Financial Control of British Forces Germany', published in November 1988.)

Indeed, the past year or two have witnessed rumblings that might portend something tantamount to a revolution on the part of Army wives. Many are angry at the Army's attitude towards them, which seems to be one of manipulative indifference requiring the officers' wives to act as unpaid social workers and then claiming the credit for providing help to soldiers' families. Four years ago Colonel Mike Gaffney was commissioned by the Army to write a report on the state of morale among Army wives. He found that it was low. 'We concluded that the root cause was a feeling of dissatisfaction with the Army itself,' he says. Although Gaffney is reported to have written his paper in an extremely tactful manner to ensure it was not dismissed out of hand, the report has not been published outside the Army itself.

Both in BAOR and in the UK there is often an atmosphere of barely repressed violence in the block and in the NAAFI: it is as if something is constantly bubbling just below the surface, and inevitably it sometimes boils over. Conversations between soldiers are characterized by the use of aggressive or foul language (the phrase 'swearing like a trooper' is an accurate simile) and often consists of little other than exchanged ego-challenges. In these circumstances relatively small quantities of alcohol are capable of catalysing an almost demonic savagery. The days when combatants would 'step outside' accompanied by seconds to hold their coats and ensure a fair fight have long since passed. Nowadays, broken bottles are wielded without compunction and when a man is down he is likely to be kicked repeatedly in the head and kidneys.

Possibly more worrying still is an increasing tendency for soldiers to 'drop' one another 'in the shit'. This is the habit of leaving undone some task that is, strictly, the responsibility of a colleague, and then, with no small measure of *schadenfreude*, sitting back to observe the consequent disciplinary action taken against the man who, for whatever reason, has failed to carry out the task in question. Not so long ago such a thing would have been unthinkable: there would have been too strong a sense of team loyalty. If one member of the platoon had failed to do something, others would have stepped in to see it performed. This is of particular concern because it suggests that the moral foundation of the Army's ability to fight may be being eaten away by a selfish worm.

The Army is, by nature, slow to right wrongs or initiate reforms. It took pressure from the Prince of Wales before anything was done to recruit a few black soldiers to the Guards and such steps as have been taken to deal with its institutionalized racism have been tentative. Largely, this has been because the Army refuses to recognize that it has a specifically racial problem. As is so often the case, it blames the outside world. Officers undergoing instruction on the Junior Command and Staff Course are taught that '. . . it would be odd if racial tensions from the wider society did not impinge on the military establishment, and there have been occasional allegations of racial disharmony within the armed forces.' Racial tensions have not 'impinged' on the military establishment from the outside: they are another part of the cult of intolerance and violence that the Army does too little to expunge from its ranks.

Anyone who has ever met many soldiers would know, by the simple expedient of listening to the way they speak about 'coons', 'niggers' and 'Pakis' that they are among the worst racial bigots to be found in society. If a policeman were to be heard expressing the sort of attitudes to blacks that are voiced every day by the average squaddie, he would soon be dismissed.

Richard Stokes, the first black Guardsman in the Grenadiers, was subjected to intense pressure to leave. He was sent to Coventry, anyone who associated with him was threatened, and he was victimized by the junior NCOs. It should not have taken a great deal of imagination on the part of the authorities to anticipate this problem and to take steps to pre-empt it. Clearly, if anything was done, it was not enough. Although Guardsman Stokes himself deserves most of the credit on account of the courage and tenacity he displayed, it is unlikely that he would have managed to find himself on parade outside Buckingham Palace in May 1988 had he not been the adopted son of a middle-class company director who was willing and able to confront the authorities and, when necessary, go to the newspapers in order to ensure that his son was treated fairly.

An investigation into racism in the Army carried out by Paul Lashmar and Arlen Harris of *The Observer* in 1986 uncovered evidence of widespread discrimination in promotion practices.

> Our enquiries reveal that black and Asian soldiers are subject to frequent personal abuse and discrimination; are much less likely to be promoted to NCO ranks; and stand virtually no chance of becoming officers.

One white Guards NCO told *The Observer* that it was well known that blacks were only promoted in regiments with the least prestige: 'Fish and chip regiments have black NCOs. The more fish and chip the regiment, the higher the rank [they reach].'

The journalists were forced to rely on the anecdotal evidence of past and serving black and Asian soldiers because the Army had kept no relevant statistics. The Army argued that it had no figures because it treated every individual alike, irrespective of race or colour, is somewhat disingenuous. It is one thing to avoid positive discrimination and be even-handed in matters of recruitment and preferment, but for an organization to prejudice its own ability to identify or plan for a potential social problem by denying itself essential management information is foolish.[1]

Even if the Army feels uncomfortable about acknowledging that it has racial problems, it should recognize that it has a duty to deal with the disciplinary problems caused by racial antagonisms. A serving black corporal complained to the *Observer* team:

> When I joined, I was asked if I was an animal and I was told I needed to be. I learnt it was true because everybody called me a black bastard. I used to sleep with a cricket bat under the bed because of attacks.

1. In Feb 1988 the Army commissioned a report from the management consultants Peat Marwick McLintock into the attitudes of ethnic minorities to the Army. This action was prompted by the realization that only 1.6 per cent of applications to join came from members of ethnic minorities, which account for 5.7 per cent of the population in the 15–24 age bracket. At the time of writing it is not known what the report will say, but fear of persecution and discrimination is sure to figure as a major factor. The Army is now keeping some statistics on its ethnic minorities.

The Army would like to claim all this has changed. Yet there is still only one black Guardsman, Stokes. One of his white colleagues told Kate Muir of *The Independent* (feature article, 19 June 1989) what he thought of a recent tour of Belize: 'We didn't really like Belize because of all the coloured people . . . notice that I say coloured people not Pakis and wogs. That's because the Army isn't racist any more.'

Towards the end of 1987, the newspapers were also full of stories of bullying in the Army which had no racial undertones. It seemed as if the publicity given to one or two incidents had given many victims the confidence to come forward. In October, Private James Guthrie of the King's Own Scottish Borderers claimed that his testicles had been burned, a broomstick had been thrust up his anus and that he had been dropped from a window 20 feet above the ground. On 5 November Lieutenant-Colonel Miles Frisby of the Coldstream Guards announced that he was confining his entire battalion to barracks whilst an investigation was mounted into a series of attacks on a young soldier. Patrick McGowan of the *Evening Standard* managed to trace a soldier from the unit who had been given leave to visit his pregnant wife in hospital. The journalist was told that the man who had been attacked was a 'bit of a brat' and that he had 'brought the attacks on himself. He was merely taught a lesson by some of the lads that he shouldn't go round shooting his mouth off.' On this occasion the Battalion Adjutant was unusually frank: 'This sort of thing has been going on quite a lot in the Army and we must take steps to stamp it out.'

This view was not reflected in the answer given by the Armed Forces Minister in December to the Labour MP, Jack Ashley, who had called for an independent ombudsman to investigate bullying in the Army:

> When considered in the context of an Army of almost 140,000 men and several hundred major units, they represent sporadic instances rather than any general, endemic cause for concern.

Jack Ashley was not satisfied with this answer, which he called 'one of the worst bromides I have received in twenty years in Parliament', and presented a dossier to the MoD detailing seventy letters of complaint he had received. The allegations these revealed involved officers as well as other ranks. They included the claim that young officers arriving in the Queen's Dragoon Guards (considered a very good regiment and the one in which Captain Mark Phillips served) had been stripped naked and been forced to drink cocktails containing urine, and an anonymous account, allegedly given by a serving soldier, who said he had been beaten, bound and thrown into a water tank where he almost drowned.

Not all the complaints made at or about this time could be investigated and some of those that were could not be substantiated, but the large number of cases being reported should have been a clear indication to the authorities that they were facing something more serious than isolated breakdowns of discipline.

It might be argued that, regrettable though such incidents are, some degree of violence should be expected in the armed forces since violence is not unknown in civilian society. However, the Army has important reasons for making sure that a soldier does not come to fear or distrust his fellows. On operations soldiers have to rely on one another, sometimes in extremely dangerous situations. Teamwork is vitally important and a *sine qua non* of teamwork is mutual trust. John Keegan writing in the *Sunday Telegraph*, argued that this means that bullying by equals is more, not less, serious than bullying by superiors. 'A bullying sergeant or corporal is a man who has broken the rules. A bullyboy gang is the enemy within – as seditious and destructive as the terrorists the Army is trained to fight.'

The Army's response to the problem of bullying has been, predictably, limited. Many officers believe that it is a problem that can be contained but not eradicated. It is probable that more effort will be devoted to ensuring that it is not reported in the newspapers again than to finding some long-term solution.[1] The latter challenge is a great one and would require the modification of the entire value system that has evolved in the Army and which is chiefly perpetuated by the NCO cadres.

This value system has its roots in the working-class culture of our industrial cities and is as clearly manifested on picket-lines and football terraces as it is within barracks. It equates strength with brutality, masculinity with a lack of sensitivity, and individualism with deviance. Outside the Army, these values are being challenged. The decline in size of the industrial proletariat and the increasing influence of women in the mainstream of society have led a large number of people to re-evaluate what constitutes male

1. The MoD possesses a large PR staff that often seems more concerned with 'perception management' than with telling the facts or assisting journalists. Its head, Hugh Colver, recently complained that journalists who had been given facility visits were not writing the sort of 'puffs' expected of them, but were artfully discovering their own unofficial stories – which often cast the Army in a poor light!

identity. The Army does not recognize the problem and has, accordingly, done nothing towards resolving it. Indeed, it continues to foster attitudes and assumptions that will have no place in civilian society in the future and increase the Army's isolation from the wider community.

Women Soldiers

The least macho, least problematic and arguably the most efficient soldiers in the Army are women. The Women's Royal Army Corps (WRAC) makes up about 4 per cent of total numbers. This may sound a small proportion but compares favourably with other countries. (Even in the Israeli Army, where women's roles have been much publicized, only 5 per cent are women.) It is a common misconception that women soldiers perform only routine, clerical tasks. In fact they work full-time in such diverse units as the Royal Engineers, the REME, the Royal Signals, the Royal Army Education Corps as well as in the Ordnance, Catering and Transport Corps. They do not, however, take part in direct combat (although women members of the Royal Military Police face considerable risks in Northern Ireland).

At present, the WRAC suffers from a rapid turnover of personnel, not least because a servicewoman is discharged if she becomes pregnant and there is no possibility of reinstatement. There is certainly an arguable case for recruiting more women and demographic trends is forcing the Army, which has hitherto been reluctant to increase their numbers, to rethink its policy. Women of the age groups from which the Army recruits have been found to be better educated, quicker to learn and even (according to studies carried out in the United States) better able to adjust to military discipline. Moreover, many civilian employers have found that women often prove more reliable workers, losing fewer days through alcohol abuse, minor illnesses and unexplained absenteeism. It could also be argued that the Army is in great need of those qualities generally held to be feminine, such as intuition, a tendency towards reconciliation in the resolution of conflict, sensitivity, and a willingness to discuss openly difficulties and concerns. The presence of greater numbers of women might also have a civilizing effect on those soldiers who persist in patterns of behaviour they consider impressive, other men find threatening, but which women very often find merely silly.

There would, however, be problems to be resolved. Where should the line be drawn? Should women be involved in combat? A number of practical arguments have been raised in relation to their relative lack of physical strength, but there would seem to be a wealth of opportunities for using more women in quasi-combat roles such as operating artillery computers, manning signals communications facilities and organizing re-supply.

One of the more interesting arguments for keeping women out of the fighting was raised by John Keegan in an article in *The Observer* of 15 November 1981. He suggested that the presence of women in the combat area might undermine the process of male bonding which he says is vitally necessary in battle. Keegan doubted whether that 'mixture of affection, dependence and desire to preserve face' could be sustained towards women since 'they [the soldiers] cannot risk the dependence because they have no experience of how far a woman can be trusted to sustain the terror and hardships of battle. They will not fear loss of face . . . because women react to moral collapse in men with tenderness rather than contempt.'

A new generation of soldiers, however, might have a markedly different attitude to women and to one another, which would rob Keegan's argument of some of its persuasive force. Moreover, women have proved themselves adept at certain kinds of warfare – guerrilla operations and sabotage, for instance – which may well become increasingly prominent in future conflicts. Whatever women's role in combat in the years to come, there would appear to be no good argument for not promoting a senior WRAC officer to sit on the Army Board.

The Future

On the threshold of the 1990s, the Army requires a radical change in outlook to ensure that its soldiers do not continue to be brutal, drunken and racist. The Army depends upon popular support for its funding, indeed for its continued existence, and there is bound to be an increasing reluctance on the part of taxpayers to pay for an Army that has allowed itself to become a social dinosaur.

Moreover, demographic trends imply that, in the years to come, the Army will be forced to accept for basic training a soldier of lower quality than it has been used to in the period of high unemployment in the 1980s. Whereas in many countries the Army is an important force for social development – for instance, in many Third World states it is where many men learn basic principles of hygiene. In Britain, as one senior officer told us, 'The Army is no longer a philanthropic organization.' At a time of far-reaching economic and social change which is seeing the emergence of an under-class of barely educated and barely employable youth, where the institution of the family is breaking down and where social alienation is setting in, perhaps the Army *ought* to become a philanthropic organization once more.

No doubt many will question the need for the sort of renewal of the Army's moral values that we are advocating in this chapter. If a soldier's function is to kill people, it will be argued, surely we don't want them to be nice guys? We would ask anyone who is inclined to advance such an objection to ponder the following points:

* It has been the commercial experience of many companies which have adopted 'ethical management' that being good leads ultimately to greater efficiency and success.
* A common feature of many of the world's great religions has been a recognition that there is something approaching a causal relationship between purity of motive on the one hand and outcome on the other. For instance, Catholics might argue that those things done 'for the greater glory of God' tend to be successful whilst man is always ultimately frustrated when he embarks upon a course of action for essentially selfish reasons. Buddhists have developed the idea of 'karma' whereby individuals always reap the rewards of good acts and find that wrongdoing rebounds upon them.
* So strong have been the associations of the profession of arms with spirituality that in many cultures soldiering and priesthood have been seen as parallel paths towards self-perfection.
* If lethal weapons are to be entrusted to a number of fellow citizens, it is surely preferable that they be given to the best men and women in society rather than the dross.

In short, what we are arguing for is an Army that does not judge its priorities on the narrow grounds of immediate utility but, realizing that its main assets are human beings, adapts its policies to the aim of developing the whole soldier.

5

A Game of Soldiers

'The grand old Duke of York,
He had then thousand men,
He marched them up to the top of the hill
And he marched them down again.'
Anon (18th C)

One of the most important dates in every Army unit's calendar is the annual 'Fit for Role' inspection.[1] This is an occasion when a senior officer will visit a regiment or battalion with a team of assessors to evaluate its readiness for battle. It is, at root, a dishonest affair which is covertly acknowledged by assessor and assessed alike to give an unrealistic picture of the unit's normal state of tactical preparedness. For example, much work goes into making ready for the inspection: vehicles that have not functioned properly all year are hurriedly fitted with the spare parts that have previously been 'unobtainable'; soldiers who have been detached from their normal duties and officers on extended leave are recalled to perform their proper functions.

The day can involve any number of inspections of men and *matériel* and, on some occasions, a surprise attack mounted at considerable expense from helicopters by a neighbouring, rival battalion who see it as its job to show up the incompetence of the unit under inspection. As soon as the attack is launched, some quick-thinking officer invariably ushers the visiting brigadier into a command post made ready for such a contingency and begins to

1. The name of the inspection changes from time to time and command to command – but every unit has one.

issue orders over the radio. The brigadier, for his part, takes out his notebook and records the promptness of the officer's appraisal of the unfolding attack and the effectiveness of his command of the defending forces. At this stage, the men engaged in the mock battle become confused. Why, they ask themselves, is the officer at RHQ having a conversation with himself? And why is he ignoring all the contact and situation reports being sent to him? The answer is, of course, that the orders being given over the radio bear no relation to conditions on the ground; the officer has recognized that he will make a better impression on the brigadier if he makes a confident pretence of being in command of the situation than he would if he were to make a genuine attempt at dealing with the emergency. On many such occasions very high marks are awarded for actions which, under combat conditions, would have resulted in humiliating defeat.

The Fit for Role inspection does, however, serve one useful purpose: it concentrates the minds of all ranks on the fact that beyond the daily drudgery of servicing vehicles and performing barrack duties there is a purpose, there is an enemy. On this one day of the year, a regiment is as ready for war as it is ever likely to be. The annual inspection is intended to test the individual unit's ability to carry out the role with which it is tasked, and consequently both officers and men will have been briefed about the particular threat they face in their theatre of operations.

In this chapter we will consider the Army's principal commitment – the defence of a portion of NATO's central front in Germany. It is there, beyond a fortified fence dotted with watch-towers, that the formidable forces of the Warsaw Pact have for more than forty years been deployed in a configuration that suggests an aggressive intent.

To prepare to do battle with the Group of Soviet Forces in Germany (GSFG), the British Army of the Rhine (BAOR) spends much of its time on manoeuvres. These take place at every level of command and can involve anything up to 100,000 men moving through the towns and villages of the North German Plain. Often dismissed as war-games or 'playing soldiers', these mock battles (or even mock wars) do have a rationale. For the generals and brigadiers, for example, it is the only chance they get to practise their trade – the command and control of thousands of men in a fast-moving and fluid situation. But to other participants they can seem silly.

It would be comforting to believe that these exercises went as smoothly as the MoD PR people lead journalists to believe. The 'official version' is that every exercise is a success. If mistakes are made (and it is admitted that they are), these teach valuable lessons for the future and, of course, the same mistake will not be made a second time. However, the overwhelming impression gained from the personal testimony of past and serving soldiers of all ranks is that many major exercises in Germany are chaotic.

The Army's equipment is generally as good as, if not better than, that possessed by other armies, but despite the enormous amount of time that is spent servicing Army vehicles – both by the units that operate them and by the Royal Electrical and Mechanical Engineers (REME) – an extraordinary number are unable to sustain more than a few days of use without requiring recovery or repair in the field.

Indeed, considering the cost of modern equipment, outsiders might well be amazed by just how unreliable much of it is in practice. One former officer told us 'exercises were always something of a joke, but they brought home a serious message – if we can't keep more than 60 per cent of our vehicles going in a couple of days of pretend war what on earth would happen in a real one?

Moreover, for soldiers of all ranks exercises have something of a party atmosphere. It is astonishing how many cans of beer for consumption by the troopers can be carried in the ammunition racks and even down the barrel of a Challenger tank. Nor do the officers go without their creature comforts. On one famous occasion in the early part of this decade one colourful cavalry colonel had a marquee erected in the middle of a field in Germany. Having decked it out with damask table cloths, fine glassware and Mess silver, he entertained all the officers of the brigade to drinks. When reproached for such frivolity by a more serious-minded colleague from the infantry, the colonel is alleged to have replied that it was 'the cavalry's traditional role in war to lend a little tone to what otherwise might degenerate into a vulgar brawl'. He was paraphrasing a much-celebrated remark made about the use of cavalry in the First World War.[1]

Besides parties, the main fun to be had on manoeuvres arises from the opportunities to do damage. If a soldier is asked about the high point of his service in Germany it is quite likely that he will tell you a story about driving a tank through a barn wall, or flattening all the crops in a field. Every major exercise has its damage allowance, sometimes running into millions of Deutschmarks. Its existence is widely known amongst our soldiers, who comfort themselves with

1. Its origin is sometimes said to have been a *Punch* cartoon.

the myth that the farmers prefer to collect the compensation rather than gather in their harvest.

But there is one thing that sours the jollity of the Army's war-games: the way in which they almost invariably end. Once 'Orange' Forces have invaded and 'Blue' Forces have withdrawn and then counter-attacked, been successful for a time but finally fallen back, unable to withstand Orange Forces' overwhelming numbers, the order comes authorizing the use of tactical nuclear weapons. In some brigade headquarters the watchkeepers have grown so used to this that they take it as their cue to stand down, so that when the order *ENDEX* is transmitted, bringing proceedings to a formal close, there is no one there to receive it.

At such times soldiers wonder if there is any purpose in what they are doing. Because they know the awesome power of the weapons they have been trained to use, they are aware of the futility, for both sides, of modern war. In his book *The Face of Battle* John Keegan wrote:

> It remains for armies to admit that the battles of the future will be fought in never-never land. While the great armoured hosts face each other across the boundary between east and west, no soldier on either side will concede that he does not believe in the function for which he plans and trains. As long as states put weapons in their hands, they will show each other the iron face of war. But the suspicion grows that battle has already abolished itself.[1]

Soldiers today are in the business of deterrence. They prepare for war in order to prevent war. They become expert in the handling of weapons they are never intended to use. They know that if they believe in the impossibility of war, that belief will make it possible. In order properly to understand the world of paradoxes in which the Army is required to function, we need to examine the origins and changing nature of the challenge posed by the Warsaw Pact armies, and assess the responses that NATO has developed to counter it.

The Strategic Perspective

When NATO was set up in 1949, the Soviet Union posed a real and, some thought, immediate threat to the security of Western Europe. As early as 1946, the Foreign Secretary, Ernest Bevin, had advised

1. *The Face of Battle*, John Keegan, p. 343 (Penguin edn., 1978).

the Cabinet that 'The danger of Russia has become certainly as great as and possibly even greater than a revived Germany.' Soviet forces had taken up a threatening posture along the borders of the Eastern Bloc countries and when they sealed off Berlin in 1949, it required an enormous airlift by the Western powers to supply the city with food, fuel and essential supplies. At the same time, the Soviets launched an ideological offensive against the capitalist world, and its proclaimed doctrine was to undermine or destroy Western society.

In 1948, Britain, France and the Benelux countries concluded the Treaty of Brussels, a mutual-aid pact designed to last for fifty years. A shortcoming of this agreement was that all the signatories had been economically exhausted by the war. The realization that it would be necessary to harness the United States to the cause of European peace led, in 1949, to the North Atlantic Treaty.

The strategy the North Atlantic Treaty Organization (NATO) adopted to meet the Soviet threat was one of forward defence. This was agreed at a meeting of the North Atlantic Council (a colloquium of the foreign and defence ministers of all the NATO countries) in 1950 and remains one of the main planks of our defence strategy today. The Germans were particularly keen to emphasize that any war fought in Europe should be fought as far to the east as possible. As Germany's Defence Minister, put it in 1963:

> To regard the Federal Republic, or even a large part of Western Europe solely as a battlefield, which NATO forces would have to liberate afterwards, would forecast the total destruction of Western Europe. This appears to be hardly a valid objective of defence policy.[1]

Of course, Germany's concern stemmed from the fact that approximately 30 per cent of its population, together with a quarter of its industry, lies within 100 km of its border with the Eastern Bloc. It would, consequently, have been politically impossible to persuade the Germans to co-operate in any policy which involved abandoning them in the event of hostilities breaking out.

Military factors were also adduced by those in favour of the forward defence option: the ground close to the Inner German Border (IGB) is cut across by rivers, canals and forests, is marshy in places, and features some sizeable towns which give the defence natural advantages. It was further argued that it would be sensible

1. Von Hassel, speech, 1963.

to deny the Soviets the psychological advantage that would accrue from a rapid, unopposed drive through miles of NATO territory.

West Germany was allowed to join the alliance in 1954 and in the following year its army, the *Bundeswehr*, was established. Britain chose to maintain a substantial number of soldiers in Germany, and this force became BAOR. Despite its name, it is not stationed on the banks of the Rhine; rather, most of its fighting units are sited well forward to the east, some right on the border such as those at Celle and Wolfenbuettel.

Although it became the corner-stone of our post-war defence policy, the forward defence doctrine has never been universally accepted. Some have argued that it is contrary to one of the main principles of warfare: that defence should be organized in depth. Others have pointed to the political difficulties of a strategy that could, in the hands of a skilled propagandist, be made to appear an aggressive disposition of forces. NATO has always made it clear that its armies will only be used in the event of an attack and it is doubtful whether they would make much headway if they did launch themselves across the border into East Germany. Nevertheless, their deployment so close to the IGB has consistently been used to justify the presence of substantial Soviet forces in the Eastern Bloc and may give rise to genuine fears among the populations of the Communist countries. Though we persist with the policy of forward defence, it is commonly accepted that its utility is chiefly political rather than military, its primary purpose being to keep West Germany inside the alliance.

However, defence technology has changed considerably since the doctrine of forward defence was first agreed, particularly in the area of mobility, and some strategists now believe that Germany's security would be better guaranteed by a more mobile defence, offering the added dimension of depth. Forward defence, they argue, is too vulnerable to attack in rear areas by airborne forces (which the Warsaw Pact has greatly expanded in the past twenty years) and is far too static – making attempts to manoeuvre involving withdrawal, with its attendant damaging effects on morale, extremely difficult. The anti-forward-defence lobby's counter to the Germans' objection that their cities would be ruined in the event of invasion by the Warsaw Pact is that a more credible defence would effectively deter such an invasion in the first place.

Moreover, the British Army claims that forward defence does not necessarily imply static defence. The official line is that the need for mobile operations is recognized and that ground would have to be conceded in the event of a strong Soviet thrust across the IGB. The enemy would be engaged by a delaying force once reconnaissance elements had been able to identify the main direction of attack. This delaying force would be tasked to keep the enemy occupied for sufficient time to allow the main defence forces to prepare strong positions, making the best use of obstacles such as demolished bridges, tank-traps and minefields, so that the invading army would be broken up into manageable packets which could then be engaged by highly mobile counter-attack forces from the flanks.

The acknowledged weakness of our defence plan is its reliance on rapid reinforcement with reserves. We would have to move enormous numbers of men and quantitites of *matériel* by sea (where they would be vulnerable) and difficult political decisions would have to be made if the Soviet leadership, at a time of escalating tension, were to declare that they regarded any such reinforcement as provocative and likely to bring about war more speedily.

But a factor explaining the endurance of forward defence in the face of technological change and the scepticism of strategic analysts is France's position outside the integrated military command structure of NATO since 1966. According to the 1988 UK Defence White Paper:

> The absence of France. . . means that all Western forces on the central front, with their associated airfields, ammunition dumps, support and other facilities, are located in a narrow corridor 250–350 km wide, consisting of the Federal Republic and the Benelux Countries.[1]

The danger that these assets might be quickly overrun, it is argued, makes forward defence inevitable.

Within this context our troops on the central front have two inextricably linked tasks. The first is, simply by being there, to deter an invasion. If they fail in that (or, more likely, if the politicians fail for them), then their role is to buy time for political negotiations to bring about peace. Accordingly, policy-makers need to keep asking themselves three key questions: what level of forces is needed effectively to deter an invasion? If deterrence fails, how much time do we need to buy? What bargaining counters will need to remain in our hands to secure a reasonable deal at the negotiating table?

1. HMSO. Cm. 344–1.

Estimates of the amount of time our current level of defence spending will buy us vary between four days and three weeks but most strategists agree on a fortnight. The cold fact of the matter is, then, that the greater part of the British Army is dedicated to *losing* a two-week battle in Europe.

This situation has arisen purely because of the existence of nuclear weapons. It is now broadly accepted that the actual use of nuclear weapons would be a disaster for all concerned; that it would be difficult, if not impossible, to restrict their use to the battlefield; and that once the nuclear threshold was crossed, both parties to any conflict would suffer such great damage as to render the original decision to take up arms counter-productive. However, it is also recognized that NATO forces in danger of being overrun might have no option but to resort to tactical nuclear weapons in the hope of bringing hostilities to a close by forcing the enemy to parley. The role of NATO's conventional forces is, therefore, to enable the use of nuclear weapons to be delayed for as long as possible in the hope that the threat of nuclear release will bring the enemy to the negotiating table.

However, there is by no means complete unanimity within NATO as to how much time we will need to buy nor even whether the approach will be effective since ultimately it depends upon convincing the Soviet Union that we are prepared to make first use of battlefield nuclear weapons. It is possible that they will not believe us, not least because so many of our own strategic thinkers have so publicly warned against it. According to Field-Marshal Lord Carver:

> So far as redressing any conventional imbalance goes, reliance on the early use of nuclear weapons is no answer. The facts of the matter are that, if NATO initiated the use of nuclear weapons, it would suffer proportionately more damage than the Warsaw Pact and its forces, so it would be cutting off its nose to spite its face.[1]

We seem to be saddled for fundamentally political reasons with a doctrine of forward defence that gives us a military disadvantage, and with a theory of nuclear deterrence whose credibility, and therefore effectiveness, is increasingly in doubt. In *Choices*, Oliver Ramsbotham contrasts the arguments of two strands of analysis of this and related questions. The case against relying on battlefield nuclear weapons he puts thus:

1. *Choices*, ed. Ramsbotham, p. 177 (Brasseys, 1986).

> NATO's reliance on the illusion of nuclear deterrence means that there is no incentive to plan for adequate non-nuclear defence. It is a counsel of despair. And yet the great wealth, manpower and technical superiority of the nations of the Western alliance make it unnecessary and absurd that NATO should still be clinging to this traditional mixture of belligerence and defeatism. There is simply no reason why the Eastern Bloc's conventional threat, such as it is, should not be met by Western conventional forces. Particularly today there are a large number of possibilities to be exploited, which include a more effective use of reserve manpower, the construction of proper defensive fortifications and the application of those advanced technologies in which the West has a commanding lead. The opportunity is there to be seized as new technology threatens to make capital intensive systems such as tanks . . . decreasingly cost-effective and vulnerable to cheaper, precision guided missiles and rockets, some of them hand-held.[1]

With the emergence of these gnawing doubts about the credibility of our battlefield nuclear weapons, greater emphasis has begun to be put upon the need for deep strike or Follow-on Forces Attack (FOFA). A capability to strike deep into the enemy's own territory is desirable in order to break up his second- and third-wave formations, to disrupt his re-supply and logistics elements and to neutralize his airfields. In 1985 NATO adopted FOFA as part of its strategic doctrine but left each national contingent to decide how to use it in its own way. Some strategists are now arguing that the development of FOFA could add a new dimension to deterrence in that the Warsaw Pact might be less willing to launch an attack into West Germany if considerable damage might be done to Eastern Bloc territory as a consequence. However, it is most unlikely that we could develop our land forces to the point where they would be capable of striking far into East Germany and FOFA would seem, therefore, to be better suited to attack-aircraft. This is an area in which technology is developing very rapidly and a new generation of ground-to-air missiles might limit the usefulness of aircraft over enemy territory considerably. The deterrent value of FOFA would, then, be rather short-lived. FOFA capability also has an attendant political disadvantage in that it provides the other side with a good excuse for maintaining strong forces. While the West is demonstrably incapable of launching any attack on Warsaw Pact soil, the bankruptcy of the Soviet Union's case for stationing enormous armies along the borders of the Eastern Bloc countries is easily

1. Ibid.

exposed, but if the Soviets can point to a genuine threat, they can justify keeping large numbers of troops in Europe.

Underlying all these considerations is NATO's governing strategic principle: flexible response. According to this doctrine NATO should maintain an appropriate set of counter-measures to match any foreseeable Warsaw Pact initiative. Chiefly, it is a policy designed to avoid full-scale nuclear war by ensuring that strategic nuclear weapons are not all that remains in our arsenal to meet a conventional or limited nuclear attack. We have been able, broadly, to match the Warsaw Pact weapon-system for weapon-system in the nuclear field (nuclear weapons are relatively cheap), but NATO countries are constrained by the democratically expressed wishes of their citizens from spending as much on conventional weapons (as a proportion of GDP) as the Soviet Union and her allies. This means that our response is not as flexible as we would like it to be and that the main danger of a nuclear war starting lies not with some madman pressing the button to launch an all-out strategic attack, but with the West starting to lose what would begin as a conventional conflict. If we were to start losing, it would not be because the quality of our manpower or our weaponry was lower than that of the enemy's. It would simply be a matter of numbers.

One of the problems that has frustrated objective assessment of the strength of the Warsaw Pact's conventional forces has been that the figures quoted by analysts are arrived at on the basis of different counting methods. Since the Warsaw Pact releases very little information about its force levels, most estimates in the West are gleaned from the International Institute for Strategic Studies' (IISS) annually updated publication *The Strategic Balance*. However, in November 1988, NATO published figures of its own which it said were based on intelligence unavailable to IISS and were consequently more reliable (figs. 2 and 3).

It is difficult to tell quite how realistic these figures are. At first sight a 3:1 superiority in tanks might seem alarming, but how many of the Soviet tanks counted are modern? How many may be more than twenty years old? The United States has estimated that only about 40 per cent would qualify as modern but warns that there is a fairly advanced programme of refitting and regunning the older tanks. However, even if a degree of over-enthusiasm on the part of the NATO staff who compiled the figures were to be taken into account, they cannot be said to produce an encouraging picture. On the basis of the NATO figures, the Warsaw Pact enjoys a superiority in personnel of 1.4:1, in artillery of approximately 3:1, in anti-tank

Fig. 2: Conventional Forces in Europe, January 1988.

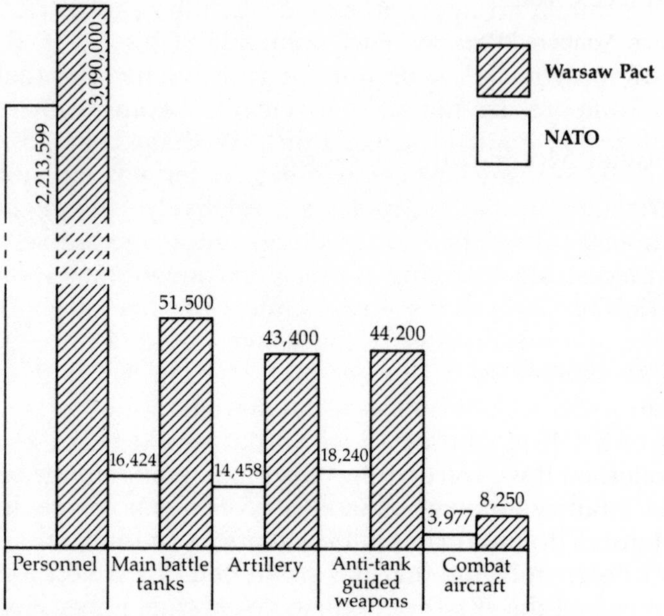

	NATO	Warsaw Pact
Personnel	2,213,599	3,090,000
Main battle tanks	16,424	51,500
Artillery	14,458	43,400
Anti-tank guided weapons	18,240	44,200
Combat aircraft	3,977	8,250

Note: these figures cover forces deployed between the Atlantic and the Urals.

Fig. 3: The Current Balance of Forces on the Central Front.

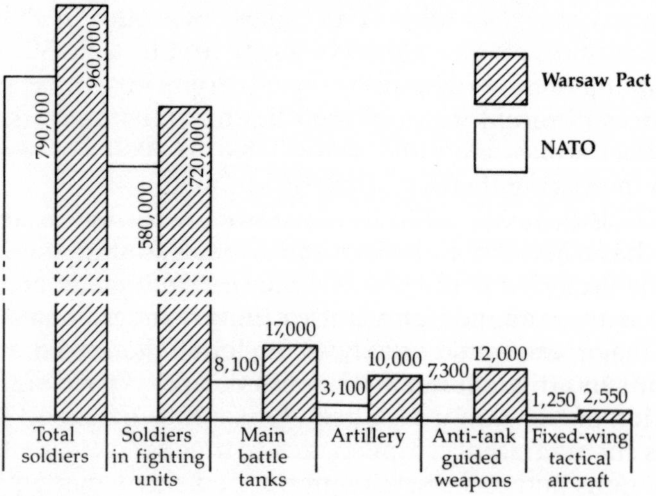

	NATO	Warsaw Pact
Total soldiers	790,000	960,000
Soldiers in fighting units	580,000	720,000
Main battle tanks	8,100	17,000
Artillery	3,100	10,000
Anti-tank guided weapons	7,300	12,000
Fixed-wing tactical aircraft	1,250	2,550

Fig. 4: The Soviet Tank Division

Tanks: 330
APC/IFVs: 255
Artillery pieces: 165

Note: APC = Armoured Personnel Carrier; IFV = Infantry Fighting Vehicle

Fig. 5: Soviet Motor-Rifle Division

Tanks: 270
APC/IFVs: 680
Artillery pieces: 215
Troops: 13,500.

Source: *Soviet Military Power*, US Secretary of Defence Frank Carlucci, April 1988.

weapons of 2.4:1, in combat aircraft of 2:1 and (according to other figures released by NATO) has more than five times as many armoured infantry combat vehicles. The Soviets, of course, argue that the figures do not include US forces stationed in America who would be flown to reinforce Europe in time of war; however, it might not be possible effectively to deploy those reinforcements – at least not in the potentially decisive first few days of battle – if the Warsaw Pact were to launch a surprise attack from a standing start.

Not only have the Warsaw Pact countries been expanding their armed forces in recent years (though at the time of writing certain Warsaw Pact armies are announcing troop reductions), they have also been improving them in terms of equipment and organization. Since 1980 the Soviet Division has undergone a facelift: tank divisions have had extra artillery and mechanized infantry (motor rifle) elements added to them whilst motor-rifle divisions have been equipped with more modern vehicles (figs. 4 and 5).

Other major improvements have included the replacement of towed guns in artillery units with tracked, self-propelled guns; the introduction of two new attack helicopters (HAVOC and HOKUM) as well as the upgrading of the existing HIND and HIP helicopters with new guns and rockets. Moreover, the Soviets possess and are trained to use chemical weapons which most Western countries would not countenance using.

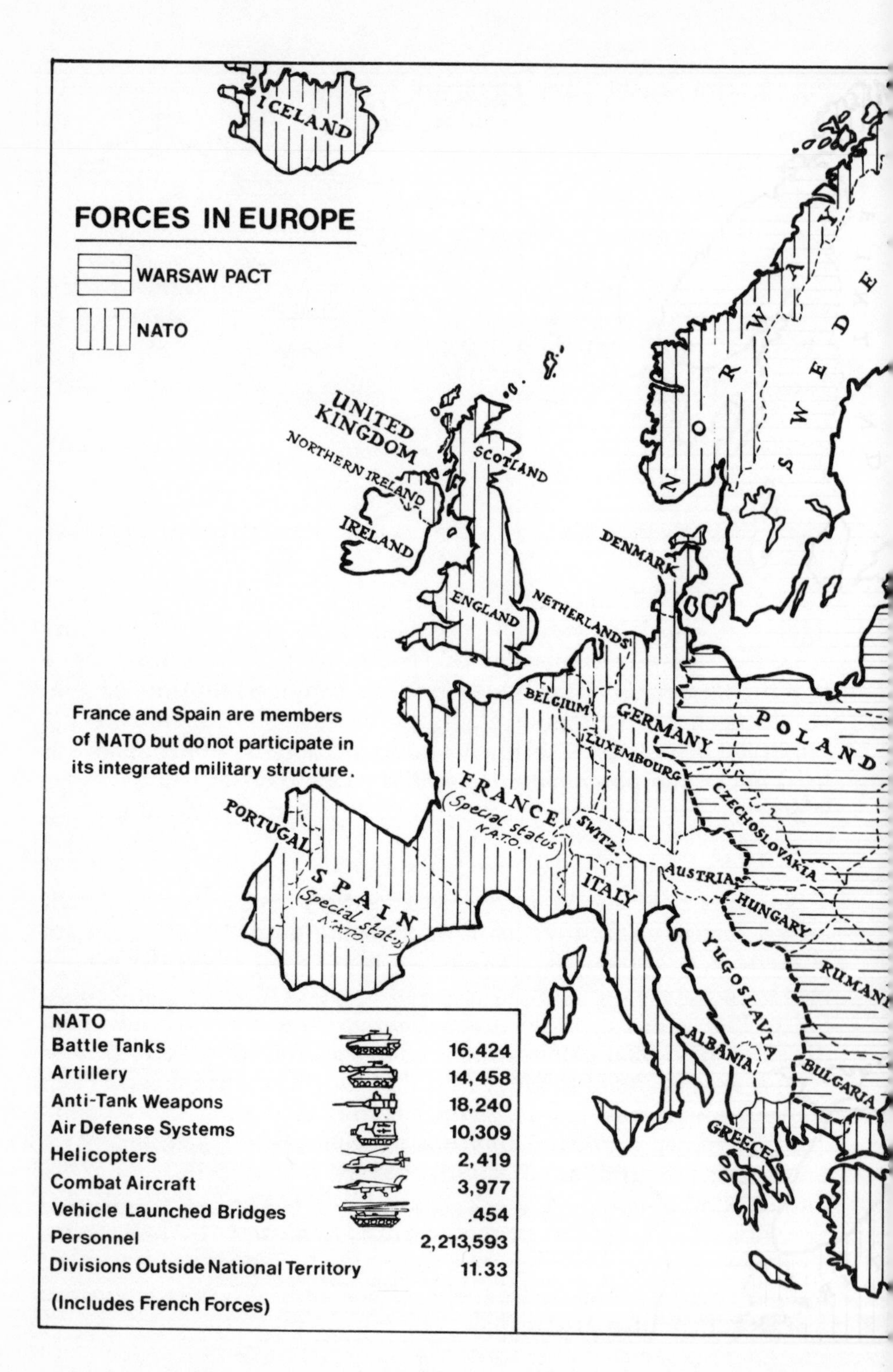

NATO	
Battle Tanks	16,424
Artillery	14,458
Anti-Tank Weapons	18,240
Air Defense Systems	10,309
Helicopters	2,419
Combat Aircraft	3,977
Vehicle Launched Bridges	.454
Personnel	2,213,593
Divisions Outside National Territory	11.33

(Includes French Forces)

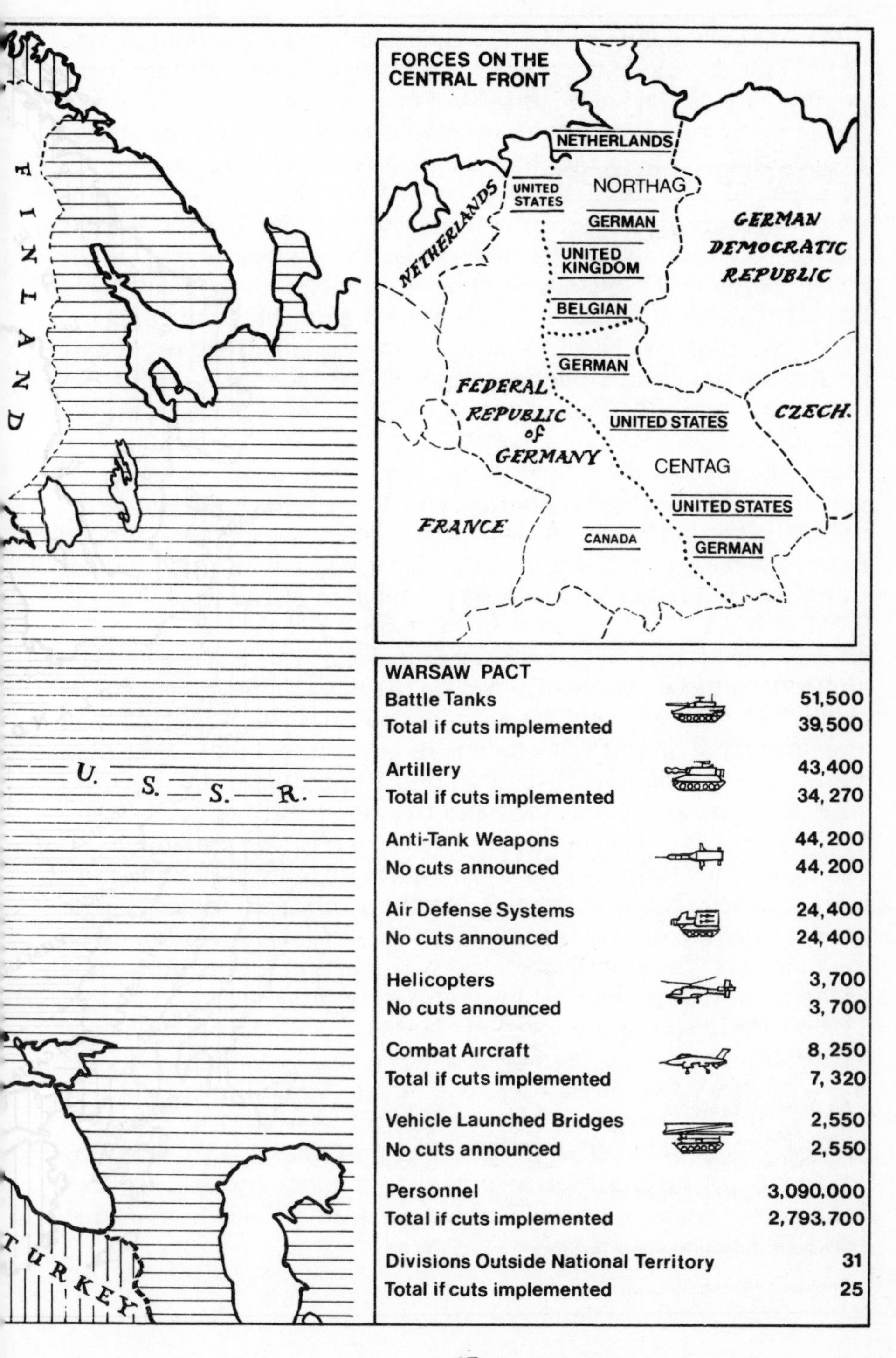
FINLAND
U. S. S. R.
TURKEY
FORCES ON THE CENTRAL FRONT
NETHERLANDS
NETHERLANDS
UNITED STATES
NORTHAG
GERMAN
UNITED KINGDOM
BELGIAN
GERMAN
GERMAN DEMOCRATIC REPUBLIC
FEDERAL REPUBLIC of GERMANY
UNITED STATES
CZECH.
CENTAG
UNITED STATES
FRANCE
CANADA
GERMAN
WARSAW PACT
Battle Tanks 51,500
Total if cuts implemented 39,500
Artillery 43,400
Total if cuts implemented 34,270
Anti-Tank Weapons 44,200
No cuts announced 44,200
Air Defense Systems 24,400
No cuts announced 24,400
Helicopters 3,700
No cuts announced 3,700
Combat Aircraft 8,250
Total if cuts implemented 7,320
Vehicle Launched Bridges 2,550
No cuts announced 2,550
Personnel 3,090,000
Total if cuts implemented 2,793,700
Divisions Outside National Territory 31
Total if cuts implemented 25

When, in December 1988, Mikhail Gorbachev announced unilateral cuts in conventional forces in Europe, it seemed that many politicians were taken by surprise. Some welcomed the move as a turning-point in world affairs as significant as any since the start of the cold war. Others said that the cuts were not large enough as they would still leave the Warsaw Pact with an overwhelming preponderance of forces. The Gorbachev proposals included the pledge to withdraw 10,000 tanks from the european part of the Soviet Union and from eastern Europe. Some of these tanks would be part of six tank divisions to be removed, probably from Hungary, Czechoslovakia and East Germany. These six tank divisions are said by the Soviets to account for about 50,000 men and 5,000 tanks (although on NATO's usual accounting basis they would normally be made up of 1,900 tanks and 72,000 men, which suggests that there will be some simultaneous reorganization of Soviet divisional structure). The Soviets cannot achieve these reductions simply by retiring older tanks. According to the American specialist, Phillip Karber, some 3,000 of the most modern will have to go, and Mr Gorbachev has indicated that he is prepared to withdraw as many as 5,000 of these. Also included in the Gorbachev package are 8,500 artillery pieces and 800 combat aircraft. However, it has also been argued that these cuts, which reduce the Soviet tank superiority to about 2:1, may well not be as unilateral as the manner of their announcement implied. Certainly it is expected that West Germany's forces will be reduced by up to 10 per cent in the next few years for demographic reasons and the new United States Defence Secretary may be expected to come under increasing pressure to cut Pentagon spending as part of the plan to reduce Washington's budget deficit. NATO responded to the Gorbachev initiative with proposals of its own, for instance, the establishment of a ceiling on the number of tanks in Europe for each side and for the proportion of the total that can be held by any one country.

The withdrawals announced in New York still leave the Warsaw Pact outnumbering us in conventional forces, but at least they set the scene for talks on further reductions. Attention now will be focused on the progress of the Conventional Armed Forces in Europe (CFE) talks. The declared aim of these talks was 'the elimination of disparities that prejudice stability and security and the elimination, as a priority, of the capacity to launch a surprise attack or large-scale offensive actions.'[1]

1. *CTE Handbook*, US Information Agency (March 1989)

NATO wants to see asymmetric cuts designed to achieve something as close to parity between the conventional forces of East and West as can be negotiated. The Soviets, for their part, do seem to have accepted the principle that their forces should become 'clearly defensive' and have underlined their willingness to remove weaponry of an obviously offensive sort, such as assault bridging equipment. This implies fundamental changes both in the way the Soviet Union looks at the whole question of defence and, consequently, in the West's assessment of the Warsaw Pact threat. In order to judge which way those changes might go, we need first to look at the coherent doctrine that the Soviets have developed over the years to lend their military planning purpose and direction.

Soviet Military Doctrine

> In the West, the concept of strategy, as a plan of action for the conduct of war, has a long and distinguished history. We have not, however, developed any universally applicable theoretical structure for the organized study of war. In the West the term 'military doctrine', if it is used at all, generally means tactical principles and regulations, a set of guidelines for the tactical commander, or a list of principles to stimulate original and creative thought. In contrast, the Soviet concept of military doctrine . . . is both systematic and markedly more comprehensive in its scope.[1]

Like everything else in the Soviet Union, military doctrine is heavily politicized. An ambitious person in a Marxist-Leninist society soon learns to frame the justification for any actions or proposals in ideological terms. After a while it seems as if all areas of human activity have a set of rules, based on sound ideological principles and apparently immutable. The interpretation of these obscure charters has provided fertile ground for academics in the West, some of whom have tended further to obfuscate the already obscure. We have, for example, been told that the reason the Soviet Union maintains an enormous army (which swallows up a hefty slice of the 15 per cent of GDP spent on defence) is not that it has any ideas of extending its hegemony westwards but is related to 'Marxist-Leninist principles' and a sort of folk memory of the Second World War in which more than 20 million Soviet citizens

1. Statement on the Defence Estimates 1988.

lost their lives. That may be the case, but does it mean they will be more likely to invade, or less likely?

There is a strong case to be made that what has really governed Soviet military doctrine in the past has been grim economic realism, a sense of vulnerability created by geography (the USSR has the longest borders of any country in the world), the position of influence enjoyed by the military within the ruling élite, and an awareness of a real technology gap *vis-à-vis* the West. Moreover, in the age of *perestroika* military doctrines will change, and change fast. No better proof of this can be required than the Soviet Union's decision to implement unilateral cuts. In his speech to the UN, Gorbachev seemed to imply that there would be major changes in terms of defence thinking as well as actual cuts in the numbers of conventional forces.

The Soviet *Military Encyclopaedic Dictionary* defines 'military doctrine' as:

> a system of views, adopted in a country at a given time, on the nature, aims and character of a possible future war, on the preparation of the country and its armed forces for it, and of the methods of waging it.

Soviet military doctrine remained fairly rigid and mechanical throughout Brezhnev's 'years of stagnation' and it is likely that the Soviet Army will be slower to embrace the ideas associated with *perestroika* than other sections of society. The Soviet Union's analysis of war has always been conducted in economic and numerical terms. It holds that in a war of long duration, the side which is economically stronger must eventually prevail. The immense economic resources of the United States combined with those of Western Europe give NATO a clear advantage according to this analysis. Consequently, the Warsaw Pact policy-makers have determined that they should avoid involvement in a long war, but should hostilities become necessary, be prepared to win a short one. Gorbachev gave some indications in New York that he may be about to abandon this traditional analysis. Chief amongst these was the commitment to ensure that the Soviet Union's force dispositions become 'clearly defensive' (though we have yet to see whether the Soviet Union will accept the interpretation of that phrase that we would put upon it in the West).

Whatever emerges from the CFE talks, the mere concession of this principle could have very far-reaching implications. For instance, it would imply that the old doctrine of the need to win a short war by maintaining the capability of mounting an invasion from a standing start will have to be abandoned. One Soviet analyst, Colonel Vladimir Chernyshev,[1] has set out a number of possible courses for defensive defence. One would be where 'both sides would have to work out means for immediate counteractions [strategic offensive operations] in case of war, trying to move military operations into the enemy's territory and air-space as quickly as possible'. If the Russians adopt this approach little will change as they will claim that forces capable of sustained offensive operations are in some perverse way defensive. The second possible course Chernyshev examines is one in which 'each side would confine themselves to defensive operations at the initial stages of the conflict, relying on deep, layered and well-prepared defences'. However, in this scenario there comes a stage where, 'having warded off the attack, the defensive troops would mount a counter-attack developing it until the aggressor is routed in his own territory.' Again this would imply that the Soviet Union would need to maintain forces which could invade Western Europe.

Chernyshev does, however, look at possibilities which involve the defeat of the intruder on the defender's own territory. One of these is a strategy consistent with the idea that troop configurations should be clearly defensive. 'In this case,' Chernyshev argues, 'the armies should have neither strike aviation nor the destructive means for a surprise attack. . . neither should be mobile or have strike potential (tanks and assault aviation) or the possibilities for penetrating attacks.' He lists the most destabilizing weapons systems as tactical strike aviation, tanks, long-range artillery, multiple-rocket-launcher systems, and the main classes of warship, and concludes: 'The reduction and elimination of these forces would largely preclude dangerous plans and provocations'.

The radical nature of Chernyshev's suggestions can be appreciated by contrasting them with current Soviet operational principles, in which particular emphasis is placed upon:

* Surprise and deception
* Speed
* Concentration
* Deep battle
* Air superiority

Surprise and deception: The Soviets regard surprise as a 'force multiplier', the effect of a surprise attack with forces of a given size

1 . *Janes Defence Weekly*, vol. II number 4.

being equivalent to the effect of a much larger force where surprise is absent. Most strategists agree that an attack on the central front would probably be made only with those forces currently deployed in Warsaw Pact countries: this is the so-called 'standing start' attack. In order to gain surprise the Soviets would rely on a process they call *maskirovka* – a combination of security measures and deception techniques designed not only to mask their preparations for attack but also to lead the West to be deceived as to the timing, the scale and the axis of the offensive. These activities would involve not only military personnel but also diplomats and intelligence operatives abroad. (The KGB defector Gordievsky who worked for many years for MI6 recently made public details of procedures whereby a watch would be kept on buildings in Whitehall so that, by counting the number of lights burning at night, Soviet analysts would be able to monitor whether the Western powers had found out about any planned attack!)

Speed: The Warsaw Pact invading forces would try to advance at a rate of approximately 50 km per day. Their main aim would be to intermingle their forces with those of NATO so that governments would be reluctant to authorize the use of tactical nuclear weapons for fear of killing their own troops. Moreover, an advance at this rate would be bound to create an atmosphere of defeatism and panic and put political pressure on Western leaders to accede to Soviet demands as the price of peace. On the battlefield, the possibility of such fast-moving operations makes rapid intelligence-gathering and analysis, plus the ability to react quickly, vitally important.

Concentration: If surprise is to be achieved, the Soviets would not have at their disposal the enormous forces they possess because these could easily be seen coming during a prolonged mobilization. Accordingly, they would seek to compensate for this by acquiring local superiority in particular sectors at key moments during the battle.

Deep battle: The Soviets do not believe in fighting only at the front; rather, they would seek to disrupt the defence by striking throughout its depth. This is why they have made a high priority of developing their airborne forces, which could be landed in rear areas simultaneously with an armoured strike across the IGB. Other methods of conforming to their deep battle principle would involve the use of ground-attack aircraft, long-range artillery and rockets, and special forces trained as saboteurs. In recent years the Soviet

Army has concentrated on developing the facility to strike deep into the rear of NATO's defence with mobile armoured forces. This has led to the development of the Operational Manoeuvre Group (OMG), usually a tank division or a motor-rifle division with extra armour, which would seek to bypass main defensive positions and press on towards NATO's rear, leaving follow-up elements to engage the defences.

Air superiority: The Soviets have developed a far better working relationship between their air and ground forces than has the West. From the outset, they would seek to establish local air superiority at certain chosen sections of the front so that their ground-attack aircraft and helicopters could operate in relative safety and to best effect. Moreover, on the larger scale, they would be seeking to destroy NATO's ability to deliver airborne nuclear weapons by carrying out offensive operations against NATO airfields.

It is interesting that the Soviets have been far more active than we have in developing the potential of the helicopter. The Hind D (the 'flying tank' as the Soviets refer to it) for which we have no equivalent, is regarded with awe by British soldiers who have read about it in magazines or who listen to the 'threat' lectures which are a regular feature of battalion or regimental life. The Hind is armed with four anti-tank guided weapons, four 32-shot 57-mm rocket pods and a 12 mm Gatling-gun. The Hind is used in close support of attacking ground troops who are accompanied by a forward air controller who directs its fire.

Having seen how the Soviets would approach a war, if one were to start before the implementation of any conventional arms limitation treaty were to circumscribe their ability to undertake operations of this sort, we now need to examine how our Army would respond.

The Tactical Perspective

In line with the strategy of forward defence, the first task British troops would perform in the event of war would be to engage the enemy as soon as it crossed the border. This would be done not only to reassure the Germans, but also to try to identify exactly where the enemy is attacking in strength in order to predict his likely axis of advance. In addition, it would be necessary as a means of gaining time to prepare a strong defensive position further back.

When this phase of operations is practised on exercise in Germany, the covering force fights a highly mobile withdrawal action and just succeeds in retreating across a set of bridges which are blown up as soon as the last man is over, leaving the advancing Warsaw Pact forces stranded on the far bank. This has struck many observers as being highly optimistic: a more realistic game plan would leave the covering force destroyed or captured in its entirety. Clearly, because they would be fighting close to the border, covering force troops would be vulnerable to artillery fire from prepared positions inside East Germany and would, therefore, need to be armoured and mechanized. An added complication would be the need to co-ordinate the withdrawal of the covering force with our allies to the north and to the south so as to stop the enemy taking advantage of a vacuum suddenly being created along one part of the front.

While the covering force engages the enemy, the bulk of 1 Br Corps will be busy preparing the main defensive position. This will be on ground chosen by the commander well in advance and numerous plans will have been prepared for the siting of minefields and demolitions. Obviously, the place where the main force will stand and fight needs to be sufficiently far back from the border to minimize the use that the enemy can make of artillery and rocket positions in his own territory, particularly of permanently sited ground-to-air missiles. Fortunately, the area of Germany which we are responsible for defending is covered with a network of towns and villages which form a natural barrier to an invading force. Clearing urban areas of defenders is a time-consuming job and simply bypassing them leaves one open to guided weapons fire from the flanks. However, the area that will need to be covered is large and a completely static defence will not be possible. Troops will be required to move at high speed over distances of many miles to respond effectively to enemy incursions. Moreover, in order not to provide an easy target for Soviet tactical nuclear weapons, they will have to be spread out in relatively small concentrations which can be brought together for maximum effect only at key moments during the battle. Activities in this defensive area will not simply consist in holding ground but in turning the enemy's flank as well. This sort of warfare requires well-trained forces, many of whom will have to be in a mechanized role, and explains why it has successfully been argued that it is vital to maintain a large force of regular troops in Germany. However, in the event of war the size of BAOR will more than double and a large proportion of the reinforcements will not be regulars but territorials and many of the infantry battalions will be non-mechanized, lorry-borne infantry.

What are these troops supposed to do? Certainly there is a role for them in the protection of key points, particularly in the rear area, but there is some disagreement within the Army about their usefulness in the main battle. One group of theorists has taken as its model Operation Goodwood, an action that took place on 18–20 July 1944 when Allied forces sought to break out of the Orme bridgehead in Normandy.[1] The lesson of Goodwood was that three armoured divisions were brought to a halt by an inferior German force which relied largely upon non-mechanized infantry with anti-tank weapons. Moreover, part of the ground over which the battle was fought bears some resemblance to that part of Germany where British forces would have to engage an invading Warsaw Pact force, particularly in that there was a web of villages in which the Germans had set up a defensive framework. The German anti-tank weapons, guarded by small numbers of infantry, were deployed in the villages themselves and had orders to let the British armour go past before engaging them in the flanks and from the rear. It worked. The largest armoured operation that had ever been mounted by the British Army ground to a halt.

One of the foremost enthusiasts of the Goodwood concepts has been General Sir William Scotter who prefaced his examination of Goodwood thus:

> I was trying to find ways in which non-mechanized infantry could be used to advantage in the main defence and help to give that defence enough elasticity and depth consistent with the spirit of forward defence: to ensure that the momentum and depth of a major Warsaw Pact thrust could be absorbed and disrupted whilst powerful armoured forces, sufficient to destroy the penetration were deployed against it.[2]

If the Goodwood theorists are right and a Warsaw Pact armoured thrust could be significantly delayed by a small, lightly armed force, vast savings could be made in the costs of our conventional defence. Some writers have gone even further than General Scotter (who had only argued that Goodwood shows that non-mechanized infantry have a part to play in support of mechanized and armoured units) and have suggested that the Goodwood concept opens the way for a defence using part-time forces, perhaps even German civilians. If all that is required is a few days' delay, they say, this could be achieved by training the civilian population in basic infantry tactics and by

1 . Three armoured divisions were deployed in operation Goodwood. They had about 750 tanks with a further 250 in II Canadian Corps and I Corps on the flanks, in total about 1,000 tanks of which 413 became casualties during the operation, most on the first day.
2 . *RUSI Journal* 125, 41, pp.59–62 (1980).

distributing light anti-tank weapons at village level. Certainly, the idea has its attractions: Germany, having had national service for so long, now possesses a huge pool of civilians with military experience. Rather than treat them as reservists, why not organize them into some sort of Home Service Force operating in and around their own villages on ground they know intimately?

Other commentators, however, have cast serious doubts on the validity of the Goodwood case. Charles J. Dick has argued that Goodwood is not at all representative of the sort of action contemplated; indeed, that it is almost unique in the annals of battles involving non-mechanized troops against armoured divisions, in that the infantry succeeded in stopping the armour. Close studies of Goodwood have pointed to shortcomings on the part of British Intelligence and to the unfortunate creation of a traffic bottleneck (which prevented the armoured divisions deploying to best effect) as being the main causes of the failure of the armoured thrust. Dick also points out that the Germans in 1944 had the benefit of knowing from which direction the attack would come and had weeks to prepare for it; we may well be denied those advantages in any future conflict. He does, however, see other roles for non-mechanized infantry:

> They are ideal in very broken or heavily afforested terrain, or in major towns (a very different, more complicated problem for the Soviets than little villages). They are needed in the rear areas for important security missions and to meet the airborne threat. In unit size, they can be useful in the forward area, for instance defending key defiles or protecting vital and vulnerable targets such as HQs or nuclear delivery means. However, commanders who, through an amalgam of politicians' parsimony and their own self-delusion, find themselves trying to stem a Soviet armoured onslaught across the North German Plain with an infantry formation may find that they are saddled with a military dinosaur – an anachronism, ponderously slow to react and more, severely limited in capability and expensive to feed.[1]

It seems that for the foreseeable future commanders will have to assume that much of the fighting in the main defensive area will be carried on by highly trained professionals in expensive tanks and APCs; whilst there may be a larger role to be played by lightly armed men, the Goodwood concept does not provide all the answers. As far as the use of reservists is concerned, the sceptics point to their immobility as a decisive weakness, saying that their

1 . *RUSI Journal* 127, 1, pp.22–27 (1982).

static positions could be quickly swamped in one sector, allowing the main armoured force to pass through.[1]

This objection, however, is primarily one against using such forces *instead* of mechanized infantry working closely with armour; there may still be case for using small, possibly 'irregular' bands *as well as* highly mobile regular forces equipped with enormous firepower.

The Future in Perspective

There is an understandable inclination in all of us to plan for what we would like rather than for reality. Military planners are not exempt from this tendency. Most of the preparations for war on the British side are directed towards setting up a main defensive position, behind a covering force, as described above. The hope (and to some extent the expectation) is that we will be successful in this, forcing the Soviets to try to gnaw slowly through our defences, thereby achieving our aim of delay. The Soviets, for their part, are keen that any battle should proceed rapidly and that their Operational Manoeuvre Groups should circumvent our relatively static defences. As all soldiers know, battles seldom go according to plan.

The following is a definition from an American translation of a Russian military dictionary:

> *Vstrechnoye Srazhenie* – encounter battle. A clash between two opposing sides when they are simultaneously striving to fulfil assigned missions by means of offensive actions. An encounter battle may occur during a march or in the course of an attack mounted to repel enemy counter attacks, and also when reserves or second echelons move up to counter attack or to inflict counter blows when in defence. An encounter battle is characterized by obscurity of the situation and by abrupt changes in it, by the rapid movement to contact of the two sides and by the decisiveness and dynamic nature of their encounter, by rapid changes of march, approach march and combat formations, by the swift build-up of effort from depth, by an intense struggle to gain time and to seize and hold the initiative and by the presence of open flanks and free manoeuver.[2]

Clearly the Soviets have been thinking about such things for a long time. We are only just beginning to come to terms with the idea and

1 . For a fuller account of this objection see *Warfare as a Whole*, General Sir Frank Kitson (Faber and Faber, 1987).
2 . *Dictionary of Basic Military Terms*, A. I. Radzievsky, trans. 1965, USAF.

have not yet developed the skills and the capability to deal with a situation such as might well develop if our forces, finding the Soviets advancing on an unexpected axis, are consequently slower to arrive in the main defensive area than expected and are forced to engage forward elements of the Soviet attack before arriving at their pre-planned battle positions. Moreover, the development of Soviet command and communications is likely to mean that, even within a set-piece defence, encounter battles on a fairly significant scale will be at least a daily occurrence almost from the outbreak of hostilities.

It looks as though the strategic picture will be radically changed in the coming years by such factors as:

* the partial withdrawal of US forces in Europe;
* an agreement of limits on the number of tanks held by alliances/ member countries;
* the establishment of a tank-free zone in border areas;
* the restriction or abolition of any FOFA capability.

Since it would be unrealistic to expect that, even in exchange for bargaining away all these familiar deterrents, we would secure the complete removal of the Soviet Union's capability of waging war in Europe, we would still face, and therefore still need to deter, some threat or other. Western Europe after the arms talks might be safe from the armoured thrust but is likely still to be vulnerable to airborne assault mounted from deep within the Soviet Union, the infiltration of *spetsnaz* forces with limited but important objectives, and state-sponsored terrorism on a large scale, possibly in conjunction with domestic insurrections and/or strikes. Moreover, depending on who wins political power in Britain (and of course in Germany), we may well see an interim stage in the 1990s where theatre nuclear weapons are either being phased out, or have simply lost any credibility as a deterrent, before conventional reductions on the part of the Warsaw Pact have gone far enough to convince us that keeping strong conventional forces is no longer necessary. In such circumstances we could face the problem of trying to *increase* the size of the Army in a political climate in which it has come to be regarded as largely irrelevant.

The growing perception of Mikhail Gorbachev as a peacemaker is not the only reason why so many members of the British public are sceptical about any suggestion that the Warsaw Pact poses a threat so serious and immediate that it needs to be countered by £19 billion a year of taxpayers' money. There are elements in the concept of deterrence itself that cloud the defence issue and thereby undermine the nation's will to protect its way of life.

At root, deterrence is a method of avoiding war by indicating to a potential enemy that if he were to attack he would suffer such damage that it would not be worth his while. In the context of the rivalry between NATO and the Warsaw Pact, it has taken the form of requiring the West to maintain a range of possible counter-measures to any possible Warsaw Pact initiative (the doctrine of flexible response); ensure the credibility of weapon-systems (out-of-date or unreliable equipment or nuclear weaons no one has the will to use have no deterrent value); and, to get the best value from the range of counter-measures that adherence to flexible response provides, to breed uncertainty among Soviet decision-makers about quite what the West's reaction would be to any hostile act they might contemplate. This last element was spelled out by the Secretary of State for Defence, George Younger, when he gave evidence to the Commons Select Committee on Defence in May 1988:

> . . . the more uncertainties that a possible adversary has to take into account, the more types of threat he has to consider and the more centres of decision he has to assess, the better is the effect of the deterrence . . .[1]

Yet, in order to keep an enemy guessing about its possible responses in some hypothetical circumstance, a state will also have to keep its own citizens, Parliament and most of its servicemen uninformed. This exchange from the Defence Secretary's evidence to the Select Committee illustrates the point nicely:

> *Chairman:* Have the United States indicated that they would be ready to use their chemical weapons in response to a chemical weapons attack on one of the European allies? . . .
> *Mr Younger:* . . . the American weapons are not assigned to NATO so they are American weapons. They have not committed themselves, as far as I am aware, on how or when they would use them, but clearly as allies they would be open to be requested.[2]

The uncertainty that flexible response engenders in the minds of Soviet planners is of two kinds: firstly, they must ask themselves

1 . 18 May 988 Q341.
2 . Evidence to the Select Committee on Defence 18 May 1988 Q89/90.

which of the West's rich diversity of weapon-systems we will be most likely to use; and secondly, whether we would ever use those, such as nuclear or chemical weapons, whose use would be morally repugnant to the overwhelming majority of our people. It is not only the Soviet planners who ask themselves the latter question: our own citizens and our own soldiers also wonder. Because of the need to keep the Soviets guessing, our political leaders can offer little guidance; they cannot even say that such weapons would be used only in the last resort.

Consequently, many people are alienated from a defence policy which they perceive as at best, amoral, and at worst, positively immoral. Their feeling rests on a belief that the politicians know what will happen but are keeping it secret. The fact is that there are no definitive plans. In the event of a conflict, the decisions about which weapons to use – and whether to use the most horrifying ones – would be taken by frightened political leaders under immense pressure to act quickly.

Another result of this climate of uncertainty is a failure to distinguish between those weapons that are of deterrent value and those which would be most valuable if deterrence fails and a war starts. It does not necessarily follow that the weapons which have the greatest deterrent effect in psychological terms would be of the greatest practical utility on the battlefield. This is particularly the case with certain high-tech systems whose potential may terrify a prospective aggressor, but which, if they were ever fired in anger, might well fail the supreme test of battle. This begs the question, where should we apply our resources – to projects in never-never land or to the real world? Within the current framework of strategic thinking, there is no clear answer.

6

Participatory vs Delegative Defence

'A well regulated Militia, being necessary to the security of a free state, the right of the people to keep and bear Arms shall not be infringed'.

2nd Amendment to United States Constitution

Britain is the only major European power without conscription. Nor do we have a true militia. Instead, the defence of the modern realm is principally entrusted to the *Professionals* – indigenous mercenaries – as one military man recently joked. The rest of us, apart from a few in the Territorial Army, are not encouraged or inclined to take much interest in matters military. As long as we consume passively, pay our taxes and have our bomb, we may relinquish responsibility and leave the whole nasty business of defence to an expert élite who appear to have the matter well in hand and who can be relied upon to keep it out of sight as much as possible.

There is a price to pay for this convenient delegative approach. No one could question the oft-proven courage of our professional servicemen and women, but the professional system in which they operate, so often described as the acme of perfection by those who have led a comfortable life in its upper ranks, has some very serious and under-publicized limitations:

1. The Army, the largest service, is distanced from the body of the nation. This separation not only limits informed debate on defence policy but it also encourages the Army in thinking of itself as an élite, sanctioned to maintain an out-dated social structure.

2. The expense of the professionally orientated system dictates that only a relatively small army can be maintained.
3. The deterrent value (not to mention the actual combat value) of small professional forces is limited.
4. In-depth defence of our own and our allies' territory, however prudent, is not seen as a viable option because it is assumed that there are insufficient personnel to achieve it.
5. The system tends to produce an army of specialists dependent not just on nuclear weapons but on a whole range of complex high-tech paraphernalia. In the event of a prolonged conventional war – which the wisdom of the day does not expect – the training of replacements or reinforcements is made impracticable. At the moment we are forced to resort to nuclear weapons or accept defeat.
6. Despite reduced manpower levels, the professional services of today have a perennial problem recruiting and retaining suitable personnel; job security does not offset the lure of the higher material rewards and greater freedom offered elsewhere. In 1988 some Army units suffered a 10 per cent drop in recruiting.[1] The projections for the 1990s are even worse, since it is expected that the number of male adolescents in Britain will fall by 15 per cent or more. So serious is this projected demographic trough that the army has set up a special programme to meet it – Manpower And Recruiting in the Lean Years of the Nineties (MARILYN).

Though all these problems deserve the most careful consideration, it is the exclusivity of the delegative approach which should be a particular worry today. Throughout the fifties, sixties and seventies in Britain there was no great division of political opinion on defence policy, but during the eighties the parliamentary consensus that once existed broke down amid squabbles about which sort of disarmament we should pursue – unilateral, multilateral or 'reciprocally unilateral'. Neil Kinnock appears recently to have brought the Labour Party back to the multilateral mainstream. Nevertheless confusion remains. Meantime outside Westminster people vote for a strong defence policy at general elections but call for defence cuts in mid-term. Fear of nuclear holocaust goes hand in hand with pride in being a member of the nuclear club. And all this is the case at the very time when our potential enemies have never been stronger militarily or politically less stable.

1. *The Daily Telegraph*, 24 October 1988.

Within this context, the divorce of responsibility for defence from the body of the nation is not only strategically unsound, but also socially and politically debilitating. Apart from ensuring the numerical inadequacy of our armed forces, it prevents most ordinary people from confronting the practical problems of defence, and helps to foster ignorance, apathy and reaction. The situation amongst our young people should be of special concern. They have been excluded from participating in their nation's defence, but have grown up in the shadow of its bomb.

Some might argue that the system of delegative defence arises out of our status as subjects of the Crown rather than citizens of a national community. Our sense of subjection to the executive certainly seems to have intensified in recent years despite the increased choice that greater affluence has brought us. A note of authoritarianism has crept into the language and practice of government, encroachments have been made upon the freedoms of the media, and the government has centralized many powers in order to press through its programme of radical reform. Feeling robbed of power, many seem to have abandoned responsibility. Amidst the materialism, despair, reactive apathy and latent aggression common in Britain in the late 1980s, the tendency towards self-delusion is all too evident. The facts of the continuing Soviet threat are restructured into a more palatable form, just as comforting stories develop to justify our growing dependence on an increasingly 'nannyish', state. Repeated like mantras, the wish-dreams ward off the evil spirits of individual doubt and common sense that might otherwise lead us to question and change. In the case of the Army one of the favourite refrains goes something like this:'The number of our regular forces may be relatively small but their quality is high, and as long as they have the right kit they will be able to cope. Anyway, who beat the Argies and stormed Prince's Gate?'

However, we have now reached a time when we have to re-evaluate many of our traditional attitudes. And, however much the defence establishment might like to maintain the status quo, one thing above all others is clear: we can't afford it. The costs of suporting a professional Army which has a seemingly insatiable appetite for high-tech weaponry are growing too fast to be sustainable. A manpower crisis is imminent. The political situation in Europe is changing fast. We need to examine a wide range of options for the future. Later in this chapter we will look at the possibility of re-introducing some form of National Service – albeit a rather different from that we have known before. We will also look at how a more participatory approach to defence might stimulate greater social cohesion. But first, in anticipation of the argument that only the delegative approach would be practical in Britain, we will examine how National Service has fared here in the past and what lessons there are to be drawn from the experience of other countries.

A Brief History of Conscription

In English law the obligation on all able-bodied men to serve in an emergency can be traced to the 'great fyrd' of the Anglo-Saxons. Similar traditions exist across Europe. Indeed, the notion that every adult male member of a society has the right or obligation to serve in its defence goes back at least to the city states of classical Greece. It has both competed and coexisted with the concept, currently in vogue in Britain, of a separate warrior class or caste defending the State. The first true conscription of modern times was the *levée en masse* of Revolutionary France in 1793. Significantly, the Revolutionary Assembly felt the need to legitimize its action by quoting ancient custom, in this case, the *arrière-ban* of medieval France which required the peasantry to turn out in a military emergency. The *levée en masse* of 1793 led to the rapid creation of an army some 750,000 strong, but administrative difficulties soon pruned it to a more manageable 400,000.

Although the Revolutionary French government tried to use historical precedent to justify its conscription policy, there were two features which were significantly different from anything previously attempted. Firstly, the number of men involved was huge by any standard (and far greater than anything yet seen in Europe); secondly, the earlier examples had usually been designed to raise a body of men only for a relatively short period. In contrast, the new mass conscription, made possible by the centralized bureaucracy which had developed before the Revolution, was conceived as a way of raising a large standing army to engage in a form of war which would involve the whole nation.

A proclamation of August 1793 exhorted: '. . . every French person must stand ready to support her armed forces. Young men will go to fight, husbands will forge weapons and manage the transport services; wives and daughters will make tents and uniforms and will serve in the hospitals; old men taking their stand in public places will inflame the bravery of our soldiers and preach the hatefulness of kings, the unity of the republic.'

However, following the bitter experiences of the Thirty Years War (1618–48), there had been an unspoken agreement on the Continent that war would be used only for the pursuit of limited interests, and not to disturb the existing system of states. The France of the Revolutionary Assembly, of course, did not feel itself bound by such conventions. The revolutionaries wanted to destroy the existing order, so had no motive to fight by its rules. The new France, united under arms via conscription, revolutionary propaganda and genuine external threat, fought with tactics which were as novel as they were aggressive. The result (as it would be for Hitler's blitzkrieg a century and a half later) was a string of victories against disorientated opponents. However, such dynamism could also rebound.

After Napoleon crushed their military power in 1806, the Prussians adopted and improved upon the French military innovations. History shows there can be risks in emulation – acceptance of an enemy's new practices might compromise the very conventions of the society which one had been fighting to preserve – but the Prussians were not deterred. Conservative in one sense, they were also innovative and fiercely ambitious.

By the middle of the nineteenth century Prussia had developed a military system which had as its corner-stones a period of short service for most men (typically two years), a lifelong liability to call-up, and a vast, all-pervasive military machine. This capability profoundly affected the development of the State. Indeed, so completely were military, industrial and administrative assets combined that the dividing lines between the Prussian State and its army are hard to draw. Militarism coloured all aspects of life. It would become a prime catalyst of Pan-Germanism (and later of Fascism).

Meanwhile, the French, as they would have some cause to regret, had been forced to give up their great armies after the overthrow of Napoleon. Conscription remained, but it was limited, and based on lottery, the aim now being to provide a relatively compact force of long-service regulars rather than vast revolutionary or imperial armies. However, the die had been cast by the French themselves in 1793: only massive military might could now protect a nation.

In the war of 1870–1 Prussia defeated France with an army of more than a million men (France had a 'mere' 555,000). After this decisive Prussian victory, the basic concept of their military system – mass conscription – was adopted throughout continental Europe.

The political will to do this was augmented by the widespread growth of centralized bureaucracy and technical advances in the fields of communication, transport and hygiene (the latter making possible the maintenance of standing mass armies that were not to be continually decimated by disease). By the start of the First World War the armies of every major European country, except Britain, were composed of millions of short-service conscripts. Concomitant with the advent of these huge forces was the search for weapons to decimate them rapidly and, as the next logical consequence, for devices powerful enough to destroy the very communities from which they were raised.

Conscription and Britain

Britain resisted conscription until the First World War, for two basic reasons. Firstly, she had no frontiers and hence no need for a massive standing army (except in India, where the bulk of the troops were themselves native Indians). As long as the Royal Navy ruled the waves, invasion was impractical. If ever Britannia needed to interfere in a European war, she could always improvise an army after it had broken out, a luxury not shared by the states across the Channel. In dire straits the county-based militias and Yeomanry (and from 1859, the rifle volunteers) could be called out; meanwhile only a compact force of long-service regulars was needed to act as the armed police force of the Empire.[1]

The second major reason why Britain had not introduced conscription was related to our national character. We British, like our American cousins, have traditionally been wary of centralized state power. The idea of standing armies, let alone peacetime conscription, was thought to be unconstitutional by many British and American writers well into the nineteenth century. This was the view of William Cobbett, who wrote in 1816 criticizing the rapid build-up of the standing army, ' "The English Constitution", says Blackstone, "knows nothing of standing armies . . . no fortresses, no barracks; nothing to keep soldiers distinct from the people – nothing of this sort belongs to England." Alas! . . . what would this great commentator on our laws have said if he had lived to this

1. From 1815 British soldiers enlisted for life, and were discharged only for infirmity. The 1847 Army Service Act introduced service for 10 years, extended to 22 to qualify for a pension. The Army Enlistment Act of 1870 reduced this to 6 years with the colours and 6 years with the reserve (changed to 7 and 5 years shortly before the First World War).

day?' Despite Cobbett's warnings and those of others like him, the power of the Regular Army grew throughout the nineteenth century at the expense of the old local militias. Although some local militias had given reasonable service in the Napoleonic Wars, by the beginning of the Victorian era the militias were badly organized and woefully undertrained. A number of different systems operated – ordinary 'conscripted' militia, volunteer militia (who might serve abroad), yeomanry (who might best be described as mounted volunteers) and 'Fencibles' (regulars but enlisted only for Home Defence).[1]

Paper service in the militia (i.e. nominal membership implying few duties) was obligatory for all those whose names appeared on the Militia Ballot (administered by the Lord-Lieutenants), and there were also volunteer members (under a statute of 1852 the volunteers were to be called out first in any emergency). Their main use was as a sort of emergency police (police forces in the modern sense not being established in the counties until 1855), but in serious internal emergencies regular troops were used.

The militias were not a wholly volunteer force, but the ancient obligation of periodic emergency service to the local community should not be confused with the European conscription of the nineteenth century, which was designed to raise mass standing armies, and took the individual away from his family for a year or more initially and for annual training camps and periodic service thereafter. The militias were truly local forces representative of their own communities and, until 1871, came under the control of the Home Office rather than the War Office. The professionals claimed (with some justification) that the militias were incompetent, and robbed them of recruits at a time when there were already too few men available. The Regular Army campaigned relentlessly, and in the 1860s the process of bringing the militias, together with their more fashionable cousins, the mounted Yeomanry and the rifle volunteers, under the control of the regulars was begun with the affiliation of all volunteer units to regular regiments. It was completed by the creation of the Territorial Force in 1907.

The typical nineteenth-century Briton's reaction to any suggestion of conscription would have been much the same as that which

1. The word 'militia' is derived from *Milites* – the plural form of the Latin word *miles*. *Miles* meant 'soldier' to the Romans but by the Middle Ages it had increasingly come to mean 'knight' and the stock phrase for describing a medieval army was *milites peditesque* – 'knights and footsoldiers'. Nowadays the word has taken on the meaning of a part-time, community-based force or 'citizen army'.

greeted the new police service; a potentially dangerous and expensive French import. Moreover it was noted that continental radicals favoured obligatory military service, believing it gave workers a new and more powerful role in society, as well as technical education, and military training which would be useful in the event of revolution.

Although the British were opposed to conscription, the need for larger armies was quite clear by the middle of the nineteenth century. And so, as a supplement to the militia, a new movement, the rifle volunteers, was formed in 1859 (in response to a short-lived French invasion scare) by a joint private and governmental initiative. The aim was to generate enthusiasm for the new sport of target rifle-shooting and turn it into a national military asset.

The rifle volunteer scheme was remarkably successful. The idea was to make voluntary part-time military service not only enjoyable, but fashionable. The Secretary of State for War became the first president of the National Rifle Association (the body set up to develop military shooting skills amongst civilians via the volunteer movement), and the Queen herself opened the first competition at Wimbledon (the forerunner of Bisley) in 1860. Joining a rifle volunteer corps became 'the thing to do'. A year after the scheme's inception 161,000 men were under training and 140,000 officially designated 'efficient'. By 1900, when Lord Salisbury made his famous comment that he looked forward to the days when there was 'a rifle in every cottage', well over a quarter of a million men were involved.

The rifle volunteers were an extraordinary and most imaginative group. Though some of their ranks were recruited from Chartist strongholds just a decade after the revolutionary explosion of 1848, and though Victorian Britain experienced industrial and social disturbances more serious than those of recent years, the private possession of military small-arms by the members of the rifle movement occasioned no problems whatsoever, and ensured that Britain was much better prepared for the First World War than would otherwise have been the case.

Britain adopts conscription

At the start of the First World War Britain relied entirely on her regulars and part-time volunteers. There was still no conscription. However, the new war of attrition with its trenches and massed frontal attacks finally brought an end to the great tradition. Conscription was introduced for the first time in Britain (but not in

Ireland where the political situation was judged too tense) by the Military Service Act of 27 January 1916. All fit, unmarried men between the ages of 18 and 41 became liable to military service, save those in reserved occupations. About 300 men who felt honour bound to resist Lord Kitchener's pointing finger went to jail rather than serve King and Country more conventionally, for the first time raising the issue of conscientious objection in Britain. In May 1916 conscription was extended to married men, and in 1917 further legislation was introduced to reduce the number of reserved occupations. In April 1918 the upper age limit of draftees was raised to 50. By the end of that year conscription was halted and demobilization begun, even though the fighting did not entirely cease with the Armistice. British troops were still engaged in the war of intervention in Russia. When the decision was eventually made to withdraw, it was in large part due to the so-called 'soldiers' strikes' which had erupted as a result of the popular opinion that the unspoken contract of conscription was for the duration of the world war alone.

By the end of 1919 the Army was once again an all-volunteer force, and remained so until 1939. In May of that year the National Government introduced peacetime conscription for the first time in British history. Initially, 6 months' military service for young men of 20 and 21, save those in reserved occupations, was stipulated. The scope was widened on the outbreak of war to include men between the ages of 18 and 41. In December 1941 women between the ages of 20 and 30 who were not engaged in essential war work were also called up, albeit as non-combatants. They could choose between the auxiliary services – the ATS, WRNS or WAAF – or bodies such as Land Army or Women's Voluntary Service. By the end of 1945 the Army had nearly 3 million serving men and women.

The problem for the Army after 1945 was the same as that which faced it after 1918: the peace was far from secure. Male conscription was retained, although in 1947 it was reduced to 12 months' service. Its retention was not a major political issue, the only opposition coming from the extreme left. In 1949 the Army Service Act was passed, requiring a year of service from the age of 18 to 19. By this time the Army had been run down to 380,000 personnel – roughly a tenth of its wartime strength. Moreover, over 40 per cent of its manpower was now involved in administration and supply. This was partly a result of the demands made on the system by the large turnover of conscripted recruits. During 1949 the period of National Service was increased to 18 months, and with the Korean War in

1950 it was further extended to 2 years. The Army's strength rose to 440,000.

How the system worked

It was the responsibility of each individual male, on reaching the age of 18, to register for National Service, usually at a branch of the Ministry of Labour. (Those few who did not were usually tracked down through income tax or social security records.) After registration, the candidate was summoned for a medical examination. Failure to attend the medical could result in a fine of £100 or up to 2 years in prison, with no loss of liability to National Service afterwards. Recruits were graded into one of four categories, the fourth being 'unfit for military service'. About 16 per cent of recruits were rejected on medical grounds.

A study in 1955 showed that doctors tended to pass significant numbers of young men who were medically unfit, and eventually a more stringent fitness requirement was introduced. Exemption from National Service was given not only to the medically unfit, but to British subjects in government posts abroad and to clergymen. Indefinite deferment was given to coal-miners, seamen, agricultural workers involved in essential food production, graduate science teachers, and police cadets. Eight-year deferments, which in practice were indefinite, were given to apprentices completing indentures, students on courses, and to those who could prove exceptional domestic hardship. After the Korean War the paper exercise of increasing the 8-year deferments to 12 years was made, and then repeated in 1955 when the deferments were extended to 18 years.

Recruits were consulted as to their choice of service and arm, but the reality of National Service was that this preference was often disregarded. Five or 6 weeks after the medical examination they were sent on a basic training course lasting 10 weeks. The regimen was spartan and designed to break down personalities quickly, and reshape them as the service thought it wanted. After basic training national servicemen were sent on to the units which would become their home until the day they returned to the civilian world.

Special schemes existed for potential officers and NCOs. A public-school or grammar-school education was usually a prerequisite to becoming a National Service officer. All candidates for a commission in the Army would have to pass a War Office Selection Board Interview (WOSBI), a set of tests and tasks very similar to today's Regular Commissions Board (RCB). National Service officer cadets went to Mons or Eaton Hall training schools whilst regulars went to Sandhurst. The scheme seems to have worked well, and newly minted National Service officers were usually assimilated into their regular units without difficulty. The same could not be said of National Service NCOs. After their training, usually as technical specialists, they often received a very frosty reception on posting, the older and less well-educated regular NCOs resenting their rapid progress.

It was theoretically possible to register as a conscientious objector and be offered alternative non-military service, but the number doing so was small. Women were not required to do National Service. There was no exemption for married men, and no statutory objection to national servicemen marrying. The wife would receive a married man's allowance to which her husband had to contribute but no married accommodation was available.

There was considerable debate as to the ideal age of induction. The government would have liked young men to enter the scheme as soon as they left school, while the Army preferred a more mature candidate. A white paper re-evaluating National Service early in 1955 made several criticisms of the system, but accepted the Army's argument on the age issue, noting the immaturity of many entrants. This led to 19-year-old conscript recruits becoming the norm by the spring of 1955.

National servicemen were integrated at all levels with regular soldiers, but the regulars were paid considerably more. In 1960 it was calculated that, in total, a regular soldier cost the Army four times as much as a conscript. After discharge the national serviceman could choose to be registered in the Army Emergency Reserve or, if willing to undertake annual camps and the odd weekend, the Territorial Army. However, the introduction of National Service had almost killed the TA as a reserve force. When the government called a state of emergency during the Suez crisis, serious deficiencies in its training and preparedness became apparent. Nor did the Emergency Reserve function smoothly.

National Service was brought to an end by Duncan Sandys' controversial 1957 Defence Review, as a result of the impact of new military technology, and, in particular, of nuclear weapons. Britain now espoused the American doctrine of massive retaliation. This argued that any war in Europe would be very short, consisting of a massive 'city busting' by nuclear weapons in response to Soviet aggression. Conventional troops would be needed only as a 'trip-wire' to delay Soviet forces if they attacked. Also, according to the review, the air defence of Britain could be left principally to missiles rather than aircraft, and British interests overseas could be protected not by maintaining permanent garrisons but by using jet air transport to move forces to the trouble spot from the UK at high speed. The Army could therefore be reduced to 180,000 regular troops, 55,000 of them in BAOR.

The final National Service intake was drafted in 1960 to be discharged in 1962. However, at the last minute it was discovered that an error had been made and that some 9,000 conscripts would have to serve an extra 6 months. The last national servicemen were 2319209 Private Fred Turner, Army Catering Corps, discharged on 7 May 1963, and Lieutenant Richard Vaughan, Royal Army Pay Corps, who left his unit in Germany on 7 May 1963 and was officially discharged six days later.

What is the verdict on National Service? The Army, whatever it might later say, considered that national servicemen, once trained, were as good as regulars. They served side by side in many of the post-war counter-insurgency operations which were no less complex than similar conflicts today. The reactions of the national servicemen themselves were mixed: some detested it, most endured it as a necessary evil in an unstable world. In the process they made friendships which would last a lifetime, grew up faster than they might otherwise have done, and, if they were lucky, saw a little of the world. Opinion polls in the mid-1950s showed that between 55 and 60 per cent of people thought National Service should be maintained. By the 1960s the tide of public opinion had turned against compulsory National Service.

The British Home Guard

So far we have considered in the British context only compulsory regular service but there are alternatives. One interesting example is the war-time Home Guard whose membership was made up both of volunteers and regulars.

The British on 14 May 1940, four days after the German attack on France and the replacement of Neville Chamberlain's government by a coalition led by Winston Churchill, the new British Secretary of State for War, Anthony Eden, made a BBC radio broadcast calling for men between the ages of 17 and 65 to join the Local Defence Volunteers (LDV), later known as the Home Guard. Something less ambitious had existed in the First World War as the Veterans'

Volunteer Association, or less politely, the 'Gorgeous Wrecks', a nickname derived from their armbands emblazoned GR – Georgius Rex. Their Second World War counterparts would soon become the butt of similar jokes but, in the early days of the new Local Defence Volunteers, enthusiasm was almost universal. The first men were reporting to police stations before the end of the broadcast, and within 24 hours a quarter of a million had volunteered – a number equal to the entire strength of the regular peacetime Army. By the end of June there were over 1½ million members.

Officially the force was part of the armed forces, and its members wore uniform and carried weapons. Not surprisingly, the majority of volunteers were old soldiers, simply because the majority of men in their forties and fifties in Britain in 1940 who were not already in uniform were veterans of the last conflict. No medical examination was required, and the upper age limit was rarely enforced. Theoretically, recruits were screened locally to make sure that no German spies joined up.

Any member could leave at two weeks' notice. Strictly speaking everyone was subject to military law, and an individual might be expelled without reason under the formula 'services no longer required'. In practice the early LDVs operated more or less autonomously, the movement developing regional and local variations.

This was not quite what the government had intended. On 30 May 1940 a Major-General was appointed by the War Office to provide an element of centralized control, and the decision was taken to link the Local Defence units to the County Territorial Associations (there being a ready supply of empty Territorial Army drill halls and similar facilities because of the war) under the Lord-Lieutenants. The latter were given the task of selecting senior Local Defence leaders, who would then select or approve local leaders.

The seven Army Commands into which Britain (excluding Ulster) had been divided were sub-divided into Local Defence Areas, each further divided into zones. Within each zone a Local Defence battalion was set up, each with 4 companies, each company with 4 platoons, and each platoon with 3 sections. The size of company, and consequently of the local battalion, often varied; it might be anything from 600–1,600 men, but the norm was about 1,000. Initially, former senior officers were selected as battalion commanders (soon tagged 'Blimps') with no pay and minimal expenses acting as a battalion commander was effectively a full-time job for someone of independent means.

LDV recruiting was strongest in the area which was expected to be in the immediate path of any invasion – the south-east. Initial enthusiasm was somewhat dampened by a chronic shortage of equipment and uniforms. By the end of the summer of 1940 most units had been issued with basic uniforms, but weapons were still scarce (some volunteers were actually taught to drill and fight with pikes). Meanwhile, there appeared to be a genuine nervousness in the government that it had inadvertently created a potentially revolutionary 'People's Army'. This fear was partly reinforced by the enthusiastic endorsement given to the LDVs by certain British socialists. One, Tom Wintringham, a veteran of the Spanish Civil War, even set up his own independent training school at Osterley Park in the western suburbs of London. The school was eventually taken over by the Army, but Wintringham did succeed in training thousands of civilians in the techniques of urban guerrilla warfare. His writings of 1941, coloured by his radical socialist perspective, shed some light on this extraordinary episode in British history:

> In May and June 1940 British finance capital met with severe defeat. Its army was unceremoniously bundled out of Europe. . . . This defeat of the British bourgeoisie led to a great increase of the possibility of turning the war into an anti-Fascist war. It became necessary for the British bourgeoisie to take steps towards the arming of the civilian proletariat. It became necessary for them to appeal to Social-Democracy for its aid, and to take Labour leaders into the Cabinet. . . . It became necessary for them to appeal to the industrial proletariat for unexampled efforts in the production of armaments. . . . This was the period in which J. B. Priestley began his 'Postscripts' on the wireless, and I helped to found the Osterley Park School for the Home Guard, to which thousands of armed civilians came to hear the tactical instruction of International Brigadiers. During this period the London *Evening Standard* became at intervals a revolutionary socialist paper . . .[1]

When Churchill renamed the Local Defence Volunteers the Home Guard on 14 July 1940, and added they were as much a part of the British Army as the Grenadier Guards, he was making three points. Firstly, it was an attempt to convince the Germans that the Home Guard were to be regarded as combatants (they had publicized their view that they considered them to be irregulars, outside the laws of war and liable to summary execution); secondly, it was an attempt to improve the new force's public image; but thirdly, and as importantly, it was a reminder that the Home Guard was subject to

1. *The Politics of Victory*, Tom Wintringham, p.28 (George Routledge and Sons, London, 1941).

military law. On 6 August, to remove any remaining doubts, the War Office issued a formal Army Council instruction placing the Home Guard firmly under Army control: there would be no more Wintringhams pursuing their own ends.

In spite of Wintringham and his comrades' efforts, the actual fighting value of the majority of the rapidly constituted early LDV/Home Guard units was very low (the psychological value cannot be discounted so easily). The most militarily valuable units were probably the Auxiliaries, the parties of volunteers who, in the event of invasion, would have carried out selective assassination and sabotage from hidden bases in the south-east (some of which were kept replenished years after the end of the war). The potential effectiveness of these units was in great part due to Wintringham; his politics might have been considered suspect, his private school for covert operations became War Office School Number 1 and was used to train regulars as well as members of the Home Guard thereafter.

The Home Guard's great moment came on the evening of 7 September 1940 when the Chief of Staff issued the code word Cromwell to all units. This meant that a German invasion was imminent. But in several places it was taken to mean that invasion had actually begun. Something of a mild shambles ensued, but one thing at least was not in doubt – the willingness of ordinary men, somewhat ridiculed subsequently, to die in defence of their country.

In October 1940, by which time the Home Guard had become a far more serious military force, recruiting was temporarily suspended. There were nearly 2 million members in 1,200 battalions. In December 1940 the Home Guard was put on a completely military footing with the introduction of formal military ranks (which had been in use anyway), the reduction of the less useful of the routine guard duties, the promise of better equipment, and of more and better training. A Director-General of Home Guard was established with a War Office staff, answerable to the CIGS (Chief of the Imperial General Staff). Formal commissions were issued in February 1941, when existing officers had their appointments confirmed or rejected by Army Selection Boards. There were some resignations over the regularization of the Home Guard. In November 1941, with membership falling back to 1½ million, conscription to the Home Guard was introduced. One of the provisions of the National Service (Number 2) Act of December 1941 was that men who were too old or unfit for normal military service, but who worked less than 60 hours a week, were required to undertake some form of community service, one option being the Home Guard.

After the summer of 1941, the threat of German invasion having subsided, the Home Guard was used as a training unit for adolescents waiting to join the Army. By 1943 the Home Guard had an average age of 30, made up principally of adolescents and men in their forties; old soldiers now represented only 7 per cent of the total. From April 1942 members of the Home Guard were recruited to serve in anti-aircraft batteries; 142,000 had done so by 1944, and another 7,000 in coastal artillery. There were even Home Guard cavalry units, marines, and in Scotland, mountain units. On 28 October 1944 the Home Guard was ordered to stand down. By this time it numbered 1,727,095 excluding female auxiliaries. The annual cost to the country was a mere £16.6 million. Home Guard casualties during the war were 1,206 killed on duty, or from wounds received on duty, and 557 injured. They were awarded 2 posthumous George Crosses and 13 George Medals. The Home Guard was formally disbanded in 1945, but its spirit lived on in the many Home Guard rifle clubs which were formed around the country, some of which still exist. Perhaps the greatest lesson of the Home Guard is that it takes time to organize any force. In any war threatening the UK today, a Home Guard would have to be already constituted or done without.

Conscription in Other Countries Today

The practice of conscription is still retained by many of the European nations. Their experiences offer a number of useful insights into strengths and weaknesses of different kinds of national service.

FRANCE

France has a population of 55,996,000, of whom 15,118,920 are under 20. The total active armed forces are 553,696 including 20,721 women and 255,000 conscripts. For the Army alone a total of 292,480 personnel includes 8,820 women and 186,350 conscripts. Army reserves total 305,000. Terms of service for other ranks are either as volunteers for 5 years or as conscripts for 12 months. The Army then encourages conscripts to extend their service for a further 16 or 24 months. Conscripts cannot be sent outside the borders of France, except to West Germany, unless they volunteer. Conscripts and

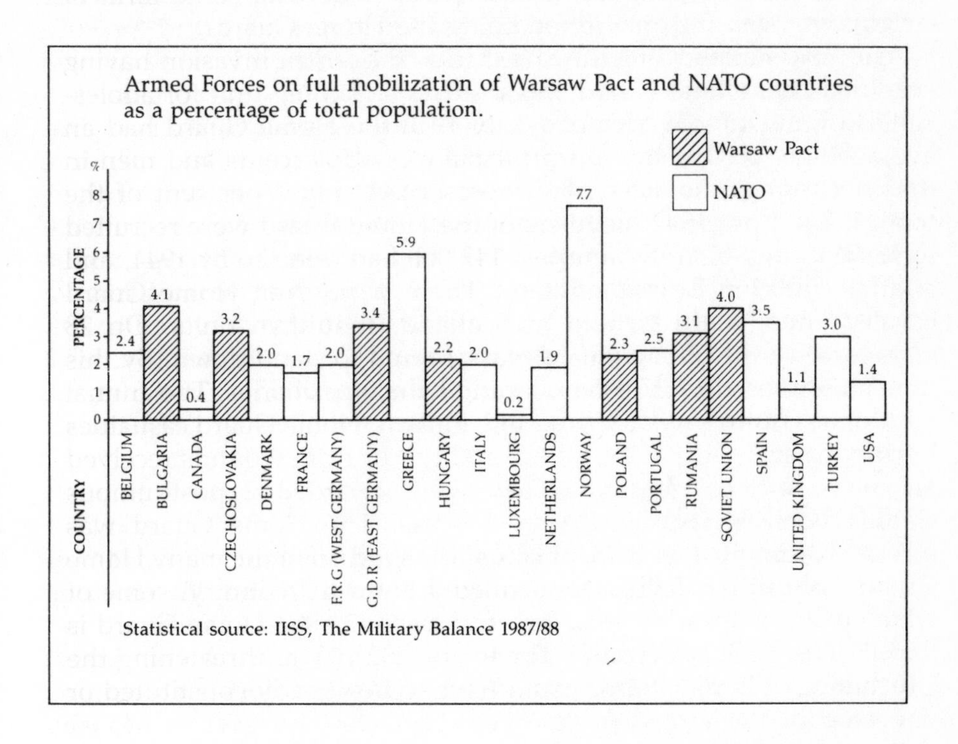

volunteers serve alongside one another except in the technical branches, the Marines, the Foreign Legion and the Paratroops, who are all required to be volunteers by reason of their more complex training. The French consider that a conscript is fully trained after 6 months, whereupon he helps train the next intake until his year is completed. So one half of the conscript Army is always training the other half.

Officer cadets, who must be volunteers, take a two-year preparatory course followed by a three-year course at St Cyr, which is now at Coetquidan in Britanny. Also at Coetquidan is the École Militaire Inter-Armes which trains selected NCOs as officers. Officers then take a one-year special-to-arms course. The whole process takes five years.

France has the only Western European army structured for offensive action in a short war. This is because the French believe that a long conventional war, and a war fought on French soil, would be disastrous to France. An early use of nuclear weapons is encouraged and France's is essentially a doctrine of nuclear-war fighting. Even the French tactical nuclear forces are called 'prestrategic' forces, indicating the expectation that a strategic exchange will follow. As a result France has a surplus of reserves, recognized in 1984 by the introduction of a two-tier reserve system. On mobilization 50 per cent of the Army would consist of reservists: including 34 per cent of the active divisions, 76 per cent of the corps troops and 64 per cent of the support units. Members of Class 1 of the Reserve, in which conscripts serve for four years, all have specific posts allocated to them. Indeed those in the first year of reserve service go straight back to their old units. In this way France can mobilize fully in 72 hours. After four years conscripts pass to Class 2 of the Reserve for 13 years (or until the age of 55). Class 3 of the Reserve contains all serving and former members of the Gendarmerie.[1]

WEST GERMANY

West Germany has a population of approximately 61,123,000 of whom about 6,658,000 are men aged betwen 18 and 30. The total armed forces number 488,700, of whom 222,600 are conscripts and 6,600 reservists on recall. There are 332,100 men in the Army, including 175,900 conscripts. West Germany does not employ women in the armed forces. The Army has reserves of 645,000. (Reserves of all the Armed Forces total 850,000). In other words, in the event of war the Federal Republic can put more than a million men on the ground.

Officers can either volunteer for a professional career or for service up to 15 years. Officers start with 9 months training – including 3 months basic training – in a unit followed by a year and a half officers' training, a year as a platoon leader in their unit, and then, since 1973, a three and a quarter years' degree course at one of the multi-service universities at Hamburg and Munich, run on completely civilian lines. For all officers and NCOs the obligation to recall from the Reserve lasts up to the age of 60.

Volunteers can enlist in the Army for between 2 and 15 years. Virtually all NCOs are volunteers. Conscripts are called up at 18. There are some deferments, including for students, and conscientious objection is permitted. Conscripts get three months basic training before filling their posts in the same units for a further 12 months. The German Army's ideal is a force that is 55 per cent

1. Statistical source: Army Attaché, Ambassade de France, London. (Figures circa 1988–89).

regular, but it cannot attract enough volunteers and there is an enlistment shortfall of 15–20 per cent. Therefore from 1989 the conscripts' service is being increased from 15 to 18 months.

Of the 716,000 German reservists, whose obligation lasts until they are aged 45, about 180,000 receive annual training. The Ready Reserve of 21,000 men consists of people who did their conscript service in the previous year. They are, officially, still in the Army but on long leave, and receive a 10–14 day refresher course. They can be recalled without recourse to the Bundestag. From there they pass into the Alert Reserve, about 180,000 strong, for 5 years, including refresher courses of 2–3 weeks, after which they pass into the Replacement Reserve.[1]

THE SOVIET UNION

The Soviet Union has a racially diverse population of 285.2 million and a military establishment of over 5 million. At 17 every Soviet male citizen must register to join the ranks of the Soviet military. During the next two years, most will be summoned to an induction centre for processing and transfer to a training unit. Those who do not register are liable to up to 3 years' imprisonment with hard labour. To quote article 3 of the 1967 law on conscription: 'All male citizens of the USSR, regardless of origin, social and property status, racial and national affiliation, education, language, attitude towards religion, type and nature of employment and place of residence, must undergo active military service.[2]

There are five basic options for conscripts: the Strategic Rocket Forces, Ground Forces, Air Defence Forces, Air Forces and the Navy. A conscript might serve in any of them (although in an élite formation such as the Strategic Rocket Forces only the brighter conscripts would be accepted). Additionally a conscript might be assigned to military support services, civil defence duties, or, if he is politically reliable, to the 'internal army' under the control of the Ministry of the Interior, the members of which are used to guard key government buildings and as internal security police for riot suppression and the like, or to the border guards who come under the control of the KGB. Including their 6 months of basic training most Soviet conscripts would serve for 2 years.

1. Statistical source: Military Attachés' Office, West German Embassy, London. (Figures c. 1988–89).
2. However, it has just been announced (Spring 1989) that university students will no longer be automatically liable for military service – the university students always had the softer option of joining a reserve officer training unit and escaping with only one month's basic training at a conscript 'boot camp'.

It is estimated that nearly 90 per cent of young Soviet males do some form of military service (and this excludes the military component of the normal school curriculum), the common starting point for all Soviet conscript service. After 6 months' basic training normal conscripts are posted to units.

The 10 per cent or so of young males who escape military service altogether do so because they fail the medical examination or because they are granted a hardship deferment, usually because they are supporting a family. The official liability to conscript service lasts until the age of 27. Although the Soviet Union is one of the few countries to have used women in combat in war, women are not currently drafted, although some 30,000 serve in voluntary roles.

The Soviet Union is split into sixteen military districts. Under normal circumstances a Soviet conscript would not serve in his home district. Officially this is justified as an effort to familiarize the conscript with other territories of the USSR, but it also facilitates the indoctrination of national and religious minorities (the Soviet Union includes about a hundred different nationalities). National problems apart, it is clear that there have been major problems recently amongst Soviet conscripts, and that these have only been aggravated by the Afghan conflict. Yet, in some respects the future looks quite bright for the Soviet conscript army, if not for us. The Soviet Union has already suffered the decline in the pool of young men which so many NATO countries are currently anticipating; in the Soviet case the number of young men of military age is now *increasing*. Simultaneously, education standards have improved significantly. Despite its inefficiences the Soviet conscript system provides the armed forces with an awesome strength of numbers; the capacity even with announced reductions, of the USSR to field a huge army will not be radically diminished in the foreseeable future; and the members of that army are likely to be better trained and educated than ever before.

A New National Service

Objections to the reintroduction of conscription fall into two categories, practical and moral.

The Army, which traditionally always took the bulk of national servicemen, asserts that the potential conscripts of today are not sufficiently well motivated or educated to cope with the duties that they would be required to perform. A professional army would not be expected to say anything else, but the evidence of two world wars and fifteen years of peacetime National Service suggests that conscripts can achieve, and in some circumstances even exceed, the standard of regulars.

General Kitson's Argument Against Conscription

In his book *Warfare as a Whole*, former Commander-in-Chief, United Kingdom Land Forces, General Sir Frank Kitson, has presented a useful summary of current British Army thinking.[1] But his view of conscription – the typical current Army view – is one of the few areas where we would challenge his logic.

The General is firmly against conscription under present circumstances, but accepts that it also has certain advantages. On the positive side, he notes the guaranteed steady flow of recruits, the increased number of trained reservists, the possible social benefit to young people, and the strengthening of links between the Army and the community. However, according to Kitson, these advantages are outweighed by five major disadvantages:

1. Military tasks have become so complex that only 45,000 of the 157,000 posts in the Regular Army could be filled by people with only two years' experience (the most that a conscript could reasonably be expected to serve).

The point is open to some debate. Even if it is accepted that recruits of the quality currently volunteering for the Army need more than two years to learn their jobs according to current specifications, it is possible that conscripts, coming from a broader social and educational mix might do better. How do the French and the Germans cope? The proportion of conscripts in their armies is more than a third, and it is not unknown for them to out-perform us on exercise. Similarly the forces of the Warsaw Pact – about whose battle performance we can only speculate – are even more dependent on conscripts.

2. Half a million adolescent males reach the age of 18 annually, 'so it would be difficult for the Army to devise a fair system for selecting the one-tenth that the Army could use'.

There are three main arguments against this. Firstly, Kitson's assumption that the Army could only use 10 per cent of a pool of half a million – that only applies to the professional Army as it is. Secondly, many of our allies manage to devise systems of selection.

1. Op. cit.

Finally, selection would not even be a problem for a voluntary system of national service.

3. The savings to the Army in terms of wages paid to conscripts would be lost in the need to hold regulars in the Army for longer periods to train the conscripts. There would also be the need for increased accommodation, ammunition, fuel and training areas.
The French and Germans, thanks to their conscripts, mobilize armies more than three times the size of ours for a lower overall defence expenditure.

4. Low-intensity operations: an enemy in a modern war of insurrection (General Kitson uses the specific example of the Provisional IRA) could gain a propaganda advantage by claiming that the soldiers opposing them were there against their will; furthermore, any inexperience on the part of Army personnel could be exploited by the enemy.
There is some merit in this objection, but it is worth noting the success with which conscripts served in other post-war campaigns, such as Malaya, and the extreme youth and inexperience of many regular soldiers currently serving in Northern Ireland. In any case, the decision could be taken not to send conscripts to Northern Ireland – each regular regiment might have a training company for conscripts.

5. The attitude of disaffected conscripts would spread to regular soldiers, making it more likely that regulars would leave after their first three years (the minimum period of regular enlistment).
This begs certain questions. Why should conscripts be disaffected? Was this a problem in the past? Again, how do our allies cope? The object of any new National Service would be to make ordinary people feel that their Army or other service was an important, stimulating and acceptable part of their lives, not a period of state-enforced militaristic torture.

Having raised these objections, General Kitson makes a very interesting admission. He acepts that it might become necessary to introduce conscription either if the international situation took 'a significant turn for the worse' or if a total ban on nuclear weapons was reached. In the event of a ban on nuclear weapons the UK would be dangerously vulnerable unless it had a ready source of additional manpower to bolster its conventional forces.

Despite General Kitson's comments and those of other senior officers we believe there is now a good practical case for conscription but it is offset by a moral dilemma: would it be right for this country to force its individual citizens into employment, and especially into uniform? If democracy in Britain were in a better state, then there might be a better case for conscription. In the mean time one might propose the introduction not of a compulsory conscription-based scheme of National Service, but of an entirely new *volunteer* programme with three options: 1) Defence Service (Army, Navy and Air Force), 2) Police Service, 3) Hospital and Community Service. (Police service is considered a particularly important option, since it would create a bridge between young people and law enforcement.)

Could a voluntary scheme be made viable? Would enough young people come forward? If a new voluntary National Service were to succeed it would have to be very different from the compulsory service seen in the past. It would need to be seen as something worthwhile, which offered significant advantages to those who took part (such as better employment prospects). Its armed service options, which would be open to both sexes, could not be orientated to drill and 'spit and polish'. 'Breaking down' and 'building up' techniques are no longer acceptable. A new National Service would need to concentrate on building confidence, self-reliance and team spirit through adventure training and similar activities, and all the options, military or not, might begin with an adventure training camp.

A new National Service would focus of necessity on the needs of the individual as much as those of the group. It would be part of the process designed to make the individual feel valuable and purposeful. No group task, military or otherwise, can be effectively completed without such foundations.

A new scheme along these lines would only be successful if it genuinely appealed to young people, perhaps as a more interesting alternative to the YTS or Employment Training schemes, or as something exciting to do before going on to higher education, or a chance to make their world a better or safer place. The authors firmly believe that one of the prime functions of a new National Service must be to offer a real outlet for youthful idealism. This energy is largely wasted by our society. David Owen said in 1984:

> I believe there are many who between school and higher education would welcome enhanced opportunities to contribute for a year, and perhaps reinforce this with a further few weeks every year for a period.

> A potential nurse or medical student might choose to serve in a mentally handicapped hospital or hostel. A potential engineer on an environmental project. Someone going into industry might like to join the armed forces for a year, then continue as a ready reserve. An accounts clerk might well wish to administer a community project for a one- or two-year period.[1]

Others have expressed similar views. Trevor Royle wrote in his recent study of National Service, *The Best Years of Their Lives*:

> Under Margaret Thatcher's administration several community schemes exist for young people. . . . These are run by the Manpower Services Commission and include the Community Programme, Voluntary Projects Programme, Opportunities for Volunteering and the Armed Services Youth Training Scheme, all of which are designed for the young unemployed. Consequently, none have been particularly successful, mainly because there is little motivation: the Armed Services Youth Training Scheme gives boys and girls aged 16–18 training in military skills which have civilian application, but this only lasts a year. Those young people who want to make a career in the armed services prefer regular entry, and in 1985 only 1,500 of the available ASYTS places had been taken up. Another drawback is that many of the 'volunteers' frequently find themselves doing the same kind of time-wasting tasks that disfigured National Service. Because they are considered as palliatives for the young unemployed, any sense of service to the community has quickly departed from these no doubt well-meant schemes.[2]

The most important contribution of these schemes has been their demonstration of how not to attract volunteers. How many young people ever heard of ASYTS, whatever its demerits? The objection of many of the young people involved in the various stop-gap schemes to keep them out of the dole queue is indicative of their feeling that they have become second-class citizens. A new National Service scheme would have to start from a position of greater optimism and enthusiasm on the part of those running it. Advertising and direct contact with schools would be all-important. The aim would be to involve about 50,000/75,000 young people a year in the military options, with a similar number taking up police and community service.

We suggest initial entry to a new National Service might be open to all young men and women between the ages of 18 and 25 (though

1. David Owen, speech 1984 quoted by Trevor Royle, see note 10 below.
2 . *The Best Years of Their Lives*, Trevor Royle (Michael Joseph, 1986).

a preliminary scheme for 16 and 17 year olds might operate in conjunction with this, which would be largely devoted to adventure training). Under normal circumstances it would last for one year, but this might be extended to 18 months or 2 years if specific vocational training were involved. Whether the option decided upon was military or not, accommodation could be shared and payment minimal. Beyond weekly pocket money a terminal gratuity could be paid of the order of £1,500–£2,000. The success of a new scheme would be dependent on a corps of highly trained teacher-leaders (it has been argued that one of the weaknesses of 1947–63 National Service was that no special training was given to NCO instructors). Those participating in the scheme would take direct responsibility for its administration and development. Some volunteers might be asked to stay on for an extra year to take up special posts in much the same way as some university students spend a year working as students' union officers. After the first period of National Service, volunteers would qualify automatically (but with no obligation) for part-time National Service, and at five-yearly intervals, would be able to return to the full-time scheme for 6 months (employers would be legally obliged to release volunteers for this follow-up training).

As far as military options were concerned, the new form of National Service that we envisage would have no immediate officer training option. It might well copy foreign schemes which split the period of service into two parts, the first a period of training, the second a period where the recruits themselves take on the role of junior instructor to train the next generation. Bullying of any sort would not be tolerated. Apart from confidence-training, basic military skills would be taught, with an emphasis on home defence.

Any new scheme of National Service, even the limited one suggested here, would obviously require substantial capital outlay and continuing financial commitment. Chichester and Wilkinson, in presenting an argument for obligatory National Service, make points equally valid in the consideration of any voluntary scheme:

> Conscription would be an expensive step, even though once the capital costs of new barracks, training facilities, and equipment had been met, it would provide the source of less expensive manpower and the flow of reserves which the country needs to prevent the size of its forces falling to unacceptable levels.
>
> However, this would be to look at the problem within the narrow parameters of the defence budget and to consider the reintroduction of national service purely as a defence expenditure item. This would be

entirely the wrong approach to a matter of the greatest national importance affecting, as it would, the whole thrust of government policy for the administration of the country and embracing the economy, employment, education and youth training as well as national security. National service could not be reintroduced without breaking down rigidities of departmental budgets and responsibilities. . . . There is an urgent need to re-examine the whole definition of defence spending, not solely in terms of the cost of military capabilities needed for national security in all its aspects, but with a much broader consideration of the national interest in mind.[1]

1 . *British Defence – A Blueprint for Reform*, Chichester and Wilkinson, (Brasseys, 1987).

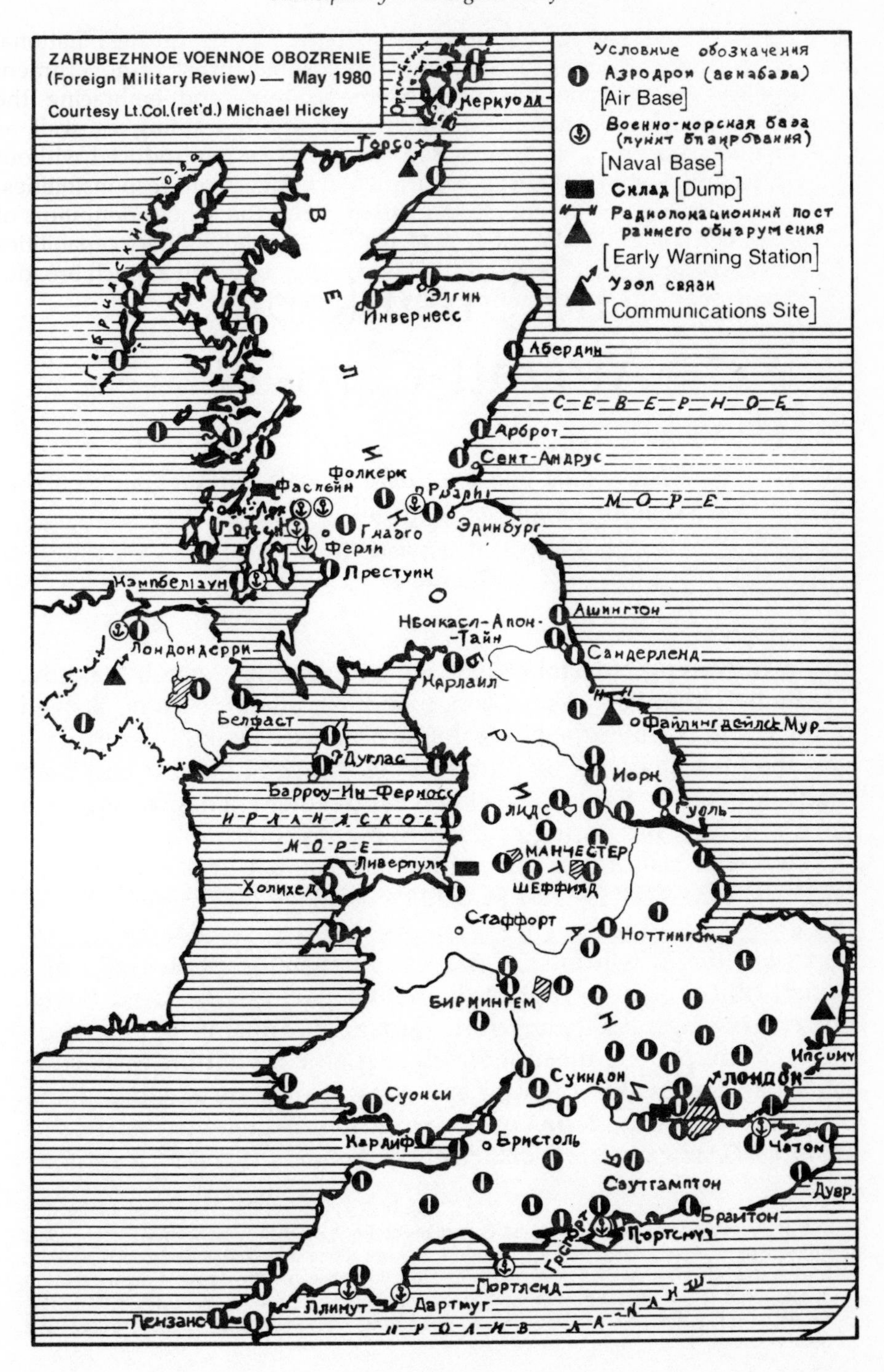
ZARUBEZHNOE VOENNOE OBOZRENIE
(Foreign Military Review) — May 1980
Courtesy Lt.Col.(ret'd.) Michael Hickey
Условные обозначения
Аэродром (авиабаза)
[Air Base]
Военно-морская база (пункт базирования)
[Naval Base]
Склад [Dump]
Радиолокационный пост раннего обнаружения
[Early Warning Station]
Узел связи
[Communications Site]
Керкуолл
Элгин
Инвернесс
Абердин
Арброт
Сент-Андрус
Фолкерк
Фаслейн
Глазго
Ферли
Эдинбург
Престуик
Кэмпбелтаун
Лондондерри
Белфаст
Ньюкасл-Апон-Тайн
Карлайл
Ашингтон
Сандерленд
Файлингдейлс Мур
Дуглас
Барроу-Ин-Фернесс
Йорк
Лидс
Гуль
Ливерпуль
Манчестер
Шеффилд
Холихед
Стаффорт
Ноттингем
Бирмингем
Ипсуич
Лондон
Суонси
Кардиф
Бристоль
Чатом
Саутгамптон
Дувр
Брайтон
Портсмут
Госпорт
Портленд
Дартмут
Плимут
Пензанс
С-Е-В-Е-Р-Н-О-Е
М-О-Р-Е
И-Р-Л-А-Н-Д-С-К-О-Е
М-О-Р-Е
П-Р-О-Л-И-В Л-А-М-А-Н-Ш

7

The Unsinkable Aircraft-Carrier?

'Tis the part of a wise man to keep himself today for tomorrow, and not venture all his eggs in one basket.'
Cervantes

At the beginning of October 1988 Soviet Colonels, Anatoli Makhov, Vladimir Greshnikov, Yuri Leonov and Vladimir Trofimov, arrived in the UK to monitor the home defence exercise Drake's Drum. This was the first such visit by officers from the USSR, and it had been made possible by the 1986 Stockholm Agreement, a new convention governing the monitoring of military exercises in Europe.[1]

The Soviet visitors, in their unfamiliar combat uniforms, striped (airborne forces) shirts and peaked camouflage caps reminiscent of those worn by American deer-hunters, received considerable attention from the British media. A Press Association photograph of a British officer with a clipboard briefing two granite-faced Soviet officers incongruously clutching Japanese cameras appeared in many of the papers, most of which also noted what the inspecting party had for breakfast (bacon and eggs). Coverage was bland and concentrated on the terms of the Stockholm Agreement itself. The *Financial Times* gave a few details of the exercise, but *The Times* alone

1. The Stockholm Agreement was signed by 35 countries in September 1986. It stipulates that any signatory planning military manoeuvres involving 13,000 or more normal troops, 3,000 or more paratroops or amphibious assault troops, or 300 or more tanks has an obligation to inform the other signatories in advance. Further, to check that the terms of the agreement are adhered to, all signatories are given the right of inspection on 36 hours' notice. The British exercise, Drake's Drum, involved only 5,000 men and 11 tanks; nevertheless the Soviets invoked their right of inspection.

reported the interesting information that one of the Soviet officers, whilst working as a military attaché in London in 1980, had been discovered taking 'voluminous notes' during a public hearing of the House of Commons Defence Committee. It might be argued that this was no more than his duty. But why did that officer and his three colleagues (another of whom had also been an attaché in London) take such an intense interest in defensive manoeuvres involving 5,000 men and 11 tanks? The importance of exercising the new rights agreed at Stockholm is part of the story; interest in our home defences is another.

Although exercises like Drake's Drum indicate a new awareness of home defence, and although there have been significant improvements recently (most notably in our aerial defences), the full extent of our unpreparedness on the home front in general and on the ground in particular is anomalous.

Nothing so perfectly illustrates our national doublethink about defence than the Army's attitude to the defence of the United Kingdom. The authorities, it seems, are unconscious of the contradiction involved in maintaining very large forces in Germany (whilst admitting that the risk of a Russian invasion there is slight) – and yet failing to do so at home. But, if arms reductions talks effectively make impossible any armoured thrust by Warsaw Pact forces across the north European plain, all traditional attitudes will need to be re-thought. Denied their tanks, might not the Warsaw Pact boost their capability for launching airborne or amphibious attack? Indeed, might they not re-think the whole way they use force for political objectives, perhaps favouring small-scale actions aimed at key industrial or economic targets? Moreover, are not the number and type of the potential threats to home security on the increase as Third-World countries or their terrorist surrogates emerge as more likely aggressors than the nations of Eastern Europe?

For the moment, suffice to say that full invasion of the United Kingdom is considered so remote a possibility that there are virtually no resources tasked to meet it; nor, more worryingly, are there sufficient resources to cope with anything but the most modest airborne or amphibious raid. (If pressed, senior officers will make comments about the possible availability of troops from the US in transit to Germany.) And even in the scenario which the Drake's Drum exercise set out to practise: that widespread sabotage and infiltration by Soviet special forces could be expected in the first days of a major conflict; there is a dire shortage of resources to meet the threat.

The accident at the Soviet nuclear power station at Chernobyl showed how even a militarized society such as Russia can find its resources stretched by a national disaster. Imagine the consequences at home of a *contrived* disaster of this sort – or even two or three simultaneously.

We cannot fully define the potential threat to the United Kingdom's home territory, but what we do know is cause for the gravest concern. In the period leading up to a war it is believed that the Soviet Union and her satelites may activate 'sleepers' in Britain to undertake sabotage and subversion operations. Meanwhile it is known that highly trained *Spetsnaz* forces, the Soviet equivalent of the SAS and SBS, will infiltrate British territory – all too easy a task since we have over 2,500 miles of coastline – to mount sabotage operations against key–point targets.

We have seen both in Ulster and on the UK mainland the disruption that can be caused by a handful of terrorists operating against limited targets. Imagine, then, what hundreds of infinitely better equipped and trained men might achieve. Or indeed, imagine what havoc one stick (four men) of our own SAS might cause in a major city and multiply it by a factor of a hundred or so: only then do we come close to understanding the scale of this threat. A paper considering the danger and how it should be met and whose authors included a former chairman of the military committee of NATO and the former Commander of Allied Forces Northern Europe noted, 'The Soviets now have special forces units (previously known as "diversionary brigades") specifically organized, trained and equipped for deep penetration operations including sabotage and disruption. Operating on the line of our SAS and Special Boat Squadrons, their personnel are highly trained. . . . A number of units of this type are known to be targeted against the UK which, as the main base for transatlantic reinforcement of NATO'S European theatre, is particularly sensitive to disruptive attacks.'

The existence of these special forces units follows basic Soviet tactical doctrine, where special emphasis is placed on deep battle – attacking the enemy throughout his territory from or even before the official commencement of hostilities – and *maskirovka* – deception[1]. These concepts, much emphasized in recent Soviet military literature, have been developed because of the Soviet need for rapid victory before the West can mobilize its full resources. As one of our

1. See Chapter 5.

military sources put it: 'If Britain could be strategically neutralized, then the likelihood of success for a Warsaw Pact conventional attack across Europe, especially one taking advantage of the momentum of the running start afforded by a mock training exercise or annual "roulement" of Soviet forces to and from East Germany, would be dramatically increased. A primary means to achieve such a neutralization would be *Spetsnaz*.'

The targets of the *Spetsnaz* in the UK would probably include military headquarters, air-force bases, political and military leaders, the requisitioned ferries being used as troop-carriers, transmitting stations and other communications centres, bridges, railways, key roads, dockyards and ports, major generating stations, oil and gas pipes, water supplies, and whatever else the Soviet command believed would cause maximum disruption and loss of morale. The possibilities are all too numerous. The *Spetsnaz* who have recently seen much action in Afghanistan are the very best troops the Soviets have. We may assume they will be experts in all forms of demolition, infiltration and ambush. They will be able to provide intelligence via long-range high-frequency radio sets and they will be able to tap into our radios. They will probably be dressed like us – for example, as fishermen, policemen, ambulancemen or soldiers, according to their task – and they will sound like us, speaking our own language, some even having mastery of regional dialect and idiom.

It is accepted by Western intelligence agencies that at any given time there will be a significant number of *Spetsnaz* troops in Western Europe on surveillance and acclimatization missions, with the occasional operational dummy run. It is suspected they have crossed the borders from Eastern Europe in TIR lorries, the number of which altogether overwhelms the customs and intelligence services, and of course, they may also be easily infiltrated as tourists or members of trade delegations or arts companies. One former officer told us that it was believed that *Spetsnaz* members may have been present in the UK during September 1985 to 'take part' in the home defence exercise Brave Defender. At the other end of the Soviet Empire, there have been persistent rumours that *Spetsnaz* commandos killed a member of the Alaskan Scouts (National Guard) who happened upon one of their patrols. The US government firmly denies this, but admits that some Soviet military equipment has been found on the Alaskan coast.

The KGB defector, Stanislaus Levchenko, recently revealed that before he joined the KGB he was a member of *Spetsnaz* (which is under the command of the GRU – Soviet military intelligence) and received special training for an operation he would be called upon to perform in time of war. He would be sent to Liverpool to monitor the movement of any shipping in the area of the docks there, and was particularly briefed to observe the movements of any nuclear submarines. It was clear from the instructions he received and the communications equipment he was trained to use that the Soviets envisaged that, if necessary, he would call down a nuclear strike on targets he identified, even though he would surely perish as a consequence. Levchenko said that much of the early training of *Spetsnaz* forces conditions them to accept that theirs might often be suicide missions. In briefings for such operations no mention is made of any provision for recovery.[1]

The Soviet threat to the UK only begins with the *Spetsnaz*. As their sabotage and disruption progress, concurrent aircraft and missile attacks on vital military, naval and air-force installations would be expected. Such conventional action would greatly facilitate further *Spetsnaz* operations. Escalation beyond this point is harder to predict, since the options are so numerous. Six of the Soviet Army's seven airborne divisions are deployed in European Russia and would, potentially, be available for operations against the UK (these were not affected by recent announcements of cuts in other units, but their effectiveness is limited by Soviet airlift capability). Each is made up of three brigades with air-portable support weapons and light armour. When considering what other resources the USSR has for a conventional attack against us we must also take into consideration the fact that all of the Soviet Union's front-line motor-rifle units can act in the air-landing role without any major reorganization, and that both the Baltic and Northern Fleets of the Soviet Navy have a brigade of specially trained naval infantry equipped to act in a role similar to our Royal Marine Commandos. Then there is the threat posed both by Soviet bombers, with their chemical, nuclear and conventional munitions, against massed civilian and military targets, and by the Soviet Navy which would try to isolate us with mines and submarine activity.

The country would also have to deal with a variety of internal threats. Apart from the possible activation of Soviet sleeper agents, mentioned above, it is possible that the Provisional IRA and other terrorist groups might assist the enemy.

1. BBC Radio 4, *My Country Right or Wrong*, June 1988.

Even in the days of *glasnost* the potential threat from the forces of the Warsaw Pact cannot be denied: intentions may have changed, reductions may be in progress, but the *capability* remains. Moreover, there may now be other potential threats; this chapter focuses on the Soviet threat, but other countries, for example, Iran, have large numbers of special forces. Whilst any potential aggressor has the capacity to cripple us in the sort of ways described above, we need to retain a capability to defend our home effectively.

Home Defence Resources

Britains Civil Defence Corps was disbanded in 1968, a casualty of the general rundown of conventional defence which came with the Mutually Assured Destruction (MAD) nuclear doctrine of the late 1960s. (It was then believed that countries with nuclear weapons, threatened by others with nuclear weapons, felt themselves more secure by being less well defended; the basis of this paradox was that stable relations between such countries were only possible if both believed that a nuclear strike would effectively wipe them out.) Some civil defence responsibilities were handed over to local government overseen by department F6 at the Home Office, but the capacity for helping the civil population on a large scale was eradicated.

The situation in Britain today is the complete opposite of that in the Soviet Union, where a comprehensive civil defence programme even includes instruction in Nuclear Biological and Chemical Warfare (NBC) drill as part of the school curriculum. In Switzerland, Scandinavia and some parts of the US (all less at risk than 'airstrip Britain') there are also comprehensive preparations. Although the most extensive protection cannot offer insurance against all-out nuclear attack, even a modest scheme could offer significant protection in a limited nuclear war (precisely the sort of war military strategists appear to be planning to fight in the era of flexible response), in conventional war, and against the chemical and biological threats which the Soviets have put so much effort into developing.

One area where the British authorities have acted is in secret measures to preserve their own control in the event of war. These have been considered in great detail. We do not deny the vital importance of maintaining internal security in war, but we would question whether it is possible without some sort of civil defence programme. Nor do we believe that real internal security can be maintained by the secret machinations of an over-centralized bureaucracy. A diffuse system with a fully informed and co-operative public is so much stronger. When we questioned the Home Office on civil defence we found them less than forthcoming. The whole subject is under review, they stated, and on further questioning it emerged that it had been under review for some years. As one of their Press Officers told us the priority since 1979 has been building up a new administrative structure so that 'flesh can be put on the skeleton'.

Police

There are approximately 125,000 police personnel in England and Wales, and another 13,000 in Scotland. They would have a very active role to play in a war and in any period of escalating tension that might preceed it. Their duties would include: crowd control – because it is assumed there would be panic among a potentially hostile civil population; traffic regulation – because it is assumed there would be streams of people trying to flee from actual, or potential targets; and many other tasks normally associated with the police in a country on a war footing. Additionally, in recent years, the police have taken on some responsibilities which were once the preserve of the military. Precisely what these are remain secret, but it is known that it is the responsibility of individual chief constables to create contingency plans for war and major national emergencies. Amongst the resources that may be deployed are the 8,000 or so police officers who have had some training in basic firearms use. This group might be of particular importance in any war where there was internal threat to the UK. However, the police are often over-stretched in peacetime – fewer than ten per cent of burglaries are fully investigated, let alone solved – and it is likely that lawlessness and public disorder will stretch them further in time of war.

The Army

The Regular Army has approximately 157,000 personnel of whom 56,000 are permanently based in BAOR and 3,000 in Berlin. In the event of war, or the threat of war, about 30,000 regulars would immediately be sent out to Germany. With the 11,000 in other garrisons overseas, this would leave about 55,000 in the UK. Of that number a significant proportion – perhaps 20 per cent – would be committed to mobile operations in NATO's Northern Region (which some authorities believe is the weak point at which the Soviets might try to break through), and many of the remainder would be tied up in logistical operations in the UK in support of the general war effort or raw recruits essentially unemployable in any useful military sense. It is most unlikely, therefore, that there would be more than an absolute maximum of 20,000 regular troops available for defensive operations at home, indeed a very senior serving officer recently told one of the authors that the typical allocation for a mobile reserve (i.e. other than key points) was one infantry company per *county*, i.e. about a hundred men.

The Territorial Army, has 76,000 members and there are 3,000 men in the new Home Service Force (HSF). (This sub-unit was created in the early 1980s specifically for key-point protection. It requires less commitment of time than the TA, and accepts older recruits. Although the intention was to form a force of 4,500 – which critics have suggested was far too small – the HSF still has only 3,000 members. Little attempt has been made to advertise its existence, possibly because there is a worry that it might poach recruits from the TA.) The Defence Estimates 1988 note: 'On mobilization and in war the TA would provide more than 50,000 troops to BAOR including two infantry brigades as part of I Br Corps.' Furthermore, the Defence Estimates 1989 confirm that 29,000 TA and HSF members would be left for Home Defence duties. Thus after commitments to administrative support it is most unlikely that there would be more than 20,000 TA soldiers available for combat or security duties at home, and 3,000 of them would be in the lightly armed HSF.

Finally, although it is likely that it would largely be a paper asset in a short war, there is the Army's Regular Reserve. Nearly everyone who leaves the Regular Army has a theoretical commitment to the Regular Reserve. Until recently it has lasted, typically, for 3 or 4 years; for those who enlisted after 1986, however, there will be a commitment for 6 years.[1]

At the moment there are theoretically about 150,000 names on the list. Legally they could be called out for 15 days of continuous training and an unspecified number of 36-hour periods a year, but this does not generally happen. Instead, some regular reservists are invited for one week's training in their third year on the reserve, but to date less than 10,000 have received this training. Only about one-

1. For those who enlisted before 1986 the commitment is as follows: if they have served less than 7 years they must complete the balance on the Regular Reserve list; if they have completed more than 7 but less than 12 years they must complete the balance to 12 on the list; and if they have completed more than 12 they have no liability.

third of the total pool of reservists have an annual obligation to present themselves for a day to their local Reporting Centre, and, we were told by the MoD in 1988, the Army has allocated specific wartime tasks to only 35,000, their jobs split between BAOR and the UK. Yet the Defence Estimates 1989 now say that it is intended that some 45,000 'ex-regulars' would have home defence roles. Arrangements for their training remain unclear. The Army certainly assumes that it will be able to call upon all its reservists in the event of war. Moreover, it well realizes the limitations even of those that are employable. Major D.G. Benest of the Parachute Regiment, writing in the Winter 1988 issue of the Royal United Services Institute Journal, noted: 'Historical evidence suggests that Reservists may be rapidly assimilated back into service life, although deterioration in physical fitness and the requirement to overcome "skill fade" or train on new equipment point to the necessity of an initial retraining period. Steps are in hand to improve this situation . . . but Regular Reservists cannot legitimately be regarded as a fully-trained reserve of immediate availability.'

It is clearly difficult to predict how the Regular Reserve would function in practice. Even if the Army were able to track down the majority of its reservists – and it had great difficulty in recalling reservists when they were needed during the Suez crisis in 1956 – the men could not be put in the field without arms and other equipment and some refresher training. Realistically, the time taken to achieve this might exceed the conventional phase of a future war. We may thus conclude that without a reformed and practised scheme for their training and reinduction into the Army the Regular Reserve are largely a wasted asset.

What about the available manpower from other services? There would be elements from the Regular and Royal Auxiliary Air Force, Royal Navy and Royal Marines, but these would be entirely occupied with the defence of their own services' major installations, and in the case of the marines, our oil rigs. They would not even be able to consider other potential targets. Indeed, so serious is the shortage of personnel to guard RAF stations (there are only the 2,800 members of the RAF Regiment and 900 auxiliaries tasked to defence duties) that it probably prompted the decision to arm female RAF personnel in 1982. According to the Defence White Paper 1988: 'On the ground the task of protecting vital military bases and installations falls mainly to the Army and RAF'; it would be more informative and honest if it continued, 'and as things stand they do not have anything like the number of personnel to do the job properly.'

In conclusion, although the Defence Estimates may claim that 'Over 100,000 ground forces are available for the defence of the UK,' we have seen that only a small proportion of them are really available to fight the enemy. Colonel Michael Hickey, a lobbyist for improved home defence and formerly an operational requirements specialist at MoD, comments:

> 'This figure of 100,000 is rather misleading. Very few of these 100,000 will be first line combat troops, those that are will need to be held in reserve for rapid deployment to meet unforeseen emergencies.
>
> There will be nowhere near enough to protect several hundred 'designated' key points, let alone the thousands of others which in fact exist. Pipelines, water and electricity plant, road and rail bridges, hundreds of disused airfields and likely landing grounds. Compare even the MoD's official figure of 100,000 with the total number of policemen in England, Scotland and Wales. They would find themselves very stretched. . . .'[1]

Although it is accepted that the defence of Britain may begin off our territory, surely the prudent protection of our home base should be our first priority, especially as it appears that strategic thinking now assigns much greater importance to areas outside the Central Region of NATO. The Soviets might, in the event of war, attack NATO in its all-too-vulnerable forward base – the UK. After all, we have become not only an 'unsinkable aircraft-carrier' for the alliance but the point of embarkation for 100,000 Regular Army and TA reinforcements for BAOR, as well as large numbers of US forces, ferried via Britain to the battlefields across the Channel. The fact is that the chronic unpreparedness continues in the face of the reluctant acceptance by military planners that the conventional stage of any future war might well last longer than previously predicted.

How can we create a realistic home defence? Clearly, present resources are inadequate. General Kitson comments on this: 'Leaving invasion out of account it would seem optimistic to suppose that the infantry component of the 100,000 odd men and women [left behind in the UK from the services in the event of war] could possibly cope with the commitment. For practical purposes it is probably true to say that if current infantry strength, including members of the Royal Navy and the Royal Air Force acting as

1. Interview with authors, January 1989.

infantry, was doubled there would still be a shortage.' Those words, from a former Commander-in-Chief, United Kingdom Land Forces, should be of particular concern.

Admiral of the Fleet, the Lord Hill-Norton, and General Sir Anthony Farrar-Hockley have both campaigned for a new Home Defence Force of half a million men. Their part-timers would be arranged in a diffuse web of locally raised platoons covering the entire country:

> The Force would be formed and equipped now, its arms being held centrally in Army depots, and only called out if there is an imminent threat of war. Volunteers would be trained in peacetime but the training commitment would not be onerous. Platoons would be raised locally on a community or parish basis, or in the case of cities on the basis of factories and the like, and would only operate in their immediate area. Their biggest single asset would be their intimate knowledge of the area, including potential targets in it. Thus they would serve local as well as a national defence need. Part of the job would be to supplement the Armed Forces in the protection of potential targets for sabotage squads and raiding parties. In the countryside, however, the key task would be to detect enemy incursions, to do what is possible to pin them down to delay subsequent progress, but above all to provide timely intelligence of hostile or suspicious movements. The Home Defence Force would thus provide local auxiliaries for the Regular and Territorial Forces – an extension of the Territorial Army – into whose command structure it would be integrated.'[1]

Hill-Norton and Farrar-Hockley also made detailed costings, estimating the start-up cost *c*. 1984 for 20,000 platoons nationwide as £120 million, with running costs of about £65 million per annum – incredible value in defence terms. Their campaign, which they saw as continuing the ancient tradition of 'Watch and Ward', coincided with the government announcement of the new Home Service Force. Sadly this seemed to silence debate on the subject, even though the HSF was less than a hundredth the size of the Home Defence Force that Hill-Norton and his colleagues envisaged.

More recently a German admiral, and former head of West Germany's military intelligence, Elmar Schmähling, has achieved some prominence for promoting a not dissimilar scheme for the in-depth defence of his homeland. Schmähling heads the Office for Studies and Exercises, the prestigious think-tank of the West

1. *Defence Begsins at Home*, Information pamphlet, 1984.

German military, charged with long-term planning and co-ordination with NATO forces on manoeuvres. His comments are all the more controversial because he is still a serving officer. Schmähling wants to see American and British troops removed from Germany, to be replaced by a new integrated citizen army. Unlike the less ambitious scheme proposed by Hill-Norton and Farrar-Hockley, Schmähling's scheme would be heavily dependent on new technology. He envisages a Germany reorganized to accommodate large numbers of time-share soldiers (these would take leave from civilian employment for several years at a time), and computerized command centres built into new buildings across the country. The predicate of his proposals is the negotiation of tank cuts by NATO and the Warsaw Pact to make conventional blitzkrieg impossible.

Schmähling is a self-confessed German nationalist, and his ideas would require the most radical political and social reorganization, as well as being expensive. Nevertheless, the fact that a very senior serving German officer should discuss such ideas is significant. There are real alternatives to the way we defend ourselves at present, particularly if significant reductions in armour are successfully negotiated. Citizen involvement is not the idealistic proposal that the military establishment in Britain would have us believe.

There is a strong case for a scheme similar to the Home Defence Force proposed by Hill-Norton and Farrar-Hockley. It could be part of a new, defensively orientated, and far more flexible system of defence. Any logical analysis of our defences indicates the need for more people on the ground. This can be achieved without an aggressive stance. We suggest that 100,000 or more extra men and women could be made available for home defence and other duties at reasonable cost and another 50,000 from the Regular Reserve made far more effective by the following means (figures are approximate):

a) an element of 50,000 from the new National Service scheme discussed earlier, tasked to relatively undemanding home defence and civil defence duties in the event of war. Essentially, what we lack at the moment is an effective capability for key-point protection. This activity is best carried out by volunteer forces who live and work in the vicinity of the assets they are tasked to guard. Some may argue that volunteers will be no match for well-trained *Spetsnaz* forces. But the existence of large numbers of men who are trained in perimeter security and who are equipped with the latest intruder detection hardware will at least narrow the range of targets that a potential enemy will contemplate attacking and will force him to plan any operation in great detail;

b) a new Home Defence Force of 50,000, similar to the force proposed by Hill-Norton et al., but not under the control of the TA, with members keeping their weapons and ammunition at home as they do in Denmark and Switzerland (centralized armouries would be far less secure). It would try as far as possible to transfer the individual from his civilian job into a very similar military task. The whole organization could be structured to take full advantage of civilian skills. All members of the new militia could remain in the UK in the event of war although, as a recruitment incentive, some training might occasionally take place at regular bases abroad;

c) a Territorial Army expanded to 125,000 personnel (an extra 50,000). This might be achieved partly by better remuneration and conditions of service (including, crucially, a clear and enforceable obligation on employers to provide their workers with leave for TA duties) and partly by allocating specific TA duties to 25,000 members of the Regular Reserve;

d) as well as the allocation of TA duties to some reservists, another 25,000 reservists in addition to those 35,000 currently tasked to BAOR could be given a specific, but part-time, role in the wartime establishment of Regular Army units. They would undertake annual training and receive increased bounties. This group would become a modern Special Reserve.

Costs of the new Home Defence Force element would be modest. We envisage a scheme not dissimilar to the rifle volunteers of the late Victorian era. Members of the new rifle corps could be offered free use of small-arms (including sub-calibre training versions of anti-tank weapons) and ammunition twice a month. They would supply their own uniforms and be encouraged, as regular soldiers often are, to buy other items of personal kit, such as backpacks. To keep costs down, members of the scheme would receive, instead of cash payments, an annual income-tax voucher. A similar scheme could be introduced into the TA. It is clear that even with the impending demographic trough there would be no shortage of volunteers from the civilian target-shooting clubs for such a scheme. Moreover, potential recruits would be *more* likely to join if they could supply their own equipment without too much attendant bureaucracy. This is a tremendous resource waiting to be tapped. Some volunteers might not be quite as fit as soldiers, but they would have the benefits of experience and proficiency at arms: the standards of marksmanship among sportsmen are typically as good as, and frequently far higher than those in the military or police. The force envisaged would not try to imitate the Regular Army, but would develop its own tactics specially suited to its members' backgrounds. By developing civilian marksmanship training, the state would ensure a ready supply of volunteers.

The Home Defence Force (or Community Guards, Defence Volunteers, or Home Force as they might be called and the reformed Territorial Army could develop on rather different lines. The TA would retain and strengthen its ties to the regulars, but it would become a more equal partner. This could be reflected by recruiting equal numbers to both forces, and by abandoning the terms territorials and regulars. There would be more joint activities, with greater opportunities for members of the TA to serve with the regulars (indeed we would also like to see a broad range of civilians brought into the Army on short attachments and vice versa; this has already begun with business managers, but there is enormous scope for development). Being in the TA would become a part-time job, rather than just a hobby.

The Home Defence Force, on the other hand, could be more like a club. As it would be principally equipped with small arms, it is probable that the Home Defence Force would find a significant proportion of its volunteers from existing rifle clubs, many of which can still trace links to the Victorian rifle volunteer movement and its Second World War sibling, the Home Guard. Members of a new Home Defence Force would elect their own potential officers, who would then be sent forward to a special selection board and, if successful, for training. The force would be nationally co-ordinated and subject to periodic inspections, but the basic administrative unit would be an enlarged, substantially autonomous, company with four or five platoons of forty members each. Local variation would not be discouraged, and an effort would be made to bring in specialists such as doctors, nurses, builders and off-road vehicle and radio operators in each unit. Each platoon could also include a local policeman on attachment. There would be no ceremonial drill in the force as envisaged. As far as the proposed new National Service scheme is concerned, its military options would include some contact with the Home Defence Force. Those about to enter the age bracket for optional National Service could be allowed to join the

Home Defence Force as juniors a year prior to their induction, national servicemen who did not take up an Army service option would be encouraged to join Home Service units after their National Service.

Critics of these proposals may argue that not enough volunteers would be found. Recruiting may be a problem for the present Territorial Army which is excessively bureaucratic, inflexible and consequently not very enjoyable for those who join, as one friend serving in it told us, 'the Regular Army in disguise'. Without an injection of imagination it will continue to be undermanned (and there has been some recognition of this recently with interesting proposals such as the formation of new units in north-western Europe made of ex-patriates). The other basic problem is that it is very demanding of time for little reward – and not only material reward.

Although we propose far more Territorial and Regular Army co-operation and integration, it has to be acknowledged that there is currently no love lost between the two groups: many regulars actively dislike the TA. Part of the problem has been that the TA has been asked to do the same job as the regulars with only the slightest allowance for their reduced training time and facilities. The TA's attempt to be the Regular Army in disguise has failed, primarily because current terms and conditions of service make it an impossible aim. The only realistic options are either to make it genuinely possible for the TA and regulars to integrate or to develop a new tactical doctrine for the TA quite different from that of the regulars: the latter seems undesirable as it would create enormous operational problems.

The examples of Switzerland, Sweden and Norway

Again, our neighbours may have something to teach us. Switzerland has a system of total defence which integrates its militia with five other services of state, covering diplomacy, the economy, civil defence, information, and 'psychological defence and state security'. The Swiss conception of defence is completely different from that in the UK. For example, it includes provision for nuclear fall-out shelters for over 80 per cent of the population.

Air forces exist as a component corps of the militia, which itself has only 1,500 regular full-time members (600 officers and 900

NCOs, the majority of whom are instructors), and yet, from a population of 6 million, Switzerland can mobilize a force of 625,000 soldiers (20 per cent of the male population) and 460,000 para-military civil defence members within 48 hours.

Constitutionally, Switzerland does not have a Commander-in-Chief or a head of the armed forces until one is appointed by Parliament at the start of mobilization (there is, however, an appointed Chief of Staff and a Chief of Training). Constitutional authority for the militia rests with the governments of the cantons. Since 1970 the Central Organization for Co-ordinated Defence has supervised military defence, civil defence and 'spiritual defence', propaganda for Switzerland's neutrality and military posture.

Every 19-year-old Swiss male is examined physically and mentally for military service (women are not conscripted). About 80 per cent pass, and another 10 per cent pass for auxiliary service in medical units and administration. No conscientious objection is permitted. Although service with army non-combatant medical units is a possibility, alternative community service is not. About seventy conscientious objectors are imprisoned by the Swiss courts each year for refusing conscription.

Training takes place in the year following the medical examination and lasts 118 days, either from February to May or from July to November. Seventy days are spent in barracks, 21 in platoon and company exercises, 21 in a battalion exercise and the last 6 back in barracks. About 17,000 recruits are trained on each course.

Those recruits who do well in this training are invited to become junior NCOs, returning the following year for 27 days' initial NCO training, then leading their own squads and platoons through a further 118 days' training. Those who do well in this may be invited to go through officer school, another 118-day course. To become fully fledged platoon commanders they will have to complete another 118 days with their platoon. This relationship between the training of privates, NCOs and officers has great advantages. According to a recent Swiss Militia booklet: 'Every inductee knows that his lieutenant has already successfully completed two basic training courses and additional cadre schools. What a superior now expects others to do was once expected of him under the same circumstances. Neither background or education determines further training and promotion. It is a question of military aptitude. Promotion is never automatic.'[1]

1. Statistical source: Military Attaché, Swiss Embassy, London.

After training, Swiss male citizens are formally on leave from the Army until they reach 50 years of age. They can be recalled at immediate notice. They keep their personal weapons and ammunition in their own homes, and their units normally correspond to the cantons in which they live. From 20 to 32 they are in the Alert Force (*Auszug*) and must complete 21 days' refresher training for 8 of the 12 years. In any given year about 400,000 men are being given refresher training. Between the ages of 33 and 42 they pass into the Reserve (*Landwehr*) and do 14 days' training for any three years. From 43 to 50 they are in the Civil Defence service (*Landsturm*) and do 7 days' training every two years.

On mobilization the Swiss Army consists of 3 field corps, 1 mountain corps, and about 15 (the precise figure is secret) independent defence brigades. Current Swiss doctrine permits limited offensive moves against the flanks of an invading force (to accomplish this there are 3 mechanized divisions and 6 independent tank regiments with a total of 800 tanks including Leopards made under licence from West Germany) but the basic strategic philosophy is essentially defensive. Its primary aim is the avoidance of war.

Operationally, if Switzerland were ever involved in war, the doctrine of Combined Defence suggests action would be very flexible and mobile, making full use of the density of military forces which the Swiss have created. There is a web of prepared defensive positions, the most impressive being in the alpine regions which are seen as a final bastion. If all else failed, the Swiss would continue fighting as partisans, in the mountains and wherever else it was possible, and every Swiss militiaman is taught techniques of guerrilla as well as conventional warfare. Some years ago, the Swiss Non-Commissioned Officers' Association even published a manual of special techniques called *Total Resistance*,[1] which gave detailed instructions on forming secret organizations, eliminating enemy leaders and the destruction of railways, power stations and the like. In any other country, where there was less official faith in the people, it would be called a manual of terrorism.

Switzerland was last involved in an international war in 1815, and last fought at all in a small civil war in 1846. The current system was introduced in the mid-nineteenth century and has been refined ever since. In 1927 an American officer commented: 'The modern Swiss Army was created not to engage in war, but to keep war out of Switzerland. . . . Its military victory [in 1914–18] was so complete

1. *Total Resistance*, Major H. von Dach Bern, ed. and trans. Captain R. K. Brown, US Army Reserve (Paladin Press, 1981).

that it did not have to fire a shot. Judged from the standpoint of aims achieved, no army ever had a more complete success.'[1] What applied in 1927 is even truer more than half a century later.

For all its strengths, there are of course problems. Much equipment has to be bought from abroad. There is a small but growing anti-conscription lobby (in 1977 and 1984 referenda decisively rejected the introduction of civilian service for conscientious objectors). Moreover, no one is sure, after nearly two hundred years, how good Swiss fighting ability might be, even if the Swiss were once the most famed mercenaries in Europe. An initial training time of four months for most conscripts is far less than that of any other conscript army in Europe (but to make any comparison which does not include continuation training is rather unfair). From November to February, when no recruits are in training, Switzerland has virtually no armed forces. But the militia is so well integrated with society that it is likely that any change now could only be for the worse. It is worth adding that Switzerland achieves its most credible defence posture for only SF4.6 billion (1988) or about 2 per cent of the GNP.[2]

Sweden has a policy of total defence comparable to that of the Swiss. The country is divided into 6 regional commands consisting of 26 defence districts. These defence districts correspond in nearly all cases with the administrative counties through which Sweden is governed. Service in the armed forces is divided into four categories: civilians such as clerks, administrators and stores workers; paramilitaries such as technicians, doctors and dentists; conscripts; and senior officers and NCOs, who must be regulars. From a population of about 8 million Sweden has a normal armed forces strength of about 150,000, including 40–50,000 conscripts in training, 60–95,000 returning conscripts on refresher training, plus about 20,000 civilians in full-time support services, and a similar number of professional officers and NCOs. In 72 hours Sweden can produce a mobilized force of 800,000. Full mobilization of the country is 850,000 (of which 700,000 would serve with the Army) plus 500,000 in the auxiliary services.

All Swedish male citizens are inducted into the armed forces between age 18 and 21 (the normal age is 18 but those in higher education are granted deferment). Conscientious objection is allowed, but objectors (except for certain legally defined religious

1. *Statemanship or War*, Lieutenant-Colonel John McAuley Palmer, (Doubleday, New York, 1927).
2 . Statistical source: Military Attaché, Swiss Embassy, London.

groups) must do 540 days' civilian community service instead. About 750–1,000 people a year choose this option. Otherwise, conscripts are trained in their own military districts according to the specialization for which they are selected. Riflemen, for example, serve for 300 days; drivers for 255 days and officers for 540 days, the longest term of service. In the Army and Navy, service can last from 220 to 540 days, in the Air Force from 270 to 360 days.

After military service an obligation in the reserves lasts from age 20 to age 47. Two years after leaving the armed forces men are required to attend the first of a series of five refresher courses spaced out through that 27–year period. These courses last between 11 and 32 days depending on specialization. These specializations include officer training. On mobilization, 90 per cent of Swedish command appointments will be filled by reservists.

At full mobilization, the Swedish field army has some 29 brigades of various types and 60 independent battalions. Sweden has never been invaded in the whole of its recorded history. The country last took part in a war in the early 1800s, and declared itself perpetually neutral in 1855. More than 50,000 Swedish troops have served in the various UN task forces which has provided Swedish operational military experience in the modern world. The system of total defence, in which a large conscript militia is combined with professional high-tech military equipment and regulars appears to work extremely well. The problem is not with the men but with the equipment. The cost of maintaining the Swedish defence industry, producing Sweden's own high-performance aircraft and tanks, has been so great in the last decade that Sweden has been forced to make some purchases abroad, notably in missile technology. (Ironically, Sweden is one of the most innovative countries as far as missile technology is concerned – the Bofors Bill, anti-tank weapon and RBS 70 and 90 low-level surface-to-air missile are at the leading edge of existing technology.) Sweden now uses American missiles such as Improved Hawk, Sidewinder, and the Norwegian Penguin, and its helicopters come from Bell and MBB. This purchase of American and NATO hardware has, however, weakened Sweden's posture of neutrality.[1]

It is not only neutral countries which are heavily dependent on militias. Our NATO ally Norway has an extremely well-organized Home Guard, which has been in existence since 1946. It has 80,000

1 . Statistical source: Military Attaché, Swedish Embassy, London.

members spread throughout the whole country, which is split into 18 home guard districts, 90 home guard sub-districts, and 500 home guard areas – the basic administrative unit. Members of the Home Guard, who are both volunteers and conscripts, must attend an annual camp. Four hundred full-time personnel (soldiers and civilian instructors in the main) are part of the Home Guard establishment.

The aim of the Norwegian Home Guard is to provide 10,000 men in 45 minutes, 40,000 in two hours and 60,000 in three hours. Total mobilization can be achieved in four hours. These mobilization times are dependent on weapons and ammunition being kept at home. As is the case in Switzerland, Sweden and Denmark, criminal use of firearms held on this basis is statistically insignificant. The annual Home Guard training requirement varies, it is set by Parliament every year and currently amounts to 50 hours, which Home Guard members can do after work, at weekends or over consecutive days. Members are trained in basic military skills, and those selected for specialist or officer training must undertake an additional 14 days' training every three years. Most of this specialist training takes place locally. As well as infantry units, there is a naval branch, under the control of the regular Navy, and an anti-aircraft branch under the control of the Air Force. The Norwegian Home Guard is essentially a quick-reaction force which allows Norway to keep a relatively cheap regular army which, according to Norwegian doctrine, does not need to be combat-ready in peacetime.

The Home Guard is by its nature deeply integrated into Norwegian society and many members train far more than they are required to because they enjoy it. The most obvious example of this are the members of Norway's many Home Guard rifle clubs. The Home Guard also has special schemes for adolescents, and marksmanship training is a popular option, with annual competitions both for shooting and the combined shooting and skiing biathlon. The whole spirit of the Norwegian Home Guard is one of civil and military co-operation.

This is almost the exact opposite of the current position in Britain where the Government, with its recent firearms legislation, has taken action to discourage civilian marksmanship training. The Norwegian Home Guard also has an important role to play in giving aid to the civilian community, and organizes a variety of rescue services. The Norwegian Home Guard has a National Council of which 18 out of 34 members are representatives elected by home-guardsmen themselves. There is also a disciplinary council, at local area level and at every level a committee of ombudsmen. Finally, the Norwegian Home Guard has a special fund to aid members injured in training.[1]

The Swiss, Swedish and Norwegian military systems depend on the fullest integration of armed forces with society, in the Swiss and Swedish cases to the point where professional armed forces, as such, barely exist. Only very stable societies can achieve this. The Swiss tradition of joining clubs and associations, plus rifle shooting as a national sport, makes the idea of a militia more acceptable to the mass of the population, and conscientious objection is very rare. The Swedes have a similar tradition, and a strong sense of national identity. British society has had such features in the past, notably in the thirty years before the First World War, when joining associations and local community groups was far more common than it is today. Such groups are now being encouraged again as a way of integrating society. It was an eighteenth-century Englishman, Adam Smith, who elaborated the notion (derived from Aristotle) that the best political unit is a small face-to-face society organizing its own affairs. If there is a distinctively British character, one would expect it to hold to Adam Smith's belief. There is no good reason to believe that a localized militia, a Home Guard, would not fit the pattern of British society, nor that society would not be strengthened as a result. Yet, when during the 1987 election campaign, Neil Kinnock speculated (in a TV interview on 24 May) on the value of training large numbers of men in guerrilla tactics so that should the Soviets invade, they would be unable to establish firm political or administrative control of Britain, this was seized upon by Margaret Thatcher in a televised speech two days later: 'He has left himself no policy but to yield to an invasion and occupation and to trust in the forlorn hope that a guerrilla struggle would eventually persuade the Army of occupation to withdraw.'

One can, of course, see why Mrs Thatcher took advantage of this opportunity during a campaign to pour scorn on her rival, but what Mr Kinnock was suggesting could have a significant deterrent effect – especially if it were implemented throughout Western Europe.

The risk of starting or continuing a major war is rarely accepted unless the aggressor believes that the war will be short or victorious. Preparations for mass defence – as the Swiss already have – would

1 . Statistical source: Military Attaché, Norwegian Embassy, London.

offer the Soviet Union the very unattractive prospect of a long struggle for conquest. Moreover, without such preparations at home the rest of our preparations abroad are something of a sham. The argument has been advanced in certain quarters that no increase in the forces available for home defence is necessary as the Soviet threat to the UK (which has never been very strong) is now diminishing. Oddly this is often put forward by the same people who advocate stronger forces for NATO's central front. Surely there is an inconsistency here, as the situation requires the perception of threat to be the same? Those who object to Home Defence being treated seriously by saying 'Are you seriously suggesting that the Russians are going to invade Britain?' should be challenged with 'Are you suggesting that the Russians are going to invade Germany?'

8

The Changing Face of War

'Kill one frighten ten thousand.'
Ancient Chinese military proverb

We noted early in this book that the Army's most active role today – as it has often been in the past – is countering insurgency. This chapter will take a look in detail at the conflict in Northern Ireland, but before doing so, it is useful to consider insurgency and one form of it – terrorism – more broadly.

The British Army has traditionally been regarded as one of the world leaders in the techniques of counter-insurgency (COIN) operations. It has been involved in a number of such operations – Palestine, Malaya, Kenya, Cyprus, Aden, Oman, and twenty years in Ulster have provided a great deal of practical experience. Indeed, Britain is one of the few countries to have engaged repeatedly both guerrilla movements in the Third World and urban terrorists nearer home.

Indeed despite appearances, Britain's is not a peacetime but a wartime Army, constantly fighting these diverse and stubborn enemies. While Britain in NATO has never needed to fight on a conventional or nuclear battlefield, since the end of the Second World War, British troops have been in action in COIN campaigns constantly. As Liddell Hart wrote in the early 1960s, 'Campaigns of this kind are more likely to continue because it is the only kind of war that fits the conditions of the modern age.'

Consequently, a great deal of thought and money is being directed at countering the new threats. Indeed, a whole new counter-terrorist industry has been established. Launching their guide to counter-insurgency products, the respected military publishers, Janes, recently noted; 'The amount of effort and research being put into the defence of every realm against traditional threats is dwarfed by that going into the defence of the realm and populace against the terrorist, the insurgent, the freedom fighter or the guerrilla.'[1]

All this research has spawned a new generation of hardware: elaborate computer and surveillance systems, specialist weapons and all sorts of other high-tech gadgetry. As one former officer told us, 'CRW [Counter Revolutionary Warfare] has become big business. I think that is basically a bad thing. Although it means we have a lot of good kit on offer, it also means that certain parties have a vested interest in maximizing the threat, or pretending that their products are the answer to it – their profit depends on it.'

Good equipment is important, and the UK has been an innovator in this field, but fighting successful COIN campaigns requires far more than the right accessories – indeed, there is the danger that the sophisticated hardware currently being marketed can distract from the real business of fighting what is, above all, a psychological battle. Operational techniques which appear effective in the short term, but which address only the symptoms of the problem, may also be dangerous, lulling us into a false sense of security about the future. Dealing with revolutionaries and terrorists requires very special skills, often quite unlike those of conventional warfare, but the Army's techniques for dealing with insurgency have generally evolved in a piecemeal way, in reaction to specific tactical problems. The difficulties of immediate containment have often inhibited the development of a more strategic approach. Talk even to a member of the Special Air Service, for example, and one is likely to be told things like, 'We're just nuts-and-bolts men'; their outlook is practical rather than intellectual.

Whilst the military strategy and tactics used by insurgents are centuries old, and in fact pre-date conventional warfare as we think of it, the main difference between fighting the tribesmen, bandits, and urban rioters of the past and fighting today's revolutionaries is the latter's possession of a coherent doctrinal programme, which in many senses is itself a powerful weapon. Some British defeats at the hands of insurgents and terrorists, and many defeats of other Western armies, have resulted from failure to recognize the new force with which they were confronted. No clearer example can be offered than the twenty years of troubles in Northern Ireland. With all its skills and experience the British Army has been

1. Publicity pamphlet for Jane's 1988 guide to counter-insurgency products.

unable to defeat the Provisional IRA. Without an understanding of revolutionary doctrine, the problems and successes of the British Army in COIN operations, and the threats which it now faces, cannot be properly understood.

Terrorism and Revolutionary War

Since 1945 there have been over 400 revolutionary wars; conflicts characterized by the attempt to overturn, not just a government, but the complete economic, social and ideological structure of a nation or region. Revolutionary warfare campaigns are now the commonest form of war; a feature of many of them is the use of terrorism.

Terrorism in revolutionary war is usually employed in conjunction with more conventional forms of violent action. It is occasionally practised in isolation, either because no other resources are available and the terrorists believe their actions may create a revolutionary situation, or (especially when a sponsor is involved) because it is the only military action which can be initiated without risking escalation to full conventional war. Of course, terrorism is not only used by left-wing revolutionaries. The technique has also been employed by a wide variety of nationalist insurgents, such as General Grivas's EOKA in Cyprus[1] or the Stern Gang in Palestine, and by various nihilistic and anarchist groups.

In many ways, the inventors of modern terrorism and revolutionary guerrilla warfare were the Irish. The bombing and terror campaign practised by Fenian revolutionaries against the British in the 1880s, both in Ireland and on the British mainland, culminated in the murder of the British Viceroy, Lord Frederick Cavendish, in Phoenix Park, Dublin in 1882 and the creation of Scotland Yard's Special Irish Branch (known today as the Special Branch). The campaign of terror and guerrilla war fought by the IRA between 1916 and 1922 against the British, leading to the partition of Ireland, is regarded by many as the first true modern revolutionary war, years ahead of its time in its sophistication, and is, in fact, the only successful example of such a campaign in Western Europe. Even so, the Irish experience has had less influence on the world's radicals

1. The insurgent movement which sought to establish union or 'enosis' with Greece.

than the theories of left-wing and Communist revolutionaries who came after them.

Yet terrorism is not an inevitable response to political frustration: choosing the path of terror implies the abandonment of many generally accepted ethical principles. Though it is often said that one man's terrorist is another man's freedom fighter; this is a cynical notion based on moral relativism, suggesting that right and wrong are matters of subjective judgment or political orientation. It is important, then, to define terrorism precisely. We submit that it is essentially a matter of method rather than one of motive: a person employing terrorist means for political ends is still a terrorist, however desirable the ends he seeks. Equally, an insurgent who confines his activities to hit-and-run raids on his enemy's security forces and is scrupulous about avoiding civilian casualties is a guerrilla and not a terrorist. *Terrorism is the application of extreme violence (or the threat of it) to create psychological casualties for political ends* – and is distinguished from other forms of armed activity in that its primary targets are non-combatants. It is the fact that terrorists regard innocent civilians as acceptable targets for shooting or bombing that, above all, sets them apart from others whose business it is to kill people. Since terrorism is an activity rather than a state of being, it is possible for some groups to be terrorists at certain times but not at others. A Palestinian who crosses into Israel to attack a military checkpoint may not be involved in a terrorist act, but one who hijacks a plane certainly is.

Some people argue that in a democratic society, anyone who opts for change through violence rather than the ballot box is a terrorist; they would make no distinction between the IRA sniper who shoots at an RUC patrol and an IRA bomber who blows up a bus station crowded with civilian shoppers. Others argue about the nature of democracy. But value judgments about political context are as essentially subjective as value judgments about motive and once we find ourselves in a situation where one man's democracy is another man's tyranny, it is but a short step back to the position where one man's terrorist is said to be another's freedom fighter. It is fruitless to make one's definition of terrorism conditional upon one's definition of democracy.

Moreover, terrorism has come to be something more than the sum of terrorist actions. Adhering to the idea of terrorism are a number of associations. It can be seen, for example, as the expression of an energy intensified by frustration – an explosion of political pressure. Sometimes, as in the case of a number of middle-class

German terrorists in the 1970s, terrorism acquires a cultish quality and dubious sociological theories are adduced to give it an intellectual respectability. Even today, certain terrorist groups appear to be primarily motivated by obscure philosophical notions drawn partly from existentialism. One such is the belief in 'the purity of action' advocated by some of the European 'autonomous' groups. Some psychologists have said that terrorism can be seen as the result of unchecked and unchannelled egotism whilst others have seen its root in the phenomenon whereby the individual projects his own self-hatred onto an external group or society as a whole.

Revolutionary Theory and Revolutionary War

Few would deny the influence of Marx and Lenin in promoting revolutionary socialism, but it was Mao Tse-tung who first practised revolutionary war as we understand the term today. He developed an intially limited but gradually pervasive form of conflict which combined guerrilla and conventional action with a psychological and political offensive. (By contrast, Lenin developed the concept of a professional Communist Party, but made war with a conventional army.)

In 1927 the Communist Party in China, with the prompting of Stalin's Soviet Union, attempted a series of urban uprisings (the Autumn Harvest), which were easily suppressed. This failure of the Leninist doctrine that revolution would flow from a sudden urban coup was not lost on Mao, then a minor Communist Party official. Familiar with socialist political ideas and the military principles of Sun Tzu and europeans like von Clausewitz, he formulated a subtle but easily communicated doctrine of his own. Relentlessly patient and fundamentally political, it combined the concept of class struggle with Clausewitz's ideas on the nature of war as a political act.

Like the Prussian Colonel, Mao saw that guerrilla action could offer a chance for the materially weak to engage an enemy, more powerful in conventional terms. However, Mao never denied the importance of conventional military strength, or eschewed conventional engagements when he was in a position to win them. Guerrilla action he believed only bought time to achieve political dominance and to build an effective conventional army for the final confrontation.

He spelt out the necessity of winning over the local population so that a 'sea' could be created in which his guerrilla 'fish' could swim. Mao's emphasis was always on the peasantry as opposed to Lenin who focussed the efforts of the Party on the urban proletariat. With the backing of the rural population ensured by the well organized cadres of the party, Mao saw an initial phase of strategic defence (in which the creation of secure bases, education, and the manipulation of political resentment took precedence over military operations) passing into a period of strategic stalemate and guerrilla warfare towards a final phase of strategic dominance and conventional offence.

Mao's strategy, in direct contrast to the Marxist–Leninist model, was for a protracted war fought over an enormously extended 'battlefield'. The enemy, lacking the support of the people, might achieve tactical victories on occasion, but would never be able to bring these together into strategic success. In a country like China, Mao and his followers could trade space for time against the enemy, and use the time to create 'will' within their own supporters. So long as their political will was greater than that of the enemy, and they were prepared to outlast him, their victory was seen as inevitable. For Mao, as for von Clausewitz, war and politics were almost synonymous, which led Mao to believe that dominance on the political/moral front would naturally lead on to military victory. This is not quite as obvious as it may sound and should be contrasted to the current Western view that firepower is all important. It also raises an interesting question: does defence have to be built on firepower?

Mao's ideas had international influence even before he completed his war in China. Ho Chi Minh of Vietnam was particularly impressed, and reproduced Mao's ideas in 1941 in a book called *The Resistance Will Win.*[1] It became the basic primer for Vietnamese Communists. However, the war which later developed in Vietnam did not precisely mirror the one in China. Although it was protracted, revolutionary and anti-colonialist in concept, and although it combined guerrilla and conventional action, it also included an extra element, the widespread, calculated use of terror. The Vietnamese used terror both as a means to coerce the local population, and as a weapon against the enemy.

1. Source: *War Studies Course Handbook,* RMAS.

Giap and the 'Science' of Terror

The man chiefly responsible for the Vietnamese terror was Vo Nguyen Giap, a former history professor who, having led a band of Soviet-sponsored guerrillas against the Japanese in the closing years of the war, rose up to command the Communist armies of Vietnam. Giap stressed the importance of psychological warfare and terror in his book *The War of Liberation and the People's Army*.[1] He stated that no move should be made against the enemy until complete psychological dominance was achieved both over them and over the civilian population. Terror was the means to this. Moreover, he believed its application affirmed the commitment of those who practised it, liquidated adversaries, boosted morale and disrupted the target state. Giap did not see terror as a replacement for conventional action, but as a tool to supplement it. Nevertheless he will be remembered for his theorizing on terror and psychological operations, and may accurately be called one of the progenitors of modern terrorism.

Che Guevara: The Failure of a Theory

In 1956 a small party of revolutionaries led by Fidel Castro and including the Argentinian, Ernesto 'Che' Guevara, returned secretly to Castro's native Cuba with the object of starting a revolution there. Trained in Maoist doctrine, the party landed in the south of the island, as far from the capital of Havana as possible. After an initial setback when many of them were killed in an ambush, the survivors, about twenty men, were able to raise enough support among the people to cause the Cuban dictator, Batista, to flee the country on New Year's Day 1959, leaving Castro in charge of the country.

The truth was that Batista's regime had been so corrupt, and his army so incompetent, that almost any action against him would have led to his overthrow. Guevara, however, concluded from his experience that South American governments could be overthrown by revolution. He believed, with Mao, that revolution would begin in the countryside, but that a small band of dedicated revolutionaries could act as the focus (*foco* in Spanish) for the revolution, radicalizing the people and greatly accelerating the speed with which the revolution would succeed or even exporting it as a ready-made package. The doctrine itself became known as *focoism*.

1. *Ibid*.

Guevara's theory was put into practice in various South American countries in the early 1960s, culminating in his own attempt to create a revolution among the Indians of the Bolivian highlands with twenty followers – none of whom spoke the Indian dialect – in 1967. Like all the other attempts, this was a disastrous failure, and Guevara himself was killed by Bolivian security forces.

Guevara's approach to the revolution, and that of his friends and supporters, was by no means always a matter of politics alone. Like his associates, the Frenchman, Regis Debray, and the American political writer, Herbert Marcuse, Guevara seemed to find something morally positive, even redemptive, in the act of violence itself. This idea, whose origins can be traced at least to the anarchists of the nineteenth century, also motivated such revolutionary terrorist groups as the Bader–Meinhoff Gang in West Germany in the 1970s.

Carlos Marighela: Urban Guerrilla

In both China and Vietnam the Communists had substantial conventional resources from an early stage in their campaigns. Other modern revolutionaries have not had the same advantage (and may have failed as a result). For example, in South America in the 1960s and 1970s terrorism or very limited guerrilla action were often the only options available to those committed to overthrowing their governments by violent means. One Latin revolutionary who found himself in this predicament was the Brazilian ex-Communist, Carlos Marighela, who was killed by Brazilian secret police in 1968. From Guevara's failure, Marighela concluded that *focoism* could create a revolution, but that it should be based in the cities rather than the countryside. He articulated a desperate revolutionary creed focused on terrorist action by the 'urban guerrilla'.

In Marighela's much-reproduced *Minimanual* (an instruction book for would-be terrorists), the importance of deed rather than dialectic is emphasized. Although he rejects excessive theorizing, four themes can be identified: 1) a fanatical cult of the revolution, where violence almost becomes an end in itself; 2) a deliberate effort to push the authorities into repressive counter-measures against the population (believing that, if this could be achieved, they would be sowing the seeds of their own destruction); 3) concentration on the urban front to divert the resources of the authorities and to allow organization elsewhere in the countryside, where a genuine revolutionary base could then be built up on the classic, Maoist, pattern;

4) the use of publicity and media manipulation – 'Publicity is like a weapon in the street, anyone can pick it up and use it.'

The last point merits special attention, as so many commentators see media exploitation as the predominant characteristic of present-day political terrorism and, indeed, the reason for its existence. Within the last twenty years international air transport has made it possible for small groups to strike anywhere in the world and to seek safety and support from countries favourable to their cause. At the same time, international communications have meant that such terrorist acts will receive the greatest possible global publicity. Some terrorist strikes have been undertaken with no more than this objective, such as the seizure of the Iranian Embassy by Kurdish separatists on Whit Monday 1980. This has led to calls for the press to be curbed, to deny terrorists what Margaret Thatcher has called 'the oxygen of publicity'. Such a point of view, although demonstrating the fundamentally psychological nature of the conflict, can divert attention from the frustrated aspirations often at the root of terrorism, and the fact that terrorism is often only part of a broader campaign. The idea of denying terrorists access to the media by government decree is therefore viewed by most experts on the subject as too simplistic, and ultimately counter-productive. However, because terrorists have taken steps to develop genuinely theatrical techniques in order to appeal to the broadcasters, some measures could be taken in co-operation with radio and TV news organizations to deny terrorists the advantages of theatrical effect.

Ireland's Conflict

Though there has been a steady development of revolutionary theory, this has, arguably, not been matched by increasingly sophisticated counter-revolutionary thinking. Often politicians have preferred to deal with insurrection and terrorism on and ad-hoc basis – neither seeking nor finding a permanent solution. The conflict in Northern Ireland, for example, appears endless.

Since 1969 nearly 3,000 people have died in 'the troubles'. Although it is often said that the military situation is better than in the early 1970s, the Royal Ulster Constabulary still routinely deals with about ten bombing incidents a week, and twice as many shootings. Images of the casualties of 'an IRA bomb' or 'a sectarian killing' regularly appear on our television screens. The public has become habituated to the horror, the security forces established as 'the pig in the middle'.

This bleak situation is as confused as it is confusing. Is there a war on? The average soldier may think so as he patrols the Falls Road with rifle and flak jacket, even if the statements of the government are rather more ambivalent. Officially we are informed that there is no war: wars can only be declared against sovereign states. Yet we have also heard from those in authority of 'the war against the IRA', 'the war against terrorism', and of the IRA's 'brigades' and 'active service units'.

However, if we do describe the conflict in Ireland as a war, it is also important to make it clear that it is a limited war in which the enemy is relatively weak, and has naturally chosen the weapons of the weak: terror, subversion and guerrilla warfare. What action there is takes place on very limited fronts, as retired British paratroop colonel, John Hickey, an Irishman himself, notes: 'The media have created the impression that Ulster is a terrorist state. It is not. The troubles are confined to a relatively small area of the six counties.'[1] Indeed, for most of the people of the province, for most of the time, life goes on as normally as it does in the rest of the UK: rather more people die in road traffic accidents in Northern Ireland than are killed by the paramilitary groups. And yet, although terrorism is localized, 2,700 dead in Northern Ireland with its population of only 1.5 million is equivalent to over 90,000 casualties on the mainland. Certainly there can be few families among the Catholic community who have been left untouched by the troubles and the whole society is affected by the social and economic problems that have followed in the wake of the violence.

Any assessment of a war, and in particular one in which terrorism plays such an important part, must include a careful examination of psychological factors. For the terrorists it is not the physical but the psychological casualties which are important. Consequently, one of the most important tasks in any effective counter-terrorist action must be to reduce the number of psychological victims. However, the war in Northern Ireland is not just a terrorist campaign, but also a revolutionary war fought on many fronts.

The Background

Any attempt at exploring the British Army's future role in Ulster must also examine what the conflict there is about. The roots of the

1. Interview with authors, 1 February 1989.

present troubles are deep indeed, and the events of several hundred years ago remain of contemporary political relevance, not only because some wrought lasting change but because they have become symbols. Those who seek to understand contemporary Ireland must understand not just the literal facts of the events of Irish history, but the development, and the manipulation of the way they are perceived.

The first recorded incursion into Ireland by the English state was made during the twelfth century. Having been declared king of Ireland by Pope Adrian IV, Henry II encouraged some of his Norman warlords to settle there so that they might subdue the Irish kings and physically claim Ireland for the English Crown in accordance with the papal decree.

Henry's barons did not manage to subjugate all the Irish kings, but instead established themselves as powers independent of Henry himself. The English king was soon forced to go to Ireland with an army and invite the wayward barons to pay homage together with the Irish kings whom they had been sent to crush. The barons complied; the locals generally did not, and because of difficulties of transport and communication there was little Henry could do about it. However, one of his more faithful nobles, John de Courcy, mounted an expedition against the northern provinces. He beat the local king, Dunleavy, and was rewarded with the Earldom of Ulster.

In 1210 King John arrived in Ireland but even though he was able to put down a rebellion, he found it impossible to consolidate his rule there. After John, English kings lost interest in the troublesome isle and more than three hundred years passed before Henry VIII made a serious attempt to bring Ireland under the firm control of the English Crown. He too failed but his daughter, Elizabeth I, did not. When a small Spanish force landed at Kinsale in 1601 and joined up with an Irish rebel army led by Hugh O'Neil, she sent her viceroy, Lord Mountjoy, to crush the insurrection. After this, according to the writer and soldier, Michael Dewar, 'the tudor conquest of Ireland was complete. English Law was enforced and Protestantism declared the state religion, even though, as yet, there were only a handful of Protestants in Ireland.'[1]

Indeed, the large Protestant community in Northern Ireland was not established until the reign of James I who despatched to Ulster in and after 1607 a number of Scottish and English Protestants as part of a policy of plantation – a means of consolidating power over

1. *The British Army in Northern Ireland*, Michael Dewar, p. 12 (Arms and Armour Press, 1985).

a colony by settlement, the principles of which had been articulated by Niccolo Machiavelli in *The Prince*. In Ulster, land was taken away from the indigenous people and handed over to the Protestant newcomers who were expected to exercise social control, collect taxes and be more reliable than the rebellious Irish. The first wave of immigration, which established a new Protestant gentry, was quickly followed by a huge influx of industrious Scottish Presbyterians who built up new towns with their own schools and churches. Machiavelli may have written that the victims of such a policy 'can never do any harm as they remain poor and scattered', but he obviously had not reckoned with the Irish or their rebellious temperament. In 1641, poor and scattered though they were, the Irish rose in revolt and slaughtered 12,000 of the Protestant interlopers.

In 1649, Oliver Cromwell, already tiring of the continued unrest, mounted a punitive expedition against the Catholic Irish. The calculated brutality displayed by his troops at Drogheda and Wexford has never been forgotten and still fuels anti-British sentiments in Ireland. Under Cromwell the confiscation of Catholic land was resumed with a new vigour and the native Irish were driven to the more remote areas in the west of the island.

In 1688, following the Glorious Revolution which ousted James II from his throne, William of Orange, a Protestant, became king of England. James, meanwhile, fled to Ireland via France where he was accepted as king. In 1689 Protestant inhabitants of Derry and Enniskillen rose up in support of William. The events at Derry have subsequently entered into the mythology of Ulster Protestantism. Just as Derry was about to fall to an Irish army, thirteen apprentice boys used their initiative and shut the gates of the town. A three-month siege followed which was finally raised when one of William's ships broke through the river blockade. On 1 July 1690 William won a famous victory over James at the Battle of the Boyne. It would confirm – at least for two hundred years – the ascendancy of Scottish and English Protestants in the governance and ownership of Ireland. The victory at the Boyne during the reign of 'good King Billy' is still commemorated by Protestant Orangemen.

Relations have remained tense ever since between those who proclaim loyalty to the British Crown and those who want to see Ireland an independent nation. This mutual hostility manifests itself in many forms, often tribal, not always rational, all too frequently violent. There were major rebellions or attempts at revolutionary change in 1798, 1803, 1848 and 1867 (the latter year of troubles even included a remarkable, and remarkably ill-considered, attempt at the invasion of Canada by 800 Fenian expatriates living in the USA).

The abject failure of the revolutionary approach led to the growth of a constitutional movement for Home Rule in Ireland during the 1880s. Under the charismatic leadership of James Parnell, and with support from the British Prime Minister, William Ewart Gladstone, it looked as if a degree of independence might at last be achieved. The prospect was scuppered by the Conservative maverick, Lord Randolph Churchill, who saw that the issue could be used as a weapon against Gladstone and the Liberals. He played the 'Orange Card', deliberately inflaming Protestant opinion in the north with his brilliant rhetoric. 'Ulster will fight and Ulster will be right!', went his rallying cry.

The Home Rule movement went into decline. Gladstone lost power in 1886. A few years later Parnell was discredited by a divorce scandal involving his mistress, Kitty O'Shea. Nevertheless, the spirit of change which he had fostered led to considerable social reform and a serious attempt to tackle the emotive question of land tenure.

Though the prospect of Home Rule had become more distant, much of the tension in Ireland appeared to pass with the dawning of the new century. But, a decade later the crisis of Herbert Asquith's Liberal government brought Home Rule back into the forefront of political consideration. Parnell's old Irish Party, rebuilt by John Redmond, found itself in the position of having enough seats in Westminster to keep Asquith in power. It was not long before a deal was struck, and in 1912 the Liberals reaffirmed their commitment to Home Rule.

The reaction in Ulster was immediate. Nearly half a million Protestant Unionists signed the Ulster Covenant and a well-organized Ulster Volunteer Force (UVF) of 100,000 was raised. The Ulstermen enjoyed considerable support within the British establishment, particularly the Army. Most of the volunteer force's officers were themselves British regulars – moreover the Director of Military Operations of the British Army, Sir Henry Wilson, was an Ulsterman and particularly sympathetic. All this led to an extremely tense situation. In March 1914, in the Curragh Incident, Anglo-Irish officers serving in Ireland announced that they would resign their commissions rather than fight to suppress the Ulster opposition to Home Rule. Still confused in its details, this incident was the closest that the British Army has come in three centuries to direct interference in national politics. When the Ulster Volunteer Force managed to land 35,000 rifles at County Antrim, civil war and mutiny seemed likely. The Liberals backed down, Asquith feeling the position of his own government was too precarious to allow him to suppress the Ulster leader Carson and his Ulster Provisional Government.

Meanwhile, the political situation in Southern Ireland was confused. The creation of the UVF had been sufficient stimulus to provoke the creation of a similar, if less well managed, group of Republican volunteers. The majority of these saw themselves as a defensive force against the UVF. However, a significant minority, many with links to extremist groups like the Irish Republican Brotherhood (IRB), believed that violence was the only path to political independence.

At the outbreak of the First World War, Redmond agreed to a postponement of Home Rule. He even encouraged Irishmen to sign up with the British Army, and his own son was killed on the Western Front. Thousands of the Ulster Volunteer Force, regarding themselves as essentially patriots, had also volunteered to fight for the British Army, as the 36th (Ulster) Division. One of the hardest-fighting units in the Army, it served on many occasions alongside the 16th (Irish) Division, recruited chiefly from southern Catholics.

Though Redmond retained effective control over the majority of the southern volunteers, he could not control the extremists. In 1916 a small group of Irish Republican extremists, badly misjudging the mood of their own countrymen, attempted to take advantage of British involvement in the war by staging the Easter Uprising; 700 rebels seized the Post Office and other public buildings in central Dublin. Although these events have been subsequently dramatized and glorified, there was only very limited popular support for the rebel cause, or sympathy with its failure, until the savage over-reaction of the British government once again inflamed national feeling.

A wave of executions, arrests and general brutality fostered the emergence of a hard-core volunteer group based on the IRB. Pledged to continue the fight against the British until a republic was declared, they would soon become known as the Irish Republican Army (IRA). From the start the group was organized on two fronts, one military, one political. The political wing was built upon an existing republican organization known as Sinn Fein (Ourselves Alone, in Gaelic). Originally a newspaper, it had been founded by a printer, Arthur Griffiths, in 1907, and already had links with the IRB.

The imposition of conscription in Ireland in 1918 ensured Sinn Fein political popularity and a steady stream of volunteers for its military wing. After the elections in December of that year, Sinn Fein declared its own revolutionary government and Parliament. The party had won 73 of the 105 Irish seats at Westminster but refused to take them up (in fact 36 of the newly elected members were not even able to attend the new Parliament in Dublin as they were in gaol). By not taking their seats the Sinn Fein members set a precedent of abstention which still characterizes the party's approach to British parliamentary elections. Gerry Adams, for example, though elected an MP in 1983 has never been to the House of Commons.

The British declined to recognize the Dublin assembly and widespread insurgency followed. During this outbreak of troubles two more groups entered the demonology of Irish Republicanism: the Black and Tans (a special security force composed of recently demobbed British soldiers), and the Auxiliaries (made up of former officers). Both forces became notorious for the uncompromising line they took and both were, consequently, loathed and feared. Irish history tends to repeat itself; during the 1960s another non-regular security force – the B-Specials – was to achieve a similar notoriety in the north.

Eventually, Sinn Fein representatives were called to London to discuss a treaty. It was agreed that an Irish Free State (a state with dominion status similar to that then enjoyed by Canada) would be set up, with a provision for six of Ulster's nine counties to remain part of the United Kingdom as the province of Northern Ireland. Although two of the six counties had Catholic majorities, the area ceded to the Unionists was judged to be the smallest unit that would have an overall Protestant majority and still be economically viable.

The IRA and Sinn Fein split over the issue of participation. Michael Collins, who had negotiated with the British, declared, 'I have signed my death-warrant.' The statement was indeed prophetic. He would die in an IRA ambush in August 1922. Many members of the IRA and Sinn Fein remained committed to the idea of a republic and were willing to continue the fight. Civil war erupted from 1921 until 1923 and the extreme elements of the IRA and Sinn Fein were defeated. Repeating the error of the British, the Free State government imprisoned 13,000 and executed nearly a hundred of them, confirming a bitter legacy which divides Irish political life to this day.

By 1931 the IRA had been declared an illegal organization by the Dublin government. Bitter at what they saw as the betrayal of their cause, a disillusioned group of conspirators decided to pursue the struggle by going underground. They retained the name Irish Republican Army, though it no longer gave a true indication of their numbers or military capability.

Nevertheless, for the best part of 38 years the IRA remained a subterranean force in Irish politics, surfacing for occasional bombing campaigns in the 1930s and 1940s and mounting a border campaign in the late 1950s which was such an abject failure that what remained of the movement finally declared its disgust with the Irish public and, now entangled in Marxist dialectics, veered away from terrorism.

The beginning of the present troubles may be traced to the Civil Rights movement of the late 1960s. A group of middle-class Catholics had observed the success of the Civil Rights campaign in the United States and decided that techniques similar to those being used to end institutionalized prejudice against blacks also had potential for ending the discrimination against Catholics that was widespread in Northern Ireland. A movement with a broader social manifesto grew, gaining support from both Catholic and Protestant trade unionists.

The demands made by the Civil Rights campaigners were not extreme: they wanted the abolition of the business vote in local elections and its replacement by a one-man-one-vote system; an end to discrimination in the allocation of public housing; new laws to protect against discrimination in employment; the abolition of the B-Special police auxiliaries and the repeal of emergency legislation that had suspended certain traditional rights. However, the Protestant community believed that the campaigners had a secret agenda which included the unification of Ireland.

In October 1968 the police attacked a Civil Rights demonstration in Londonderry in full view of television cameras. One of the victims of the police violence was a Catholic MP. Despite the outrage this incident excited throughout the UK, another march was ambushed by a mixed group of police together with supporters of the Reverend Ian Paisley the following January. RUC men in uniform stood by as their off-duty colleagues (including approximately one hundred B-Specials) clubbed demonstrators to the ground at Burntollet Bridge. In April it happened again. A peaceful demonstration in Derry was attacked, but this time the Catholic community responded and stone-throwing and rioting broke out in the Bogside district. Tension mounted through the summer in anticipation of a Protestant march in August. As expected, this proved a catalyst to further rioting and the people of the Bogside declared their area out-of-bounds to the police and set up an alternative administration in what became known as Free Derry.

Now, more than ever, the Protestants believed that the Catholics were plotting the reunification of Ireland. Their mood turned ugly and they set about burning the homes of Catholic families. On 14 August 1969 British troops were ordered into Derry to protect the Catholic population.

Protestant violence was not confined to Derry. On the night of 13 August there were riots in Belfast. The following night almost fifty Catholic families were burned out of their homes and the B-Specials machine-gunned a Catholic housing estate, killing a child and a British soldier who was visiting his family while on leave.

Since the British had not yet arrived in force and the RUC appeared disinclined to intervene, anyone who had a hidden gun at home was asked, often by the local priests and community leaders, to come on to the streets to act as vigilantes. The IRA was back in business.

On the afternoon of Friday August 15, the Army began to deploy in the Catholic ghettos. There had been little time for preparation and planning and detailed local intelligence was scarce. The 1st Battalion of the Royal Regiment of Wales, who were sent to the Springfield Road area, set up a barrier in the Falls Road – dividing the two Catholic communities of the Lower Falls and Springfield but leaving Catholic Clonard vulnerable to attack from Protestant Shankhill. Similar errors were repeated across the city. On that Friday the Army was welcomed on both sides of the sectarian divide. One officer of the Royal Regiment of Wales later recalled that as his unit went through the Protestant areas there were shouts of,'Get in there and smash the bastards,' but the Catholics greeted his men with cups of tea and evident relief.

It did not take the Protestants long to realize that the Army saw its job as the protection of the Catholic estates. Then they turned on the soldiers with bricks and stones. An officer of the Parachute Regiment, which was based in a Protestant district, subsequently told the writer Max Arthur: 'It was a frightening thing . . . to watch in the Shankhill Road at night people in Territorial Army uniforms, people carrying Union Jacks, singing "God Save the Queen" and slinging petrol bombs at us.'[1]

Meanwhile, a dispute was brewing within the IRA about its response to the Army's presence on the streets. In December the organization split: the hard-liners broke away to form the Provisional IRA (PIRA) and set up its own political wing, Provisional Sinn Fein; the more moderate elements who remained called themselves the Official IRA but become more popularly known as 'the Stickies'. The Officials were as willing as the Provisionals to shoot or bomb when it suited them but were less narrowly sectarian in outlook and more markedly influenced by left-wing political ideas.

During the following year the Army saw trouble from both Protestants and Catholics but it was not until 6 February 1971 that the first British soldier (Gunner Curtis of the Royal Artillery) was killed, in the New Lodge area of Belfast. On the same day the Army shot dead James Saunders, a staff officer of the Belfast Brigade of the Provisional IRA. The shooting war had started.

In the ghettos of Belfast and Derry PIRA had found a theatre of operations for guerrilla and terrorist tactics, and went on the offensive. Many of its members naively believed that if they could kill as many British soldiers as had been killed in Aden (38), the British government would be forced by domestic public opinion to pull out of Northern Ireland altogether. In the first four months of 1971 more than 130 bombs exploded in the province. As the officials saw how successful PIRA's campaign was, and particularly how it was benefiting their recruiting, they decided to join in as well. On 22 May they staged the first ambush of an Army patrol.

Unfortunately, the very thing which should have been avoided at all costs – further alienation of the Catholic community, which might give succour to the Provisionals – was ensured with the introduction of internment without trial in August 1971. This was implemented as a direct result of pressure from Stormont. Lieutenant-Colonel Michael Dewar wrote after the event:

> Internment was a political disaster, nor was it particularly effective in military terms, yet it was inevitable given Stormont's failure to accept radical reform years before. Although internment without trial was a traditional remedy in Ireland, both North and South, for it to happen in a part of the United Kingdom in 1971, in one of the oldest

1. *Northern Ireland Soldiers Talking*, Max Arthur (Sidgwick & Jackson, 1987).

> democracies in the world, presented the Westminster Government with a conundrum it would have preferred to have avoided.'[1]

David Johnson, a former senior lecturer at Sandhurst, was equally unenthusiastic:

> This policy allowed for the arrest and indefinite detention without trial or charge of suspected terrorists; but intelligence shortcomings meant that non-terrorists were picked up in the same net. It led to great resentment among the Catholic community, which in turn only served to push the violence to new levels, especially when stories of mistreatment of detainees started to circulate. For the authorities internment was to prove counter-productive as the events in 1972 were to illustrate.[2]

Internment was very badly handled by the security forces. Operating with a list provided by the RUC Special Branch which was inaccurate and out of date, the Army failed to capture any senior Provisionals in Belfast. Of 342 men taken into custody in the initial phase of Operation Demetrius – as the Army called the round-up – 116 were released after 48 hours. Many of those arrested were old men, former IRA members perhaps, but no longer active. The Chief of the General Staff, Sir Michael Carver, was later to say that the police had 'pushed up the list to the large number they produced and were encouraged to do so for Stormont's political reasons.'[3]

Reaction in the Catholic ghettos was swift and violent. Riots broke out in Belfast and Derry and many of the young rioters offered their services to the Provisionals. The effect of internment, therefore, was to increase the numbers of fit young men willing to fight and this posed additional problems in terms of intelligence-gathering as many of the new PIRA members were not previously known to the security forces.

The Army's response was to increase its visible security measures. A heavy military presence in overt patrolling provided PIRA with a classic target, as well as one which they could exploit in their propaganda. The Army was behaving all too like an army of occupation. Meanwhile, a few months after the own-goal of internment, the Army found itself at the centre of a storm of criticism over some of its tactics, particularly 'interrogation in depth'. Following

1. Op. cit. pp.54–55.
2. *Guerrilla Warfare*, ed., John Pimlott, p.173 (Hamlyn, 1985).
3. *The Provisional IRA*, Bishop and Mallie, p. 187 (Heinemann, 1987).

the Compton Report of November 1971, which cleared the Army of the actual use of torture, the techniques of violent interrogation ceased in favour of subtler methods more easily reconciled with the Army's aspiration to win the hearts and minds of the Catholic community. In truth, the latter campaign was unlikely to succeed considering the situation on the ground and the way it was being mishandled.

Some lessons were being learnt, however, particularly in the field of intelligence. Brigadier Frank Kitson, himself a veteran of counter-insurgency campaigns in Kenya and Cyprus, had convinced his colleagues of the importance of good local-level intelligence-gathering and of the value of building up an accurate and detailed picture of the enemy and his methods.

But in January 1972 Kitson's reserve force, 1 Para, was lent to 8 Brigade in Londonderry for riot control. On 30 January the Paras shot dead 13 men, and wounded 13 others, including one woman, in what became known as 'Bloody Sunday'. The Widgery Report on this incident cleared the men of shooting indiscriminately but concluded that some of their victims had probably been unarmed. Within the month the British Embassy in Dublin was burned down and the Parachute Regiment mess at Aldershot hit by a PIRA bomb the first target hit by PIRA on the mainland.

Army morale was not high. Effective techniques to contain the violence were not yet being used. The problems went beyond disorganized intelligence and inappropriate tactics for riot control to the very basics of urban soldiering. The subject remains highly sensitive, but it appears that the Army was often inflicting as many gunshot injuries on its own men as on the IRA, and so began to rethink not only its safety procedure but also its methods for teaching basic marksmanship (much as the police have done in the 1980s). Special ranges were improvised where soldiers could practise their shooting and patrolling techniques as realistically as possible.

In March 1972 the Parliament at Stormont was dissolved and direct rule from Westminster was substituted. In an effort to win peace, special prisoner status was granted to internees and the British government let it be known that it was interested in secret talks with the Provisionals. At this point PIRA morale was high. More than ever they were convinced that they had a fighting chance of getting the British out of Ireland. In their own minds the abolition of Stormont was a direct result of their military campaign. Moreover, there were signs that the British public was wearying of the conflict: an opinion poll conducted in September 1971 showed that already 59 per cent of the population was in favour of recalling the troops from Northern Ireland.

This was a period of intense military activity. During the month of May 1972 the Army recorded more than 1,200 incidents involving explosives or firearms. No-go areas had been set up the previous month in Belfast and Derry and on June 24 the hundredth British soldier was killed.

It was in this climate that on 7 July a group of Provisional IRA negotiators, including the young Gerry Adams went to tea at Paul Channon's house in Chelsea to meet the Home Secretary, William Whitelaw. The way for the talks had been prepared by a secret emissary of the Prime Minister, Edward Heath (who is believed to have been encouraged in this direction by representatives of the Secret Intelligence Service, MI6, which was deeply involved in intelligence-gathering in Ireland, north and south, in the early 1970s). On 26 June, as a prelude to the talks, a bilateral truce was declared. When the talks proved inconclusive, the truce was scrapped and the violence was resumed.

On 21 July, Bloody Friday, 22 PIRA bombs exploded in Belfast, killing 9 and wounding over 130. The PIRA alienated the Catholic population by this action, and the Army felt that the time was right to launch a major military initiative. In Operation Motorman on 31 July 1972, 27 battalions were used to reoccupy the no-go areas. The PIRA was, apparently, given sufficient warning of the impending action to ensure their exit before the arrival of troops so that Army casualties could be minimized.

1972 was the worst year for the Army in Northern Ireland. When the figures were collated at the end of December, 129 soldiers, 17 RUC men and 321 civilians had been killed; 578 soldiers, 94 RUC men and 3,902 civilians had been injured; 1,853 bombs had been planted, of which 1,324 exploded; and there were 10,630 shooting incidents. Clearly the security forces were not dealing with a small terrorist problem along European lines; this was a revolutionary war on a significant scale.

During the next two years a political initiative was launched which, it was hoped, would bring an end both to the violence and to the frustrations that lay behind it. A new assembly was set up whose members were elected by proportional representation. A conference was convened at Sunningdale to discuss power-sharing in the assembly, but the whole process failed when the Protestant trade unions went on strike in May 1974.

In November the Ministry of Defence issued a statement that there was no war in Northern Ireland and the names of Army personnel killed in the province would not be inscribed on war memorials. Less than a fortnight later 19 civilian casualties were added to the roll of the dead when bombs exploded in the centre of Birmingham. Four days after this the British government finally decided to make PIRA an illegal organization throughout the UK and the Prevention of Terrorism Act was rushed through Parliament. Intended as a temporary measure, its provisions were described by the Home Secretary as 'draconian'. This spate of announcements is instructive: the government clearly appreciated the scale of the problem and saw that emergency measures were needed but was reluctant to admit that there was a *war* of any sort.

1975 proved to be a quiet year in which the Army lost 'only' 20 men and the number of terrorist incidents was markedly reduced. However, there was an alarming increase in sectarian killings. The reduction in pressure on the security forces was in significant part related to the fact that the Army's intelligence co-ordination was beginning to be successful. With the arrival of professionals from the security service, the RUC Special Branch was now providing information that it had formerly been reluctant to share; this was of considerable assistance to the Army at brigade level. The Provisionals were put under great pressure, at last the Army appeared to be winning its war. As in 1969, feuding split the ranks of the IRA. A new group, calling itself the Irish Republican Socialist Party, broke away and started its own terrorist group – the Irish National Liberation Army (INLA). INLA attracted some of the better educated and more politically minded members of the republican movement and soon took on the character of a Marxist rather than a nationalist organization. Although few in numbers, INLA forged links with the worldwide terrorist fraternity, receiving weapons and explosives from Libya and training and other support from Palestinian groups. INLA aimed to intensify the pace of the war and started a fresh wave of bombings and assassinations.

In 1976, with a political solution no nearer, the process of Ulsterization[1] which had begun with the expansion of the Ulster Defence Regiment continued. It culminated in the British policy document 'The Way Ahead' in January 1977, which confirmed the primacy of the police. The RUC would take the high-profile work and maintain a presence on the streets while the Army would be

1. Handing over responsibility for security to those who live in Northern Ireland.

used to support police operations and go undercover on intelligence-gathering and surveillance assignments. The pattern for the Army's new role had been set in January 1976 when the SAS had been deployed in Northern Ireland, first in South Armagh and later throughout the province.

By this time PIRA had been heavily infiltrated by British Intelligence and was in such disarray that it was forced into a complete reorganization. Its strength had always been that, unlike the continental terrorist movements, it was a genuinely popular force with strong links in the community. Now, instead of remaining a broadly based movement, it restructured itself into small active service units [ASUs] of 3–5-man cells. No longer could it present itself as a guerrilla force fighting an Army of occupation; its new structure meant that it was suited only to small-scale actions, such as those which are essentially terrorist in nature. Consequently, PIRA has been engaged in bombing campaigns and assassinations ever since, starting with the winter campaign of 1977–8, which concluded in an atrocity that alienated many supporters when a bomb was placed at the La Mon House Hotel in February. The blast killed 12 and injured 32 more.

A series of political assassinations by the PIRA and other extremist groups followed in 1979. The British Ambassador to the Hague, Sir Richard Sykes, and the Tory MP, Airey Neave (the victim of an INLA bomb) were killed in March, Earl Mountbatten in August. Also in 1979, 18 soldiers were killed at Warrenpoint in a PIRA action which revealed a sophisticated understanding of security forces methods. In 1980 a series of attacks were made on British Army bases in West Germany and since 1981 we have seen a series of major propaganda bombings on the mainland such as the Regent's Park/Hyde Park explosions of July 1982, the Harrods bomb of 1983, and the destruction of the Grand Hotel at Brighton during the Conservative Party Conference in 1984.

A lull followed and there was talk of the IRA having been defeated. In 1988 another major mainland campaign was begun with bombs at first at the Mill Hill Barracks then at Tern Hill. There were also a number of well 'publicized' false alarms. A few pounds of semtex found on the mainland achieved more publicity than the murder of three innocent civilians in Ulster, the day before.

What Next?

The key question remains, is the Army winning in Northern Ireland? On the one hand, it could be argued that the situation has been kept under control and that the killings of security force personnel in Ulster, taken with the occasional bombing on the mainland, represents what one Home Secretary, Reginald Maudling, called 'an acceptable level of violence'. However, given that we know of the aims and methods of revolutionary war, a case can be made that the terrorists are winning. It has been the IRA's aim to make Ulster ungovernable by creating a 'climate of collapse' in the province. In this they have clearly failed. But another of their aims has been to make the British public so unsympathetic towards the Northern Ireland problem that the politicians at Westminster would feel under pressure to withdraw the troops. Opinion polls have shown that in this they have been very much more successful.

There can be little doubt that the bombing campaign on the mainland has been effective in requiring the British people to make inconvenient changes to their way of life. The 1988 Conservative Party Conference at Brighton was held in an atmosphere of siege, and thousands of police took part in one of the biggest security operations ever seen, while a Royal Navy minesweeper patrolled offshore to deter an IRA attack from the sea. After the conference, when MPs reassembled at Westminster, the Home Secretary, Douglas Hurd, announced new restrictions preventing the broadcasting organizations from transmitting interviews with terrorists and their apologists. Replying to the criticism that followed this move, the Prime Minister expressed the view that we all had to surrender some of our freedoms as part of the war against terrorism. Both the added burden of security and the encroachment upon traditional rights and freedoms can be seen as playing into the terrorists' hands. In addition, the Northern Ireland Unionists, particularly the more extreme such as Ian Paisley, are not particularly popular with the British public who perceive them as intransigent and unreasonable. Consequently, an increasing number of people are beginning to take the view that Britain should withdraw its guarantee to the Protestant community in Ulster and leave Ireland's problems to the Irish.

A factor of considerable assistance to the terrorists is that the present British government's attitude towards the problem of terrorism has always been ambivalent. It is argued that the IRA are simply criminals who should be dealt with by due process of law, whilst at the same time it is said that the rights of law-abiding people should be infringed because we are effectively in a state of war. The law itself has been subject to radical revision and extension in order to deal with the terrorist threat. There are provisions in the

Prevention of Terrorism Act, in the system of Diplock Courts (where judges sit without juries in Northern Ireland), and in the broadcasting restrictions which run counter to some of Britain's most hallowed traditions of liberty. By seeking to beat terrorism within the normal civil law, we have corrupted the law itself.

Moreover, the insistence that the Northern Ireland problem is essentially one of criminality has led to distortions and contradictions within the security forces. A criminal problem can only be dealt with by obtaining convictions in courts. To secure a conviction, evidence is needed. But the processes of evidence-gathering and of sustained intelligence-gathering are not always compatible. The security service, MI5, was drawn into the Northern Ireland problem in the early 1970s and since then has gained a remarkable degree of expertise in both the acquisition and analysis of intelligence relating to IRA operations. However, for MI5 to be effective, it is vital that it does not become involved in criminal prosecutions. Sacrificing important sources or hard-won data to the short-term expedient of obtaining evidence hampers the long, slow business of building up the full intelligence picture. Moreover, by the nature of their work, Security Service personnel do not want to find themselves in the witness box making statements on oath. In these circumstances uncomfortable compromises have had to be made: if something has to give way, should it be the effectiveness of the Security Service or the integrity of the machinery of justice? Neither is desirable if we wish to remain a safe and healthy democracy.

By far the greatest victim of the political confusion about Ulster has been the Army. Subordinate to the RUC, it has never had the opportunity to fight the war that it is uniquely capable of winning. Every soldier who has served in Ulster will tell you that almost all the active PIRA cadres are well known to the Army. Each of our units is equipped with books detailing the biographies of the local terrorists. Their car registration numbers are on the Army's *Vengeful* computer, whilst other databases can provide everything down to the colour of the wallpaper in the home of an IRA man's grandmother. Many terrorists are kept under almost constant surveillance by men from specialist units such as 14 Int (Intelligence) Company (the Army's experts in the mounting and manning of covert observation posts). If the Army was allowed to act on this information, the IRA would probably suffer casualties in the region of 70–80 per cent of personnel based north of the border, including key command and quartermaster elements.

Every politician says that 'there cannot be a military solution to the Northern Ireland problem, there can only be a political one.' Most soldiers believe that without a military victory over the terrorists, there will be no political solution. The recent political history of Ulster is one of failed political initiatives. If the current policy of police supremacy were reversed and the resources of the RUC Special Branch and MI5 were put under the control of a military commander who had a clear brief to fight a counter-insurgency battle against the Provisionals on every front – military, propaganda and political – the situation in Northern Ireland could be radically altered in less than two years.

In order to achieve this, Westminster needs to recognize the problem for what it is – i.e. a war – and to abandon the policy of trying to fight terrorists with civilian means – policemen and courts. Fighting terrorism in any theatre is a process whose rules might be reduced to the following formulae:

1. **Do nothing to increase the number of psychological casualties, after all it is the purpose of terrorism to create them – physical casualties are only the means to this.**
2. **Take measures to reduce the number of pychological casualties.**
3. **Put the terrorists, especially their leaders, on the defensive by means which do not alienate the whole community in which they operate.**
4. **Address the underlying frustrations which breed terrorist activity.**[1]

In Ulster these rules could be applied as follows:

1. Minimize the high-profile security forces' presence on the streets except when riots are in progress.
2. Admit to the existence of real social problems – doing otherwise increases local anger.

1 . Some readers may wish to compare our formulae to Robert Thompson's famous '5 Principles' which might be reduced thus:

1. The government under threat from insurgency must have a clear political aim and objective.
2. The government under threat must function according to the laws of the land.
3. The government under threat must draw up a co-ordinated strategy including political, social, economic and military responses.
4. The government under threat must give priority to defeating political subversion rather than achieving military victory.
5. The government under threat should use its own military forces to secure its own base areas before attempting an offensive against the insurgents.

3. Ensure and advertise that police and military are representative of both communities.
4. Announce a timetable of a return to normality including: the phased abolition of Diplock Courts (first by increasing the number of judges from one to three, later using juries recruited elsewhere in the United Kingdom, finally bringing back local jury trial).
5. Lay out a plan for the complete harmonization of law and administration in Northern Ireland with that in the rest of the UK.
6. Hold out the carrot of massive financial investment conditional upon peace being established; giving a clear and unequivocal commitment regarding the future of the province over the next twenty-five years.
7. Mount a massive propaganda campaign in Ulster to get across the message that the Provos have a vested interest in the troubles continuing, and also in the United States to communicate the idea that PIRA are terrorists just like Colonel Gaddaffi or mad mullahs of Iran.
8. Develop small teams of counter-terrorist specialists based on the SAS model but drawn much more widely from those who have served in Ulster to undertake a *precise* offensive against the Provisional IRA and its *leadership*.
9. Close down all businesses such as drinking dens, taxi-services or demolition companies which are run by terrorist organizations.
10. Use whatever resources necessary to cut terrorists' supply lines from abroad.
11. Take effective action to prevent the Provisional IRA's further involvement in EEC farming fraud – a major source of income.

Failure to do these things, to go on the offensive so that the initiative might be seized back, and to apply 'negative reinforcement' to the IRA leadership, will ensure that the future of Ireland, north and south is jeopardized. Every day a policy of mere containment via unimaginative security is pursued, allows the IRA 'mafia' becomes yet more deeply embedded in the local community, that they increase their funds via legitimate and illegal business activities and that real democracy in Ireland becomes an ever more distant prospect.

Recently there have been signs that the Army has tried to implement – as far as the politicians will allow – some of the principles enumerated above. However, there are also signs that by once again ignoring the moral dimension, these initiatives may be self-defeating.

On Sunday 6 March 1988, three IRA terrorists were shot dead in a Gibraltar street. Within hours journalists were briefed on the type and size of bomb that they had allegedly planted. But no bomb was found on Gibraltar. Instead, some time later a car packed with explosives was discovered in Spain. The lie machine had been at work, spinning a continuing web of untruth which was to envelop the subsequent inquest into the terrorists' deaths, bringing the law and the SAS (who had carried out the operation) into disrepute. Many of those sympathetic to the Army began to accuse the soldiers of outright murder – recalling allegations of a 'shoot to kill' policy said to have been operated earlier by certain elements within the RUC and which had led to the 'Stalker affair'.[1] The public have not yet been told the full facts about either Stalker or Gibraltar. All that can be said is that neither episode can be regarded as an unqualified success in the war against terrorism.

1 . John Stalker, then Deputy Chief Constable of the Greater Manchester Police was suspended from duty when his investigations into alleged RUC wrong doing were nearing their conclusions. Stalker was subsequently cleared of allegations that he had socialized with criminals. In fact he claims no formal allegations were ever made. Stalker was made the victim of a campaign of innuendo.

9

The Future: The Challenge of Adaption

'You see, I had read a book,' the Knight went on in a dreamy far away tone, 'written by someone to prove that warfare under modern conditions was impossible. You may imagine how disturbing that was to a man of my profession. Many men would have thrown up the whole thing and gone home. But I grappled with the situation. You will never guess what I did.' Alice pondered. 'You went to war, of course —' 'Yes; but not under modern conditions.'

'Saki' (H.H.Monro), The Westminster Alice.

With the CFE (Conventional Forces in Europe) talks proceeding we find ourselves at a watershed in the history of European defence and security. The changes in the military situation that some of the proposed agreements would bring about may require a complete rethink of strategy, tactics and philosophy.When the talks began their remit was limited. Naval power was not to be considered at all and the Americans had been careful to see that the question of attack aircraft was relegated to the bottom of the agenda. Naturally, no thought of tactical nuclear weapons was supposed to intrude on the negotiators' deal-making. But at the NATO summit in Brussels in May 1989, George Bush set, if not a timetable, then, at least, a target deadline within which the talks had to be seen to be achieving something. In doing so he also made clear that the United States was prepared to budge on attack aircraft and set the talks within a wider context of possible reductions of short-range nuclear missiles.

The proposals President Bush made for conventional force reductions were received in Moscow during the inaugural meeting of the Congress of People's Deputies and were not given much detailed consideration before being welcomed as 'a step in the right direction' by the Foreign Ministry spokesman, Gennadi Gerasimov. The Soviet military, though cautious, may not have been entirely displeased by this encouraging sign from the US President as they are interested not so much in 'perestroika' as in 'uskorenye' (or technological acceleration), hoping that reductions in troops and heavy equipment would release funds for research and development towards what the American soviet affairs analyst, James T. Westwood, says they intend: 'a leaner, more defensively oriented force structure.[1]

CFE is not, though, the first attempt to limit conventional forces in Europe. The Mutual and Balanced Force Reduction (MBFR) negotiations lasted more than fifteen years, from 1973 to February 1989. No agreement was reached but, according to Stephen Ledogar, the head of the US delegation at Vienna, MBFR did, at least, 'lay the groundwork for the new talks.'

In fact, the Warsaw Pact had been trying to get conventional force reductions before Mikhail Gorbachev's speech to the United Nations in December 1988. The 'Budapest Appeal' of June 1986 called for 'mutual, negotiated cuts of 500,000 personnel but met with little response.

There are still barriers to progress at Vienna. To date East and West have tended to put radically different interpretations on the same sets of statistics. On 30 January 1989 the Warsaw Pact, for the first time, published its own estimates of the conventional balance in Europe, concluding that a rough parity existed between the rival alliances. This is not NATO's view of the situation: its own report, published the previous November,[2] had pointed up the marked superiority of the Warsaw Pact in virtually every category of conventional arms. After the various Warsaw Pact countries had announced unilateral cuts (between 27 January and 1 February 1989, East Germany, Czechoslovakia, Bulgaria, Poland and Hungary followed the lead given by the USSR in December 1988 and announced cuts in conventional forces), the US Information Agency presented a revised version of the NATO estimates to include the

1. See *Combat Arms Magazine*, p.8, May 1989.
2. *Conventional Forces in Europe – The Facts*, NATO, 25 November 1988.

position that would be reached if the declared Warsaw Pact cuts were implemented. It is worth looking at these figures (see pp. 86–87) in order to grasp the scale of the problem facing the negotiators in Vienna.

In recent months much has been made of the apparent fact that the Warsaw Pact has no intention of invading Western Europe. Why, many ask, does NATO not match the Eastern bloc arms cuts with reductions of its own? The answer, as those engaged in the CFE talks know well, is that we dare not build our strategy for peace upon Warsaw Pact intentions, but must focus instead upon their capabilities. We know that whilst the Soviets seem to be genuine about turning swords into ploughshares – or, at least, converting some of their tank factories to the manufacture of kitchen appliances[1] – their most recent announcements have indicated that planned cutbacks in tank production are not expected to exceed 20 per cent of current volume for the foreseeable future. At present, Soviet arms manufacturing plants are making enough tanks to equip a division every month: by the early 1990s there may be far fewer tanks in the Soviet Army, but those that there are will almost all be of the most advanced kind.

It is still possible that CFE could, like MBFR, end with no conclusive agreement. But there do seem very real grounds for optimism. The Soviets now seem to accept the principle that, in those classes of weaponry where they have an undeniable advantage, asymmetric reductions are a legitimate demand. This means that the CFE talks could result in major reductions in tanks, troop-carrying armoured vehicles and artillery. Indeed, at the opening session, the Soviet Foreign Minister, Mr Shevardnadze, indicated that his team of negotiators would be looking for even greater cuts than those outlined in the proposals put forward by NATO in response to the reductions already announced by Mr Gorbachev. The new proposals had called for a ceiling of 20,000 tanks each for NATO and the Warsaw Pact and huge reductions in armoured troop carriers and artillery. Mr Shevardnadze also proposed a demilitarized central zone in Europe and reductions in offensive air- and sea-power.

From NATO's point of view the idea of a demilitarized zone extending, perhaps, fifty or a hundred miles each side of the IGB is not particularly attractive at the moment. Most commentators believe it would give a number of advantages to the countries of the

1. As reported to the Congress of People's Deputies of the USSR, May 1989.

Warsaw Pact. France's stand outside the common military command structure of NATO already has the effect of bottling up allied forces in a fairly narrow stretch of territory in West Germany and the Benelux countries: any further concentration of these resources would render them vulnerable to air or missile attack and allow an invading force to make an unopposed advance on a number of significant West German cities. Furthermore, the logistical problems of reinforcement (already considerable) would be exacerbated by the need to move large forces up to the front within Germany. In addition to these problems, the Germans are likely to resist strongly anything which breaks the principle of forward defence.

A demilitarized zone may not be to NATO's advantage, but an agreement limiting the number of tanks (and possibly other classes of armoured vehicle) deployed forward could be. It would help the alliance to overcome its present structural weakness by enabling the addition of a dimension of depth to its defensive arrangements that is lacking at present.

Forward defence could become the responsibility of the infantry and engineers (who would make greater use of obstacles, especially minefields) whilst armoured and mechanized forces would be held further back, allowing them to prepare counter-attacks once the direction of the enemy advance had been established. Such counter-attacks would also be more effective as forces could be more easily concentrated than under present conditions where they are spread along the whole length of the IGB and the border with Czechoslovakia.

Such constraints on the deployment of particular classes of weapons are likely to be all the more acceptable to both sides now that early-warning measures have grown more sophisticated. In the past many ideas that might have led to enhanced security have had to be ruled out because of the problems of verification (checking that the other party is keeping his side of the bargain). Today, long-range radar, satellite observation and a multiplicity of sensors can be brought into use to monitor even small troop movements. NATO already has the ability to look deep into Warsaw Pact territory and feed the data it collects through processors which can distinguish between a tank and a civilian vehicle of equivalent size.

What is likely to happen on the Central Front? We believe that diplomatic activity either currently taking place or likely to follow the present round of negotiations will result in the reduction of Britain's armoured forces in BAOR and the redeployment of the rest further back, with an enhanced role for dismounted infantry and engineers close to the border.

Furthermore, it is probable that in the not-too-distant future NATO will have to make concessions in terms of its air-power. We appear to have the advantage in this respect although it is difficult to be certain as the Warsaw Pact has never been entirely frank about the strength of its air forces. Even though concessions are anticipated, they will not be made until both sides exchange accurate and verifiable data.

At the moment, the Soviets are, naturally enough, using their apparent weakness in the air as a negotiating ploy. Nevertheless, there are good reasons for including strike aircraft in any package: both sides are vulnerable to an air attack which takes out vital command and control assets, destroys troops on the ground and communications links and, by neutralizing airfields establishes air-superiority under which attacking ground forces will have a significant advantage. There remain great problems to be overcome in reaching an agreement about aircraft: firstly, they are easily and quickly moved, so that constraints on their siting will not suffice – a limit on total numbers held is essential; and secondly, the development by some countries of multi-role aircraft makes it difficult to distinguish between defensive and potentially offensive systems. Nevertheless, some deal is likely.

The row that broke out between Germany's Chancellor Kohl and Mrs Thatcher in the spring of 1989 was concerned with whether or not NATO should modernize its short-range nuclear missiles or enter into negotiations with the Soviet Union with a view to reducing their number. Currently, the mainstay of NATO's battlefield nuclear force is its 88 ageing Lance missiles (though nuclear weapons can also be delivered by artillery and aircraft). Of NATO's 5,500 artillery pieces, 2,500 are nuclear-capable. (The main British nuclear artillery piece for the future is the 155-mm gun. It was announced in July 1987 that Britain would withdraw completely from the 203-mm nuclear artillery role.) Aircraft are also capable of delivering free-fall bombs, and the MoD is currently studying the option of acquiring a Tactical Air-to-Surface Missile (TASM) – possibly on the basis of a joint development with the USA – which would be deployed early in the next century.

American involvement in the provision and control of tactical nuclear weapons is close: the Lance missiles held by the British Army are the responsibility of the Royal Artillery but can only be fired with the active co-operation of US military personnel who, as it were, hold the keys. However, the Lance system will soon be effectively obsolete and there is some pressure within NATO for a decision about a replacement. The range of any successor will have to be less than the 500 kilometre limit established under the INF (Intermediate Nuclear Forces) treaty and, according to the Statement on the Defence Estimates 1988: 'The most likely follow on system is the Army Tactical Missile System (ATACMS) – which is a conventional missile for use with the Multiple Launch Rocket System (MLRS). MLRS, bought from the United States, is already in service with the Royal Artillery but will not be nuclear-capable for some time as Congress has so far refused to fund the development of a nuclear warhead that can be fitted to it.

The German view was that NATO should adopt a wait-and-see approach regarding the modernization of short-range nuclear forces. They further argued that it would make little difference in terms of deterrence to do without Lance as even without these missiles, there would still be some 4,000 nuclear warheads on German soil. And Helmut Schmidt, a former Chancellor, went further. In a BBC radio interview at the height of the dispute, he said that what really deters is the fact that any aggressor would have to face more than a million German servicemen.[1]

Mrs Thatcher took a radically different line. She argued that to negotiate reductions in short-range nuclear missiles risked ending up with the total abolition of this category of weapon. This could undermine the credibility of the American strategic nuclear guarantee by leaving a gap in the range of options that go to make up flexible response. Nuclear weapons had kept the peace in Europe for forty years, she maintained, and the experiences of 1914 and 1939 should have taught us that conventional weapons alone are not enough to deter war in Europe. As far as she was concernd, it would never be safe to be without them.

While the NATO countries were squabbling over these matters, the Soviets were nearing the completion of their modernization programme – replacing the obsolete Free Range Over Ground (FROG) with the more advanced SS21. Moreover, they enjoy a 15:1 superiority over NATO in this category of weapon.

Despite Mrs Thatcher's opposition, some sort of agreement to limit or ban short-range nuclear weapons may be inevitable. Political pressure is increasingly being applied inside the various Western democracies by those who perceive that the chance of a nuclear war starting by some accident or misunderstanding is greater than that

1. BBC Radio 4, *Today*, 29 May 1989.

of any invasion by the Warsaw Pact. One can only imagine how much more widespread such a perception would be if both alliances were to agree to reduce their conventional forces drastically and if Soviet troops in Eastern Europe appeared to be deployed in an apparently more defensive posture.

Moreover, since the traditional justification for NATO's having short-range nuclear weapons has been the Warsaw Pact's preponderance in conventional forces, once parity or near-parity has been achieved between East and West in conventional weapons, the chief reason for their retention will have gone. The political debate will then centre on the question of whether keeping short-range nuclear weapons deters *all war*.

As yet there is no knowing quite how far the de-nuclearization of Europe might go. One possible compromise would be to agree to the withdrawal of all land-based systems but allow both sides to keep a small number either at sea or capable of being delivered by air. Small numbers, indeed, may be the key to mollifying most of those who are worried about nuclear weapons of all classes. Too often the pollsters ask only whether one is for or against the bomb. We suspect that most people would be in favour of keeping a small nuclear arsenal ('just in case') but are against the thousands of nuclear weapons held at present. The argument for maintaining small numbers is strengthened by the consideration that the Warsaw Pact is not the only potential enemy. Some Third World countries are thought already to have nuclear weapons and it is possible that more will do so in the next twenty years. However, as far as Britain is concerned, we should prepare ourselves for the reduction (if not the complete removal) of short-range nuclear weapons as it is unlikely that the Conservatives will remain in power for ever.

Technology is another catalyst of change whose effects will be no less marked than those of politics and diplomacy in the coming years. It is now set to revolutionize the battlefield once again. However, on the principle that forewarned is forearmed, a few caveats are in order.

Throughout history there are examples of the side with the technical advantage winning. Whether it was a case of possessing the longbow, cannon, repeating-rifle, machine-gun or Stinger missile, the principle remains the same: the right technology can make the difference between defeat and victory. Of course, the more primitive or under-equipped do sometimes defeat the more advanced and better-equipped but the winning side, at least until the mid-twentieth century, has generally been the one in possession of the newer weapons and with the greatest capacity to deploy them effectively.

Though the potential and actual advantages of technology are clear, it is also evident that technology does not automatically provide an advantage to the user. The modern and complex is not inevitably better than the old and straightforward (or indeed, than the new and straightforward). History also offers evidence of technology's limitations, its misuse and its irresistible and sometimes illogical attraction. Here are some specific cases.

A typical eighteenth- or early nineteenth-century battle involved opposing infantry 'squares' or 'lines' engaging each other at short range (120 yards or less) with smooth-bore muzzle-loading firearms. In these circumstances firearms offered no technical or tactical superiority – in terms of range, accuracy, rate of fire or cost – over the longbow (indeed, in the case of rate of fire the longbow was vastly superior). Yet, from 1500 to 1850, wars were fought with muskets. Why? One reason was technological momentum: the musket was the weapon of its day and regressing to the bow was not conceivable; another (and probably most important) was that, although the bow was a more effective weapon in many respects than the musket, its use required more skill: without a scheme of enforced practice as operated in England until the sixteenth century, there would have been considerable difficulties in its deployment especially by a rapidly raised mass Army. Nevertheless, there is a moral: *we should not always assume that new is better.*

A rather different lesson can be learnt from the example of the heavily armoured knight. In the search for increased protection, the knight and his horse got heavier and heavier and slower and slower – thus defeating the great tactical advantage of mobility that the man–horse combination had once possessed. The knight continued to be one of the primary weapons of war long after he had become a tactical liability. All the ingenious efforts to improve his equipment only made matters that much worse: misdirected technology actually succeeded in making an outdated system even less effective by decreasing the mobility which had once been the great tactical advantage of the man–horse combination. Moral: *sometimes the existence of a weapon-system, and the economic and social investment which that implies, can distort research and development and extend the life of the weapon-system even when it is tactically disadvantageous* (the British obsession with battleships before the Second World War is another example, as is, more arguably, the continued existence of leviathan-like main battle tanks).

As we may erroneously keep and develop an obsolete weapon-system (a syndrome which we might refer to as 'irrational traditionalism'), or unnecessarily opt to change an adequate system without enjoying any real benefit (which we might call 'futile modernism'), so we may sometimes create a gap in our armour by discarding a well-tried system which is still needed (which we might call 'irrational modernism'). Two prime examples of the last-mentioned phenomenon came to light in the winter of 1987 when American warships made their presence felt in the Gulf, escorting Kuwaiti oil-tankers. It was found that, for all their high-tech wizardry, the US ships could not cope adequately with an 'old-fashioned' threat posed by floating sea mines. The problems did not end there. The ships also discovered they were all too vulnerable to the tactically primitive speedboat attacks of revolutionary guards. Despite their long-range surface-to-air and surface-to-surface missiles, the big US ships had no short-range weapons capable of engaging Khomeini's aquatic kamikazes. The US warships stayed well out of their range. Moral: *Don't get rid of your old kit until you are sure that the new can fulfil old needs as well as new ones.*

In developing an awareness of technology's limitations we also come to appreciate the real nature of technology. Hardware can never be considered in isolation: it is created and used by people trying to complete specific tasks. The introduction of a new technology in any sphere of activity can change – often narrow – people's perceptions of that activity. It can also change the social relationships between the actors: technology often makes hitherto unimportant people indispensable, at the same time as relegating to marginal utility those whose roles had previously been central.

Thinking of technology only in terms of equipment makes its abuse more likely. At root, technology is much more than a group of mechanical or electronic 'things' or the programmes which maintain them. It is a method, a means which has to be constantly directed to adapt to changing circumstances. Tactical evolution is an inseparable part of the 'technology equation', as are social and political developments and ethical standards (which might prohibit the use of certain technologies).[1]

1. One might cite as an example of this the development by the SAS of new tactics to use with the'stun grenade'.

Mao showed how a side which initially had a technological disadvantage but which had a modern and appealing ideology could triumph. And the Afghan Mujahadin more recently have succeeded in their defensive guerrilla operations against a super-power. Many would attribute the Mujahadin success to their apparently primitive organization. Old fashioned though it might appear it certainly adapted rapidly to the threat posed by a large, centrally controlled army (and indeed to some modern weapon-systems like the Stinger missile if not to less manageable pieces of equipment such as armoured vehicles and helicopters). The Mujahadin are often criticized for their lack of unity, but dispersion and decentralized command has been an important reason for their effectiveness as guerrillas (even if it is proving to be something of a disadvantage as the war in Afghanistan moves into a conventional offensive phase).

However, technology can sometimes be useful strategically regardless of its tactical utility. If war is considered as being influenced essentially by economic factors, a primary aim should be to break the enemy economically. In that case, there may be a place for developing expensive technologies, which may or may not be effective, simply in order to persuade the enemy to do the same (all that is important is that they believe the systems will work). Visitors to events such as the Paris or Farnborough air shows may have been surprised at the amount of sensitive equipment on show, but the commercial interests of defence manufacturers coincide with this 'competitive strategy' policy. However, it is a dangerous game, not least because, like anything which relies upon deception, it can also engender self-delusion.

In order to prevent ourselves becoming the victims of such self-delusion it is useful to see our armed forces and the equipment they use in three ways: *as complex peacetime organizations that must be administered; as a pile of chips or tokens on the negotiating table (which may or may not represent real assets); and as the forces we actually use to fight a war*. Bearing these three concepts in mind and with some awareness of the limitations of technology, we can now turn to one of the great problems that our society faces as it approaches the millennium – the difference between the new technologies and social institutions in their rates of adaptation.

In the British Army, the effects of different rates of innovation are felt very strongly: the microchip has transformed the battlefield at least as much as it has the civilian workplace. As if to make matters worse, the challenge of technology presents itself at a time of great social uncertainty (which is probably no simple coincidence) and when political developments which must have profound effects on defence policy are following one another at an enormously increased rate. The Army, an institution characterized by a marked reluctance to change, is likely to have special difficulty in adapting to this dynamic but uncertain age. Nevertheless, although disinclined to change at some levels, it has in the past been considerably transformed when politicians have been set on reform. Politically and technologically, radical change is again unavoidable.

The designers of military equipment are now capable of delivering weapon-systems of such accuracy and with such a developed capacity to stay with a target, once identified, until the 'kill', that it sometimes seems that war must soon be rendered entirely obsolete (though it must be said that something rather similar was being said in the late nineteenth century). But each new technical development is quickly met with a corresponding counter-measure, and, each innovation is more expensive than the last. Perhaps the most significant advance in recent years has been in the field of 'smart' munitions. Here the application of computer intelligence to ammunition in flight can allow the weapons to make 'decisions' according to data received by various sensors. A recent American innovation is a missile capable of sustained flight which is programmed to wait above suspected enemy positions until its sensors detect radar emissions, at which point it will lock on to the signal, follow it back to its source and explode.

The main focus of smart munitions research has been on finding ways to defeat armour. Tanks are nowadays very well defended and modern forms of composite and reactive outer-armour have reduced their vulnerability to certain kinds of ammunition.[1] Accordingly, weapons designers have been trying to find ways of attacking tanks at their weakest points – the top of the turret and the belly-plate. Missiles have been developed which, when fired at a column of tanks, break up over the target to release a quantity of sub-munitions which rain down on the turrets from above. Early examples consisted of sub-munitions which hunted out a particular type of infra-red radiation as put out by the tank's engine but these were found too easy to hoax by infra-red screening or decoy flares. More up-to-date variants can store information relating to the radar

1. Composite armour contains ceramics which smash on impact, thus laterally diffusing the energy of the round; reactive armour contains strips of plastic explosive which explode at the moment of impact, neutralizing the effect of the round.

signatures of certain vehicles in their internal memories and hunt for targets which best approximate to the templates with which they have been programmed.

A major problem of such weaponry is that it has clearly offensive potential and can consequently be seen as destabilizing. Possession of large quantities of highly accurate missiles which are very likely to acquire and destroy important targets might tend to promote a first strike (and also a deep strike) mentality: the knowledge that the enemy had similar systems and could, if they used them first, knock out your command and control systems and destroy large numbers of your troops in a sudden missile attack, would encourage pre-emption. Accordingly, these munitions are likely to be included in the categories of those whose deployment is constrained or prevented under treaties designed to establish clearly defensive military configurations on both sides of the Iron Curtain.

Consequently, the important weaponry of the future will be that which reinforces deterrence whilst lacking offensive applications. An example of such a system is the smart mine, which is programmed to recognize particular types of enemy vehicle and which, since it is not dependent on pressure for its detonation, cannot be dealt with by the current method of clearing minefields by generating a pressure wave in the ground.

The technological challenge for the 1990s will be to develop a broader range of such systems. This would involve a complete change of direction in procurement where the trend has been to develop aggressive systems or those which are dual-capable.

A move to purely defensive systems might well be easier than some sceptics believe at present. A major untapped resource in defence technology development is that large body of scientists who have refused so far to play a part in helping to build the war machine. Some of our brightest scientific minds, for reasons of personal principle, avoid defence research. Though they might still shy away from designing a better main battle tank or attack helicopter, they might well respond to a sincere call to help make war impossible. For example, they could make the most exciting contributions in intermediate technology – controlled technology on a human scale. Small very often is beautiful, as well as ethical, flexible and economic.

One imaginative idea that has been canvassed recently and which would add to the security of post-Vienna Europe is that of burying a network of fibre-optics along the length of the IGB and stretching some kilometres back. Using low-power lasers, the grid would provide all commanders who had an access point with up-to-date intelligence about enemy troop-movements, since any significant variations in the ground pressure above the network would set off a variation in the path of the laser light which a properly programmed computer could recognize as a regiment or division of the enemy forces. Such a grid would be vulnerable to disruption by artillery, but any gaps could quickly be filled by showering the ground in the relevant areas with small sensor devices.

Another possibility is to make greater use of remotely piloted vehicles (RPVs) packed with cameras, radar and sensors which could provide accurate real-time intelligence about enemy troop-movements.[1]

High technology apart, a more effective deterrence than that provided at the moment would arise out of a situation in continental Europe and in mainland Britain where conventional war in the air or on the ground had been rendered impractical. Arguably, the most useful weapon systems of the future will not be the heavy and exclusively complex ones, but the flexible and highly portable. The development of a fire and forget, 'man-portable', ground-to-ground, anti-armour weapon capable of engaging enemy main battle tanks at 1,500 metres would change the entire battlefield – it should become a priority of our research efforts. Also, extremely simple measures could prove decisive in the event of war. Major bridges and motorways in Germany could be pre-chambered with explosives. So any aggressor would know that his progress was bound to be slow.

A multiplicity of low-level deterrents could be developed. For example, we might adopt the idea of the 'Liberator pistol' from the Second World War. This was a psychological warfare initiative in which the allies designed and manufactured a very cheap single shot pistol (with cartoon instructions for its use) which was then dropped into territory occupied by the enemy. Preparations could be made now to apply the same idea to small-arms and to rudimentary throw-away anti-vehicle rockets. A Soviet Commander would certainly have to think twice if every German civilian had a weapon capable of destroying a tank or APC.

Because air superiority is also going to be vital, the number of our portable anti-aircraft weapons should also be increased many-fold.

1. The utility of RPVs in battle was conclusively demonstrated by the Israelis in their invasion of Lebanon in 1982.

Again it would be sensible to have a mixture of high-tech and simple 'point-and-shoot' devices (the latter both for economic reasons and because of the possibility that the enemy might develop electronic counter-measures to sophisticated systems). One should even be willing to accept an increased risk of accidental engagement of one's own aircraft and make the sky a no-go area for all.

However, as we have already said, equipment cannot be considered in isolation. Nor will better access to intelligence be sufficient if commanders are not trained to use it and to act on their initiative, or if they are trapped by organizations or procedures which inhibit rapid action. Recently the planners at the Army Staff College at Camberley have come to realize that senior officers in the British Army are comparatively bad at delegating tactical command to junior officers and have (along with their counterparts in the US) begun to study the doctrine of *aufstragtaktik* (as they say in Germany) or 'mission-orientated tactics', as the Americans have renamed it. This is a system that has been applied in German armies since the Wars of Unification in the 1860s, although it only really began to emerge as a clear operational doctrine in the latter part of the First World War where it developed as a response to the problem of poor communications in certain sectors of the front.

Under *aufstragtaktik* a subordinate commander is given no specific orders but is briefed on the overall plan of his immediate superior and given a mission to execute within the context of that plan. Thereafter he is, essentially, left to use his initiative. He has been told what to do, and it is recognized that he is the one best able to judge how to do it. During the Second World War this system was used down to battlegroup or regimental level but battalion commanders were given specific and detailed orders. *Aufstragtaktik* was then reintroduced below company level. (It should be noted that *aufstragtaktik* was not applied throughout the German Army in the last war, when it was impeded by both traditionally authoritarian attitudes and National Socialist methods. The authors believe it could work well in the Army of an advanced democracy.) The British Army, by contrast, was characterized by the constant need to pass reports up and receive orders down the chain of command. It is not markedly less rigid today.

The advantages of the doctrine are that, at lower levels, orders relate more closely to the developing situation on the ground and chance opportunities are not lost because of communications failures or the slowness of higher formations to respond to requests for permission to act coming from junior commanders. The problem with seeking to introduce such a system to the British Army now is that it is not something that can simply be overlaid upon an organizational culture which has never put a particularly high premium upon individual initiative in junior officers. What would be called for is nothing short of a fundamental re-evaluation of existing power-relationships within the Army. Certainly there is a need to experiment with *aufstragtaktik* and adapt it to the conditions our forces would be likely to encounter in a high-speed, high-tech European battlefield where communications will be disrupted from the earliest moments of the conflict. It is probable that mere delegation is not enough: it must be delegation to well-motivated, broadly educated and mature individuals. There is no reason why our soldiers of the near future cannot be all these things if we want them to be.

The implications of re-examining the way in which soldiers relate to their work and one another could be far-reaching. The SAS has already set a precedent: it has been accepted that its specialized work requires the stripping away of 'bull' and the use of first names between members of the small teams who work together on particular operations. The battlefield of the future is likely to require more and more soldiers to act in small teams and to exercise a relatively high degree of autonomy. There is a need not only for increased numbers of the special forces of the type we currently possess. There is also a case for developing and maintaining in peacetime two further capabilities to disrupt the enemy: a) an 'ultra-SAS' or an 'SOE in peace' – individuals (not just the super-fit) with specialist skills for covert penetration and sabotage; and b) large platoons or companies (not dissimilar to David Stirling's original desert raiders) who could operate as mini-tactical-manoeuvre groups behind the enemy lines.[1]

Although we have the SAS, there are only a few hundred of them, their emphasis is on working in small groups (or 'sticks'), and their primary wartime role today would be long-range recce. There is a real need for other sophisticated capabilities to sever command centres, eliminate key figures, and attack economic targets.

We also feel that such forces offer a more moral way of making war since they are selective. For us it would be better to win a battle by killing the opposing general than the opposing army; it might

1. David Stirling was a young Biritish officer in North Africa in the Second World War who proposed a scheme for attacking enemy airfields with small teams of raiders in specially equipped jeeps. First called the 'Long Range Desert Group' it evolved into the Special Air Service.

also be easier. Who will deny, for example, that our failure to kill mass-murderers like Hitler or Stalin was culpably irresponsible?

There are major obstacles to developing the sort of forces suggested above, quite apart from likely political opposition on both sides of the Iron Curtain. The perception that there is too much rank-consciousness in the Army could well prove an even bigger barrier to the recruitment of independently minded people in the future than it is today, and it is independently minded soldiers that the Army will need. Perhaps it is time for the Army to consider developing some new regiments on an experimental basis (possibly of mixed arm) where the traditional distinction between officers and men is not maintained. One might also experiment with terms of address in existing regiments. Perhaps the time has come to abolish 'Sir' and replace it with rank and surname, or within platoons, rank and Christian name. This would be a signal of a broader commitment to a new less class-bound order.

There is a clear need for more cross-posting between services and arms, and the Army might also fruitfully look at its systems for appointing and promoting staff officers. Rather than merely telling people where they are to go and what they are to do it might consider the expanded use of appointment boards so that individuals can apply for the jobs which they feel offer the best opportunities for the exploitation of their particular talents.

However, there can be no simple prescription for adapting the Army's social relations to modern circumstances; a workable method will have to be found by experimenting with looser structures at every level of command. A start could be made in peacetime by giving the commanding officers of regiments and battalions greater control over the resources allocated to their unit, perhaps by giving them a budget and letting them shop around in an internal market for training facilities, supplies, transport etc. This would be likely to result in considerable savings as it would end wasteful practices that are nowadays prevalent, such as the habit in many units of firing off the remaining training ammunition in the last days of every financial year (without obtaining any significant training benefit), in order to ensure that the following year's allowance is not reduced.

If the British Army in Europe is going to need to learn new tactical doctrines and to make adaptations in traditional social relationships so as to come to terms with a situation changed out of all recognition by diplomatic initiatives and technological change, it is also going to need to reconsider its basic dispositions and weaponry. Arguably, airborne forces will be an increasingly important instrument of Soviet offensive operations in the future. These will be difficult to limit under treaty as they can be stationed well away from the theatre of operations and concentrated only in the immediate period of preparation for an attack. The world would think it unreasonable of NATO to try to reduce the troops that the Soviet Union says it needs on its eastern and southern borders as they are not obviously any concern of ours. Therefore, the Soviet Union will – whatever treaty limitations are agreed – still be able to mount some kind of action within the European theatre. Given that the ability to drive through an armoured assault will have been removed by reductions in the number of their tanks, and given that new defence technology will, in any case, make an overland attack unattractive, we must expect them to develop their capability for attacking from the air. Accordingly, we must be able to deal with incursions by *spetsnaz* forces, quickly followed by a large airborne drop designed to hit our defences throughout their depth. Guarding against this sort of threat effectively requires adequate numbers of trained men.

Troops employed in a rear-area defence role need not be so expensively equipped as those committed in an armoured or mechanized counter-attack role. In deterrence terms, the knowledge that airborne forces would be likely to encounter superior numbers of defenders within a very short time of landing would do more than make an enemy commander think twice. Currently the Army believes that such an airborne threat can be dealt with by relatively small forces, so long as they are highly mobile and can be rapidly transported to drop-zones. This is not really an effective deterrent as an enemy commander would make the tying-down of these forces while his attack goes in a central component of his plan, or would lead them off by some diversionary tactic. Arming the civilians in every German village and backing them with versatile, trained soldiers would prove a far more effective deterrent.

The Army has, of course, already begun to speculate about what the future might hold. At every level there is debate, as there always has been when professional soldiers get together. As yet, however, there is little evidence of action or positive steps towards reform. One of the current disagreements concerns the future of armour. Some officers believe that the tank has been rendered obsolete by smart munitions. They argue for the re-roling of the Cavalry in attack helicopters. Others point to the vulnerabilty of helicopters (particularly those cheaper types not originally designed with the battlefield in mind) to hand-held ground-to-air missiles, and to the need to establish local air-superiority before helicopter operations can begin. The tank, they say, is still the best tank-defecting weapon-system and is likely to remain so.

Nor is there complete agreement about precisely what a tank should be. Every tank is a compromise between the competing claims of firepower, mobility and protection. Traditionally, British tanks have tended to be very well armoured – mobility has been sacrificed in the interests of protection. German tanks, by contrast, are very fast but not so well protected. The battles that rage among the General Staff about the future of the tank are essentially battles about the allocation of resources: the RAC want the available money to be spent on expensive, modern tanks; the Infantry want the cavalry re-roled into something cheaper so that they can use some of the money for improvements to their own equipment. The result of all this squabbling behind the scenes is that politically expedient decisions are made instead of rational military ones. Too often half-measures are adopted and officers have to live with uncomfortable fictions about the utility or efficacy of both the equipment they use and the units in which they serve.

Here is a cautionary tale. In September 1988 the British Army unveiled, for the benefit of its NATO allies, a new operational force: 24 Air Mobile Brigade. An exercise was mounted on Salisbury Plain to demonstrate this new unit and three infantry battalions were lifted into positions to stop an 'enemy' armoured attack. The declared purpose of the Brigade is to provide the Commander of I Br Corps with a highly mobile team of specialists in stopping Soviet Operational Manoeuvre Groups. However, some observers of the exercise have expressed profound doubts as to whether the Brigade would be of much use in heading off an OMG. The main criticism is that it is far too small a unit for its task. The equivalent American force is 101 Air Assault Division which is made up of three infantry brigades, an artillery brigade and an attack helicopter battalion. France has a slightly smaller Air Mobile Division with two infantry brigades and four attack helicopter regiments. By comparison the British force is extremely small.

Its critics argue both that it is inadequate in numbers and that it is simply not well enough equipped. Its 30 Lynx attack helicopters are equipped with US-made TOW wire-guided missiles which are regarded as somewhat primitive on the new high-tech battlefield, and the main anti-tank capability of the infantry elements of the

Brigade is provided by MILAN anti-tank weapons which cannot defeat the improved armour fitted to modern Soviet tanks. Britain has been slow to adopt new anti-tank missile technologies. Although it has been available since 1972, it was not until 1978 that Britain adopted MILAN as its weapon for the 1980s. Currently the MoD is in the early stages of procuring a new TRIGAT (Third Generation Anti-Tank) missile system but it is not expected to be in service until the latter half of the 1990s. The TOW missile dates from 1965 and there are doubts whether it could penetrate a Soviet T80 tank. The Americans have at least 5,000 of its successor (HELLFIRE) stockpiled but the Lynx helicopters of 24 Air Mobile Brigade are not adapted to use them. In any case, the Lynx is a poor launch platform and those in service with 24 Brigade have no secondary armament of air-to-air missiles and so would be easy targets in the event of a confrontation with an enemy aircraft or attack helicopter. Arguably the Brigade's only up-to-date equipment is the LAW 80, a light anti-tank weapon which is both easily portable and accurate. Some claim that it can penetrate the frontal armour of any main battle tank now in service. However, it is designed to be carried by an ordinary infantryman who would use it only in an emergency – particularly if the enemy armour is supported by infantry – as its practical anti-armour range is only a few hundred metres.

Another criticism of 24 Brigade is that none of the 30 troop-carrying helicopters it needs to lift its infantrymen actually belongs to the Brigade, or even to the Army. The Pumas and Chinooks that would, theoretically, be tasked to 24 Brigade if ever it were deployed belong to the RAF. Indeed they represent more than half the RAF's total strength in those helicopters. It would be most fortunate if, in time of war, they survived at all, or if there was no more urgent need for them elsewhere on the battlefield. As one commentator put it:

> When Britain's Air Mobile Brigade is needed during a crisis on the Central Front to oppose and defeat three or four times its own number of Soviet armoured troops, it will be transported by those of the RAF's helicopters which have not been shot down . . . and when it arrives there is nothing it can actually do to stop the Soviet tanks in its path.[1]

The example of 24 Brigade is illustrative of a tendency found in many parts of the Army: an apparent preference for the meretricious over the genuinely useful. The underlying reason is the

1. Anon. Confidential briefing to the authors.

politicking in the background: many of those involved in the process believe that the true objective will ultimately be achieved; that, for instance, by setting up an inadequate Air Mobile Brigade, the Army has created an irresistible pressure for it to be, eventually, properly equipped. If the generals had waited until the politicians provided the money before establishing the structure, there might never have been an Air Mobile Brigade at all.

If 24 Brigade is unlikely to stop a Soviet OMG, what could we put in the way? We must resort to tanks and mechanized infantry. Fortunately, the Infantry has found a powerful new weapon in Warrior, an armoured fighting vehicle equipped with a 30-mm Rarden cannon which is effective against lightly armourd reconnaissance vehicles and APCs. This will provide good protection on the move and integrated fire-support in the assault, leaving our tanks free to engage enemy armour and make the best use of their 'shock action'.

The introduction of Warrior may well lead to increased calls for a clear distinction between light and heavy infantry, but there are also disadvantages to any increase in specialization, particularly if it creates classifications which will prove difficult to reform in the future.

Another subject about which there has been much talk but little action is Britain's capability for intervention in far-flung parts of the globe. The political instability of much of the Third World suggests that there may well be an increased requirement for British forces to undertake operations outside the NATO area during the next decade. Such activities would not always involve fighting; indeed, more often than not our troops are likely to be used to train and transform a country's own Army (as they have done in Zimbabwe) or merely by their presence deter some predatory neighbour from attacking a valued ally (as continues to be the case in Belize). Often such arrangements serve the national interest in other ways, for example, by increasing our diplomatic influence in the host country and by forging closer economic and trading links. Indeed, it has been argued that our reluctance to commit forces under such arrangements since the early 1960s has been a major contributory factor to the decline of Britain's commercial strength even amongst Commonwealth countries. By contrast, the French have retained garrisons in many of their former colonies and consequently enjoy a virtual monopoly in trading relations with much of francophone Africa.

The old colonial attachments preserved in the Commonwealth will not be the only opportunity for British soldiers to serve in far-off countries. As the European Community begins to develop a co-ordinated foreign policy (as it is enjoined to do under the terms of the Single European Act), so we can expect to see European military formations configured from elements drawn from more than one EC country deployed in places where there is a clear pan-European interest to be served. Nor can we yet dismiss the idea of United Nations peace-keeping forces which, though they have had a rather patchy record, may still prove the only acceptable form of intervention in some parts of the world.

Not all the possible tasks for out-of-area operations are ones which will be mounted by agreement with the governments of the countries on whose territory British soldiers would be deployed. The increasing propensity of certain regimes to undertake acts of 'state terrorism' means that our forces might well be required to enter the sovereign territory of other nations to extract civilian hostages or British nationals whose lives are in danger from government forces. In a number of cases it may be that our national, European, or even broadly Western interests are best served not by supporting the government side but by providing specialist military aid to insurgents as the United States chose to do in Nicaragua.

Just as the range of tasks that we might need to undertake ranges from operations like the Falklands war, through the provision of specialist aid in counter-insurgency operations, to the emergency removal of, perhaps, one important individual, so the countries in which British troops may need to serve are many and diverse. Though we still have some forces committed in Brunei and Hong Kong and still enjoy close relations with other countries in South-East Asia, the most likely areas to which our troops will be committed are the Middle East, Africa and the Caribbean. This last theatre is increasingly perceived as important by the United States and, as was demonstrated in the case of the invasion of Grenada, it is likely to be the Americans who will undertake any large-scale military operations in the area even if the country concerned has historic links with the UK. Nevertheless, instability in the region is likely to be exacerbated by mounting tension in South America and there could well be instances where the US is happy to leave the resolution of low-intensity conflicts to us whilst it contains greater threats elsewhere.

As far as Africa and the Middle East are concerned, we enjoy cordial bilateral relations with many important countries in those regions partly because of traditional ties and attachments and partly because these countries are the source of many of the minerals and raw materials that are crucial to our economic survival. If we are likely to send troops to African or Middle Eastern countries during the 1990s, it would be as well to start preparing for it now. Since we no longer possess enough ships or heavy-lift aircraft to be able to mount large operations rapidly, and since the propinquity of hostile or simply non-aligned countries could cause complications, it would be sensible to establish a number of facilities in these regions that would enable us to mount limited operations without the need for long-range resupply. This could be done by building on existing relationships such as our agreement with the government of Kenya to exercise British troops on her soil, or the special military understanding that has been established with Sultan Qaboos of Oman.

What would be needed would be to establish small bases sited next to an airfield in Oman, and another in a friendly African country. In Oman, the existing facilities, either at Masirah or Salalah, could be expanded to house a small British contingent. These mini-bases would have a very small permanent staff of intelligence, logistics and liaison specialists, possibly working under the cover of a training or advisory team, who would plan and rehearse their use in a wide variety of contingencies. Meanwhile the sovereign base garrisons in Cyprus could be modified to allow for the presence of an intervention force with a permanent and integrated airlift capability. The obvious starting-point for such a force would be adding the Ghurkas (who will soon lose their base in Hong Kong) to the Paras to create a new airborne division (currently we only have a brigade – 5 Airborne – of four battalion strength). This force (an all-arms grouping) would form, however, only the core of a much larger out-of-area force that could be reinforced with troops from Germany or the UK. This would require that training of units in BAOR was not limited to preparation for battle within the European theatre but allowed for them to be dual-roled: ready to fight wherever tension became most acute. To be effective the intervention force would have to be equipped with the most advanced weaponry and not left to become the poor relation of those troops stationed in BAOR. Indeed, we should take the view that once Europe is more stable, it will be the soldiers of the intervention force who are most likely to see action. (It should be noted that even modestly high-tech systems can be tremendous force-multipliers in the Third World: it has been argued that the provision of one helicopter during the Angolan civil war in the 1970s would have tipped the balance against the Marxist MPLA.)

We would argue that the existence of such a force – so long as it was properly constituted and was not the product of the half-measures mentality described earlier – would have tremendous military and symbolic value. Even those young people who today regard the Army as irrelevant and are sceptical about the threat from Eastern Europe can appreciate that political leaders such as the late Ayatollah Khomeini and Colonel Gaddaffi represent the kind of problem that can probably be dealt with in the long run only by armed force. They will be more likely to join, or consent to support through their taxes, an Army which they perceive to be useful.

In the longer-term this force could be integrated within similar forces in other European armies to provide a means whereby Europe could protect its own interests in areas which do not fall within NATO's remit.

But whereas European integration may still be some way off, some of the other changes we have considered in this chapter are more pressing. Now is the time for such matters to be opened up to wider public discussion. In the next few years a political debate will take place on the question of whether NATO should give up its reliance on short-range nuclear weapons. Those who argue for their removal are on notice to come up with an equally effective alternative for preventing war in Europe – a new strategy to replace flexible response.

Our view is that the sort of conventional forces we have now will not be enough and that if we are to have any chance of ensuring our security, we must develop a multiplicity of lower-level deterrents within a clearly defensive configuration.

Our hope is that those on both sides of the nuclear debate will be prompted to address themselves to these wider considerations.

Conclusion

'ill fairs the land, to hastening ills a prey,
where wealth accumulates and men decay.'
Oliver Goldsmith, The Deserted Village (1770)

On the threshold of the twenty-first century the British Army faces radical change. The impact of the arms control process and other political developments upon the nature of the Army's future commitments and upon popular perceptions of what kind of Army it will be appropriate to keep up; the effects of the demographic trough on the Army's ability to recruit and retain the soldiers it needs; the changing expectations of our citizens; the changing nature of war and of the means by which it is fought; our growing commitment to the European Community; the alienating effects of much of the Army's organizational culture and value systems – in particular its narrowly functional approach to ethical standards: all these demand action.

We have drawn special attention to the question of the Army's values and ethics, an issue which is more easily sidestepped than technology or the demographic trough. To suggest that the Army has real moral problems, and that they may in some way be related to the nature of the service is to probe a very sensitive area. It is particularly painful for many serving in the Army because so much that is familiar to them may be challenged; the possibility of change is opened up – change going beyond the more easily accepted reform of tactical doctrine, organizational structures and equipment.

Those with an emotional investment in the status quo feel threatened when they sense the wind of change blowing towards them. They become like the three little monkeys, hearing, speaking and seeing no evil. We do not deny there are many strengths in our Army – indeed it is probably one of the better armies in the world. Nevertheless, the symptoms of moral decay are also undeniable. The system rewards ruthless careerism, allows far too much off-duty drunkenness, fails to make a commitment to the broad education of all personnel, tolerates bullying, and possesses a corporate mindset rigidly opposed to individuals speaking out honestly. Such things appear in other spheres of human activity, but they should be of grave concern in an Army where individuals are involved in the business of killing other people.

We have noted in an earlier chapter the extent to which our Army might be out of step with emergent mores and values. There is another way of looking at the same notion: that any society gets the Army it deserves. The modern British Army which at a social level combines base proletarian culture on the one hand with the sillier excesses of bourgeois snobbery on the other, is tolerated by the British public. This may be partly because the public does not know what is going on, and partly because it does not particularly want to know what is going on. All that matters is that the Army appears to do its job well enough when called upon to fight.

In his essay 'On Liberty', John Stuart Mill wrote: 'The worth of a State, in the long run, is the worth of the individuals composing it, and a State which postpones the interest of their mental expansion and elevation . . . a State which dwarfs its men in order that they might be more docile instruments in its hands – even for beneficial purposes – will find that with small men no great thing can really be accomplished; and that the perfection of machinery to which it has sacrificed everything, will in the end avail to nothing, for want of the vital power which, in order that the machine might work more smoothly, it has preferred to banish.'[1]

The British State does much less than it might through its education system in terms of the mental expansion and elevation of the people. Too many are emerging from our schools with few prospects of employment or real fulfilment. They are consigned to the 'underclass' – those who, unless they have the opportunity to join something like the Army, will be perpetually dependent upon menial employment or State benefit for their survival. Meanwhile, the strong and the able – or the lucky – who might in a better world help the less fortunate within their community, prefer instead to

1. *Three Essays*, J. S. Mill, ed. R. Wollheim, p.141 (Oxford 1975).

pursue wealth and career advancement with an intensity which in other ages was reserved for religion.

'Active citizenship' has never really got off the ground as a political idea for the late 1980s. Originally conceived as a retort to those suggesting that Conservative policies were about little other than 'looking after Number One', the concept failed to receive its expected Prime Ministerial endorsement at the Party's conference at Brighton in 1988. Outside of a small circle at the Home Office, little has been heard in Whitehall of active citizenship since.

The trend in altruism such as it is discernable in modern Britain seems to be towards passive delegation rather than active participation. The increase in charitable giving, for instance, has been attended by the development of mass broadcast events where viewers or listeners telephone in their contributions, pay by credit-card, and confine their participation to the wearing of red plastic noses. Similarly, 'payroll-giving' or GAYE (give as you earn) has developed – a computerized form of philanthropy imported from the United States from which all human exchange has been removed; it is regular and automatic and there is no need for the donor to think much about or even be simultaneously aware of the transmission of his gift.

If most people are too busy working or taking part in modern 'leisure activities' to give much time to taking part in the serious business of running their own communities or defending their country, the possibility exists that this is what they really want. In such a climate, is there any future for the sort of Army that we have proposed, one truly representative of our society, relying heavily upon part-time volunteers, committed to the general education of its members and giving them a moral lead?

We believe that there is – but that it could only operate in the context of much more widely diffused power and responsibility within society. Greater effort is needed to explain the mysteries of defence to a wider public and a serious attempt needs to be made to recruit the active consent of the people to policies which they can understand. Also, we would have to dispense with the political posturing over nuclear weapons which currently obscures so much. One of the advantages that would accrue from opening up the defence debate to a wider public would be to make the Army more accountable. It would challenge the Army's reluctance to consider any course other than the one it is already set on. As we have seen, many other countries do things in different ways. Our generals should be made to explain precisely why they learn so few lessons from abroad. Is their insistence on carrying on as they have always done really in the public interest?

By involving people both in taking decisions about defence and in implementing them, we might be able to recover some of the 'vital force' that Mill held to be indispensable for the accomplishment of great things. And what greater thing is there in the nuclear age than the avoidance of war? Moreover, the growth of a vigorous consensus over defence could only strengthen deterrence.

If we cannot build that consensus our prospects are grim. We will witness the gradual run-down of the professional Army to the point where it ceases to be of much use in meeting our national commitments, either within Europe or outside the NATO area. For the first time since the pay crisis of the 1970s, the Army is already 2,000 under-strength and it has been estimated that there will be a 25 per cent shortfall in recruitment by 1992. When the supply of 16 to 20-year-olds eventually begins to increase in 1995, the Army will find itself particularly short of officers – who are taken from the 20 to 24 age group. During this troubled period industry too will feel the pinch and will be offering better salaries and more attractive conditions of service than the Army will be able to match in a straight auction.

But as the Army's existing manpower shortage makes clear, it is not only the demographic factor that is causing consternation to the Generals: retaining skilled men is a problem too. Some units in BAOR are now so short that sub-units are being maintained on a 'skeleton' basis only, whilst a number of infantry battalions are now reported to have had so many of their companies chronically undermanned that they have been forced to select one for temporary closure. The equipment is put in store, and the men redistributed among those which remain. And, with the number of applications for PVR (Premature Voluntary Release) increasing and the demographic trough on the horizon, there is little to suggest that this will be a short-term arrangement.[1]

The Army's response to these problems has been MARILYN which has been widely circulated internally. Employing more women is one of the suggestions made – but so far little has been said about bringing their terms of service more closely into line with those of their male colleagues. Another proposal is to accept a lower standard of recruit, but quite what remedial measures the Army has in mind to bring poor quality raw material up to standard remains a

1. When we began writing this book there was only one battalion which had closed down a company, as we have been writing more have followed.

mystery. Some form of territorially based 'militia' with both full and part-time elements is also said to be under consideration as is what has been called 'better dovetailing' with the Youth Training Scheme.

And MARILYN is already in danger of being overtaken by events. It has been comparatively easy until recently for the government to make its case for a substantial defence budget – the threatening posture of the Soviet forces in Europe, attempts to extend Soviet hegemony elsewhere and both the substance and tone of Marxist ideology have proved sufficiently alarming to persuade the ordinary man not only of the need for conventional forces but of that for nuclear weapons as well. The success of Mikhail Gorbachev's 'Mr nice guy' image has changed all that. The perception of any real threat posed by the Warsaw Pact is vanishing fast – and the rate at which it disappears seems likely to accelerate with every new concession – real or illusory – that Mr Gorbachev makes. This is bound to have an impact upon recruitment.

What we have called the 'delegative approach' to defence has kept the majority of our citizens largely in ignorance of defence issues for so long that the distinction between those elements of our armoury that exist principally (or even solely) to deter war and those which would be of practical use if deterrence were to fail has become hopelessly blurred. We need to spell out much more clearly how our 'three armies' – *the peacetime institution* that must be administered, *the bargaining chips* on the table at Vienna, and *the effective fighting force* we want in the event of war – fit into the scheme of things. Only by being much more open will it be possible to harness popular will to the task of defending our society.

But involving people in the defence debate must mean more than just educating them: governments must listen to what people say. As early as 1946 the American theorist Bernard Brodie wrote: 'Thus far the chief purpose of our military establishment has been to win wars. From now on its chief purpose must be to avert them.' From that time to this what has averted war in Europe has been the threat that nuclear weapons would be used – and at a relatively early stage of the conflict. Political leaders must now come to terms with the fact that an increasing number of people do not want to go on relying on nuclear weapons to keep the peace, and want a peace that means more than merely the absence of war. They are anxious to see a new order established where some settlement is made in Europe that will ensure that a genuinely co-operative relationship is built up between East and West against a background of mutual security.

Meanwhile, the model of international relations as practised by governments and taught in universities and defence colleges worldwide is still essentially that of an amoral world in which independent states must pursue their own short-term self-interest. Foreign policy, of which the use of military force is seen as a part, is conceived as taking place independently of the personal moral positions of the politicians, diplomats and soldiers who administer that policy. Indeed, both diplomats and soldiers are taught that so great are the issues involved that personal feelings cannot enter the calculations.

In the future, if government is going to ask people to risk their lives by joining armies (especially as part-timers), it must offer, in peace, something clearly worth believing in and ultimately worth fighting for. Today's young adults are perhaps more streetwise than their predecessors. Often dissatisfied with what is imposed upon them, they demand honesty and more control over their lives. They are unlikely to be won over by old 'certainties' like aggressive nationalism, Victorian Values or dogmatic religion, any more than the sort of narrow corporatism in which the individual has no significance. However, they might well take to a dynamic scheme of national defence which did not demand a compromise of their principles and which offered them opportunities to be of service to their fellow men and women.

Meanwhile, an apathetic attitude to defence can only be seen as encouraging aggression. It is a barrier to peace. It would be unwise not to keep some atomic weapons in the short term, but there is no reason why we should not immediately begin to move towards a defence of Britain and Europe based on purely defensive arrangements, with greatly devolved systems of command and organization. We need a new form of deterrence to replace the current balance of terror, and a new model Army to restore the vital force of popular commitment to the defence of the community.

Index

Units and formations are separately indexed

active citizenship, 203
Adair, Professor John, 55
Adams, Gerry, 164, 170
adaptation
  necessity for Army, 188–97
  resistence to, 188
administration and support ratios (World War II), 21n.
Allied Command Europe Mobile Force (AMF), 33
anti-aircraft weapons, 190–91
arctic warfare, 33
Armed Services Youth Training Scheme, 124
armoured fighting vehicles (AFVs), 31
armoured personnel carriers, (APCs), 30
arms (personal)
  for Home Defence Force, 140
  right to bear, 12 and n.
arms (services distinguished), 27
Army Act (1955), 26
Army Board, 26, 72
Army Council, 17
Army Emergency Reserve, 111
Army Service Act (1847), 106
Army Service Act (1949), 109
Army Tactical Missile System (ATACMS), 183
Arthur, Max, 166
artillery, 19, 27 *see also* nuclear weapons: Royal Artillery
Ashley, Jack, 69
Asquith, Herbert (Earl of Oxford and Asquith), 162–3
aufstragtaktik, 191–2
authoritarianism, 55
Auxiliaries (Home Guard), 115

Bader-Meinhoff Gang, 157
Banner, Operation, 36
BAOR (British Army of the Rhine) *see also* NATO
  boredom in, 66
  costs of, 66 *see also* expenditure
  establishment, 79
  future deployment, 181–2
    units dual-roled, 199
  maintenance of, argument for, 94
  manoeuvres, 75–7
  readiness of, 75
  reinforcements, 94
  role of, 95–7
  strain on resources, 23
  strength, 34
  tactics of, 93–7
battalions
  composition of, 28–9
  in regimental system, 38
  second (overseas), 40
  size of, 18
battlegroups, 33, 44
Belize, 197
Benest, Major D. G., 136
Berlin air-lift, 78
Best Years of Their Lives, The (Royle), 124
Bevin, Ernest, 77
Bismarck, Prince Otto von, 16
Black and Tans, 164
Blackstone, William, 106
blitzkrieg, 20, 105
Boer War, Second (1899–1902), 17
Boyne, Battle of The (1690), 161
Brave Defender, Exercise, 131
Breda, Declaration of (1659), 9
Bren guns, 21
brigades, 32–3
  structure, 44–5
British Expeditionary Force, 18
Brodie, Bernard, 205
Brunei, 198
Brussels, Treaty of, 78
B-Specials (police auxiliaries), 164, 165, 166
budget accounting for COs, 193
bullying, 61, 63, 69–71

remedying, 73, 202
Bundeswehr, 79 *see also* West Germany
Burton, Anthony, 5
Bush, George, 178–9

Cardwell reforms, 16–17, 40–41, 45
career structure, 32
Carson, Sir Edward (later Baron), 163
Carver, Field-Marshal Michael, Baron, 83
casualties
Northern Ireland, 170
World War I, 19
World War II, 21
cavalry *see also* tanks
composition of regiments, 28
officers' backgrounds and behaviour, 56–7
Cavendish, Lord Frederick, 152
Charles II, King of England, 9, 10, 11, 13
chemical weapons, 85, 99
Chernobyl disaster, 130
Chernyshev, Colonel Vladimir, 91
Childers, Hugh, 16
Chindits, 44
Civil Defence Corps, 133
Civil Power, Aid to, 26
Civil Rights movement, 165
Civil Wars (English) (1642–1645 and 1648–1649), 8–9, 39
Clausewitz, Carl von, 154, 155
Cobbett, William, 106
Collins, Michael, 164
colonial garrisons, 13–14 *see also* imperial policing
combat teams, 33
Commandos, 44
communications in the field, 19
Compton Report (1971), 169
conscientious objectors, 4, 109
conscription *see also* National Service
in Britain, 101, 108–12
in Europe, 13, 116–20
history of, 104–6
peacetime, 109
World War I, 18, 19
World War II, 20
Conventional Armed Forces in Europe (CFE) talks, 2,n, 88–9, 90, 93
asymetric reduction, 180
German reaction to, 138–9
optimism over, 180, 183–4
possible outcome, 98
defensive warfare, 189
subject of, 178–80
tanks, 180–81
conventional forces
cuts in, 88–9, 90
imbalance of, 81–9
Soviet spending on, 83
Corps, specialist, 19, 31, 43–4
counter-insurgency *see also* terrorism
experience in, 150
psychology of, 151
technology of, 151
Counter Revolutionary Warfare (CRW), 151
Courcy, John de, 160
Crimean War (1853–1856), 15
Cromwell, Oliver, 1, 8–9, 161
Curragh Incident, 162
Cyprus, 195

Debray, Regis, 157
deception techniques, 92
Declaration of Right (1689), 11–12
deep battle, 92–3
Defence Estimates, 26 *see also* expenditure
defence in depth, 102, 181
Defence, Ministry of, 25
public relations, 75
defence policy
breakdown of consensus, 102
Defence Review (1975), 32
defensive warfare, 189
delegation of tactical command, 191–2
Demetrius, Operation, 168
Derry (Londonderry), 161, 166, 170
deterrence
confusion of purpose, 100
German view, 183
as NATO's prime purpose, 77–80, 99–100
numbers required, 102, 194
Dewar, Lt Col. Michael, 160, 167
Diplock courts, 174, 176
disarmament
politics of, 102
discipline, 64
Victorian, 41
Districts (Army), 34–5
divisions (administrative), 28, 45
divisions (fighting formation)
armoured, 19
regional, 43
as tactical unit, 19
Drake's Drum, Exercise, 128
drunkenness, 58–9, 63, 202

remedying, 73

early-warning devices, 181
élite corps, 44
Elizabeth I, Queen of England, 160
Emergency Powers Acts (1920 and 1964), 26
encounter battles, 97–8
EOKA (Cypriot insurgency movement), 152
equipment failures, 76
ethical values in relation to the Army, 47–73, 200–201
Europe
alliances, 17
balance of power in, 14
European Economic Community (EEC)
integrated forces, 5, 198
expenditure on forces
increase in, 3, 4
as limit on size, 102–3
Parliamentary control over, 25
on technology, 188
value for money, 98–9
World War II, 22

Falkland Islands campaign (1982), 4, 23, 60, 198
families of soldiers, 34–5, 66
Farrar-Hockley, General Sir Anthony, 138–9
Fencibles, 107
Fifth Monarchy Men, 9–10
financial problems of soldiers, 65
first strike mentality, 189
Fit for Role inspections, 74–5
flexible response, 83, 99–100
focoism, 156
Follow-on-Forces Attack (FOFA), 82
restrictions on, 98
forward defence doctrine, 78–9, 181
France
Air Mobile Division, 195
British relations, 17, 20
colonies, former, influence in, 197–8
conscription, 116–18
levée en masse, 104
Napoleon's armies, 105
NATO relations with, 82, 181
short war strategy, 117–18
World War II, 21
Franco–Prussian War (1870–1871), 17, 105
Free Range Over Ground (FROG), 183
freemasonry, 42 and n.
Frisby, Lt Col. Miles, 69
Fuller, Major General J. F., 20, 47

General Staff system, 17 *see also* officers
Gerasimov, Gennadi, 179
Germany *see* West Germany
Giap, Vo Nguyen, 156
Gibraltar, 177
Gladstone, W. E., 162
Goodwood, Operation, 95–6
Gorbachev, Mikhail, 3, 88, 90, 98, 179, 180, 205
Graham, Major General, 52n.
Grand Hotel, Brighton, 172, 173
Group of Soviet Forces in Germany (GSFG), 75
Guards regiments
coloured guardsmen, 67
guerrilla warfare
terrorism distinguished, 153
Guevara, Ernesto ('Che'), 156–7

Haldane reforms, 17–18, 45
Heath, Edward, 170
helicopters
Hind D, 93
Lynx, 195–6
paucity of, 196
Puma, 33
Soviet, 85, 93
tanks, alternative to, 194–5
HELLFIRE missiles, 196
Henry II, King of England, 160
Hickey, Colonel Michael, 137
Hickey, John, 159
Hill-Norton, Admiral of the Fleet Peter, Baron, 138–9
Ho Chi Minh, 155
Hogg, Ian, 19n, 21
home defence *see also* Home Guard: National Service
Drake's Drum, Exercise, 128–9
Home Defence Force (proposed), 138–42
Home Service Force, 135
internal security, 133–4
invasion discounted, 129
RAF role, 136–7
regular troops available, 134–5
resources for, 133–42
sabotage, 131–2
TA role, 135
unpreparedness, 129, 136–8

Home Guard, 112–16
Home Service Force (HSF), 25, 135, 138
Hong Kong, 198, 199
Howard, Michael, 46
Howe, Stephen, 3
Hurd, Douglas, 173

imperial policing, 14, 19–20, 22, 40–41, 106
India
  British Army in, 14 and n.
infantry
  composition of, 28
  Corps concept, 45
  light/heavy distinction, 197
  mechanized, 30–31
Inner German Border (IGB), 78, 79, 80, 92
  demilitarized central zone, 180–81
  fibre optic defence, 189–90
  remotely piloted vehicles (RPVs), 190
insurgency *see also* counter-insurgency
  terrorism distinguished, 153
inter-arm cooperation, 22, 33, 44, 46
inter-service cooperation
  Soviet superiority, 93
inter-service rivalry, 27
Intermediate Nuclear Forces (INF) treaty (1987), 2, 183
International Institute for Strategic Studies (IISS), 83
international terrorism, 171 *see also* terrorism
Iranian Embassy siege, 26
Ireland *see also* Northern Ireland
  Easter uprising, 163
  Free State, 164
  history of troubles, 152–65
  Home Rule, 162–3
  partition, 164
  plantation, 160–61
  Sinn Fein, 163–4
Irish National Liberation Army, 171
Irish Republican Army (IRA)
  formation of, 163–4
  Provisional, 132, 167–77
    Active Service Units (ASUs), 172
    bombing campaign, 172–3
    broadcasting ban, 173
    declared illegal, 171
    financing of, 176
Irish Republican Brotherhood, 163
isolation of Army *see* society

James I, King of England, 160
Janes Publishing Co. Ltd, 150
Johnson, David, 168

Keightley, Major General R. C., 51
Kenya, 199
Kinnock, Neil, 102, 148
Kitson, General Sir Frank, 121–2, 137, 169
Kohl, Helmut, 182
Korean War (1950–1953), 22, 109

Labour Party
  conversion to multilateralism, 3
Lance missiles, 182–3
large regiments, 45
LAW 80 anti-tank weapon, 196
Lawrence, Lt Robert, 54
Lawrence, T. E., 5
  leadership *see also* non-commissioned officers: officers'
  checklist, 56
  teaching of, 54–5
Ledogar, Stephen, 179
Lenin, Vladimir Ilyich, 6, 154
Levchenko, Stanislaus, 131–2
Liberator pistol, 190
Liddel Hart, Sir Basil 20, 150
Local defence Volunteers (LDV), 112–14

Machiavelli, Niccolo, 161
Macpherson, R. T. S., 55
manoeuvres, 75–7
  monitored, 128–9
Manpower Services Commission, 124
Mao Tse-tung, 6, 22, 154–5, 187
Marcuse, Herbert, 157
Marighela, Carlos, 157
MARILYN (Manpower and Recruiting in the Lean Years), 102, 204–5
Marines, Corps of, 43
marital infidelity, 65
maritime defence strategy, 13, 15
maskirovka (deception techniques), 92
Maudling, Reginald, 173
mechanized infantry, 21
MILAN anti-tank weapon, 196
Military Service Act, 1916, 109
militia
  absence of in UK, 101
  Ballot, 107

Cardwell reforms, 16
local responsibilities, 107
19th century, 106–7
origins, 11
pairing with Regular regiments, 41
Mill, John Stuart, 202
Mill Hill Barracks, 172
Minimanual (Marighela), 157
mission-orientated tactics (*aufstragtaktik*), 191–2
mixed arm groupings, 32
Monk, General George, 10, 13
Monmouth's rebellion (1685), 11
morality
lack of in military ethic, 3
Motor-Rifle Divisions (Soviet), 85
Mountjoy, Charles Blount, Lord, 160
Mujahadin (Afghan), 187
Multiple Launch Rocket System (MLRS), 183
Mutiny Act (1689), 12, 26
Mutual and Balanced Force Reduction (MBFR) negotiations, 179
Mutually Assured Destruction (MAD), 133

Napoleonic Wars (1789–1815), 14
National Rifle Association, 108
National Service *see also* conscription
post-war, 48, 109–12
officers, 110–11
proposed reintroduction, 103, 120–26
Army's argument against, 120–22
as Home Defence Force, 139–42
social benefits, 125–6
voluntary element, 123–4
National Service (Number 2) Act (1914), 115
NATO (North Atlantic Treaty Organization)
air power reductions, 182
AMF, 33
armour in, 27
establishment, 77
formation of, 22
Northern region, 134–5
nuclear weapons, 2, 81–2, 92, 182–3, 200
role of, 75, 78–85
strategy
buying time, 80–81, 99
delaying forces, 80
forward defence doctrine, 78–81, 94, 181
mobile defence, 79–80
strength
cuts proposed, 89
imbalance of forces, 83–9, 179–80
reinforcements, 130, 181
Neave, Airey, 172
New Model Army, 8–10, 39
non-commissioned officers (NCOs), 60–63
bullying by, 61, 70
defined, 32
influence of, 62
machoism, 61, 63
National Service, 111
officers' views of, 61–2
promotion, 62–3
Northern Ireland
Army's role, 166–72, 174
casualties, 170
conscripts, arguments against, 122
development of troubles, 165–72
'climate of collapse', 173
direct rule, 169
District, 34
intelligence gathering, 169, 170, 172, 174–5
internment, 167–8, 169
interrogation in depth, 168–9
legal processes, 173–4, 176
psychology of, 151–2, 159
public opinion of, 173
resolution suggested, 175–6
sectarian killings, 171
war or no war, 159, 171, 175
'Way Ahead', 171
WRAC in, 71
Norway
home defence in, 146–7
Nuclear Biological and Chemical Warfare (NBC) drill, 133
nuclear weapons
conventional forces, alternative to, 22–3
dependence on, 102
doubted, 82
dilemma of, 81–2, 99
flexible response, 83
RA responsibility, 31
reduction talks, 2, 178, 182–4
total ban, effect of, 122

tactical role, 77

Officer Training Corps (OTC), 18
officers, commissioned, 48–60
careerist, 53
class resentments, 57–8
criticism, sensitiveness to, 53–4
cross-posting, 193
élitism, 101
ethics, declining, 51–2, 56, 58–60
failings of, 53–5
junior, lack of opportunity for initiative, 192
men, relationship with, 57–8
Mess life, 41–2, 51, 58
National Service, 110–11
NCOs, former, 62
promotion, 62
by purchase, 12, 39
social backgrounds, 49, 56–7
snobbery, 52
staff, 193
stereotyping of, 48–9
training of, 12, 15
types of commission, 31–2
ungentlemanly behaviour, 52
values, 49–50
welfare role, 41, 60, 65, 66
wives, 66
Oman, 199
O'Neil, Hugh, 160
Operational Manoeuvre Groups (OMGs) (Soviet), 93, 97, 195, 197
organization and control of Army, 25–7
out-of-area operations, 4–5, 33–4, 197–200
Owen, Dr David, 123
Paisley, Rev. Ian, 165, 173
Parliament
control over Army, 9, 10–12, 25
Parnell, James, 162
pay, forces, 23, 39 *see also* financial problems
police *see also* Royal Ulster Constabulary
home defence role, 134
Premature Voluntary Retirement (PVR), 53
preparedness, lack of, 74–7
Prevention of Terrorism Act (1974), 171, 174
private soldiers, 63–71
aggressiveness, 66–7
financial problems, 65
living conditions, 65
moral guidance for, 73
recruitment, 64 *see also* recruitment
team loyalty, absence of, 67
training, basic, 64
promotion, 62–3
racialism in, 68
Prussia, 16, 105–6
psychological warfare, 6, 190
Psychology of Military Incompetence, On the (Dixon), 53–5
purchase of commissions, 12, 39

racial problems, 67–9
remedying, 73
rank-consciousness, 193
Raven, Simon, 49–50
recruitment
demographic trough, 2, 4, 102, 201, 204
difficulty of 102–3
lowering of standards, 204–5
skilled men, retention of, 204
Redmond, John, 162, 163
regimental system, 37–46
county titles, 41
defined, 38–9
feudal origins, 42, 45, 49
inward-looking, 45–6
loyalty to, 38, 45, 46
origins, 12, 14
precedence, 40
raising regiments, 39–40
reforms, 16, 43–6
suggested, 46
uniforms, 39
in World War II, 22
regiments
mixed-arm, 193
Regular Commissions Board, 110
Regular Reserve, 16, 18n, 135–6
Resistance Will Win, The (Ho Chi Minh), 155
retraining, 102
Revolution, English (1688), 1, 161
revolutionary theory, 154–8
rifle volunteer movement, 106, 108, 141
Royal Ulster Constabulary, 158, 165, 166, 171
Special Branch, 168, 175
Russell, William Howard, 15n.

Sandhurst, R. M. A., 111 *see also* officers, commissioned
academic studies, 52n.
leadership defined, 55–6
social conditioning, 49, 50–51
Saxons (personnel carriers), 31
Schmähling, Admiral Elmar, 4, 138–9
Schmidt, Helmut, 183
Scotter, General Sir William, 95
'sergeant power', 62
services
arms distinguished, 27
Seven Years War (1756–1763), 14
Shevardnadze, Eduard, 180
Sinn Fein, 163–4 *see also* Irish Republican Army
Provisional, 167
'smart' munitions, 188–9, 194
society
Army and, 13, 23, 40, 47, 48–9, 101–3, 106, 202
as reflection of, 70–71
Army's view of, 52
home defence as integrating factor, 148
National Service as beneficial force in, 122–3, 125–6
participatory approach, 104
popular conception of Army, 103
unacceptable behaviour, 72–3
'SOE in peace', 192
Soldier, Soldier (Parker), 60–61
Sovereign
regimental connections, 39
as symbol of loyalty, 1, 12–13
Soviet Union *see also* Warsaw Pact
air power, 93, 182
airborne forces, 79, 92, 98, 130–32, 194
conscription, 119–20
conventional forces, 83–9
unilateral cuts in 88, 90
helicopters strength, 85, 93
military doctrine, 89–93
defensive role, recognition of, 89, 90–91
mobility, 93
operational principles, 91–3
Operational Manoeuvre Groups (OMGs), 93
short war theory, 90
uskorenye, 179
modernization of weapons, 183
naval infantry, 132
nuclear weapons, tactical, 94
perestroika, effect of, 90, 179
'sleepers', 130, 132
special forces units, 129, 130
spetsnaz forces, 98, 130–32
tanks, 180–81
threat, perceived, 3, 22, 77–82, 130–33, 194
lessened, 180, 184
Spanish Succession, War of (1702–1714), 14
Special Branch, 152
RUC, 168
Special Reserve, 18 and n.
new proposals, 140
specialist corps, 19, 31, 43–4
spetsnaz forces, 98, 130–32
Home Defence Force as deterrent, 139–40
SS 21, 183
Staff College, Camberley, 191
Stalker, John, 177 and n.
standing armies
control by Parliament, 25
distrust of, 106
establishment of, 9–11
European, 14, 104–6
restraints on, 11–12
Stern Gang, 152
'Sticks', (SAS groups), 130, 192
Stirling, David, 192 and n.
Stockholm Agreement (1986), 128 and n.
Stokes, Richard, 67–9
strategy *see under* NATO
stun grenades, 186n.
Sun Tzu, 154
Sweden
home defence in, 145–6, 148
Switzerland
home defence in, 133, 142–5, 148
Sykes, Sir Richard, 172

Tactical Air-to-Air Surface Missiles (TASM), 182
tanks *see also* cavalry: Royal Armoured Corps
anti-tank weapons, 190
armour, 188 and n.
battle, 27, 28
cost-effectiveness, 82
development of, 20 and n.
limited numbers, 98
obsolescence, 194–5
RAC structure, 43
recce regiments, 27

role questioned, 195
Soviet
capacity, 180
Division, 85
withdrawal of, 88, 180–81
tank-free zones, 98
types, 21
World War II, 21
technology
advances in, 79
anti-aircraft, 82
anti-terrorism, 151
'competitive strategy' policy, 187
counter-measures, 188
dangers of dependency on, 102
defensive systems, move to, 189–90
effect on warfare, 184–8
limitations of, 185–7
simplification of, 190–91
Ten Year Rule, 20
Territorial Army (TA)
BAOR reinforcements, 34, 94, 135
commitment, 35
formation of, 18, 107
home defence role, 135
infantry, 28
numbers, 25
officer recruitment, 55–6
'one army' concept, 35
proposed expansion, 140–41
recruitment problems, 142
Regular Army, relations with, 38, 142
UK Mobile Force, 33
territorialization of regiments, 16, 38
terrorism 150–54 *see also* counter-insurgency: Northern Ireland
combating, 175
defined, 153
insurgency distinguished, 153
psychology of, 154
publicity for, 158, 173
in Revolutionary Theory, 155
state sponsored, 5, 98, 129–30, 198
Thatcher, Margaret
on short range nuclear weapons, 182, 183
on terrorism, 158
Thirty Years War (1618–1648), 105
'threat' lectures, 93
'thrusting majors', 53, 57
TOW missiles, 197–8
tradition
as barrier to change, 2
training *see also* officers, commissioned
basic, 64–5
citizenship, 6
foreign armies, of, 33
motivation, 64
NATO, 33
out-of-area, 33–4
TRIGAT (Third Generation Anti-Tank) missile system, 196
Tumbledown (TV play), 54

Ulster *see* Northern Ireland
Ulster Covenant, 162
Ulster Volunteer Force, 162–3
United Kingdom
as vulnerable base, 130, 137
United Kingdom Land Forces (UKLF), 34
United Kingdom Mobile Force, 33
United Nations
peace-keeping forces, 28, 198
United States of America
Air Assault Division, 195
chemical weapons, 99
defence cuts, 88
NATO role, 78
partial withdrawal from, 98
and Northern Ireland, 176
nuclear weapons in Europe, 182
in World War II, 22

Venner, Thomas, 9–10
volunteer battalions, 41, 43
volunteers, 106, 107, 108

Wales, Charles, Prince of, 67
Warminster (School of Infantry)
values, 49–50
Warrior (armoured fighting vehicle), 197
Warsaw Pact *see also* Soviet Union
airborne assaults, 79, 82, 129
amphibious assaults, 129
CFR, 179
equipment, 85
force reductions, 2
helicopters, 85
imbalance of forces, 81, 83–9, 179–80
technology balance, 83–5
West Germany
BAOR sector, 94
civilians employed, 66

civilians in war role, 95–6, 194
conscription, 118–19
demilitarized central zone, 180–81
force reductions, 88
foreign troops' removal sought, 3–4
IRA attacks in, 172
NATO
membership, 79
tactics, influence on, 93, 181
reluctance by, as theatre of war, 78
time-share soldiers, 139
troop withdrawal urged, 139
nuclear weapons, wish for removal, 2, 183
Whitelaw, William, Viscount, 170
Widgery Report, 169
William III (of Orange), 11, 161
Wilson, Sir Henry, 162
Wintringham, Tom, 114–15
wives of servicemen
morale, 66
women *see also* WRAC
conscription of, 109
employment in Army, 204
World War I, 18–19
World War II, 20–22
WRAC (Women's Royal Army Corps), 71–2

yeomanry, 107
Younger, George, 99

Zimbabwe, 197

Formations and Units

Corps

Royal Armoured Corps, 27–8
Royal Army Education Corps, 62, 71
Royal Army Ordnance Corps, 27, 71
Royal Artillery, 27, 31, 183
Royal Corps of Transport, 71
Royal Electrical and Mechanical Engineers, 27, 31, 64, 71, 76
Royal Engineers, 27, 71
Royal Marines, 23, 33, 136
Royal Military Police, 71
Royal Signals, 27, 64, 71

1st British Corps, 34, 94, 135

Divisions

1st Armoured, 34, 43
3rd and 4th Armoured, 34
7th Armoured, 43
Guards, 28
Guards Armoured, 44
51st Highland, 43
2nd Infantry, 34
16th (Irish), 163
Light, 28
Prince of Wales, 28
Queens, 28
36th Ulster, 43, 163

Brigades

24th Air Mobile, 195–7
5th Airborne, 33, 199
7th Armoured, 43
22nd Armoured, 43
3rd Commando, 33
Forester, 44
Ghurka, 28, 33, 199
Green Jackets, 44
Guards, 44
Home Counties, 44
1st Infantry, 33, 34
8th Infantry, 34, 169
39th Infantry, 34, 169
52nd Lowland, 43

Regiments

Blues and Royals, 13
Coldstream Guards, 13, 69
Grenadier Guards, 13
Household Cavalry, 27
13th/18th Hussars, 27
King's Own Scottish Borderers, 69
9th/12th Lancers, 27
Lifeguards, 13
Parachute Regiment, 23, 28, 31, 33, 44, 166, 169, 199

Queens's Dragoon Guards, 69–70
Special Air Service (SAS), 28, 34, 44, 57, 130, 151, 176, 177, 186, 192
Royal Green Jackets, 31
Royal Regiment of Wales, 166
Royal Tank Regiment, 27
Ulster Defence (UDR), 25, 34, 35, 171

Other Unit

14 Int (Intelligence) Company, 174